STUDIES IN THE EARLY HISTORY OF BRITAIN

General Editor: Nicholas Brooks

Scandinavian Settlement in Northern Britain

To W.F.H. (Bill) Nicolaisen

Scandinavian Settlement in Northern Britain
Thirteen Studies of Place-Names in their Historical Context

Edited by Barbara E. Crawford

Leicester University Press
London and New York

LEICESTER UNIVERSITY PRESS
A Cassell imprint
Wellington House, 125 Strand, London, WC2R 0BB
215 Park Avenue South, New York, NY 10003, USA

First published in Great Britain in 1995

British Library Cataloguing-in-Publication Data

A catalogue record for this book is available from The British Library

ISBN 0 7185 1923 X

Library of Congress Cataloging-in-Publication Data

Scandinavian settlement in northern Britain : place-name studies in
    their historical context / edited by Barbara Crawford.
        p.   cm.
    Includes bibliographical references and index.
    ISBN 0-7185-1923-X
    1. Scotland – Civilization – Scandinavian influences. 2. England,
Northern – Civilization – Scandinavian influences. 3. Land settlement
patterns – England, Northern. 4. Scandinavians – England, Northern –
History. 5. Scandinavian languages – Etymology – Names. 6. Names,
Geographical – England, Northern. 7. Land settlement patterns – Scotland.
8. Scandinavians – Scotland – History. 9. Names, Geographical – Scotland.
10. Northmen – Great Britain. 11. Vikings – Great Britain. I. Crawford,
Barbara.
DA775.S27   1995
941.1 1–dc20   95–10299
                                                                          CIP

Typeset by Mayhew Typesetting, Rhayader, Powys
Printed and bound in Great Britain by SRP Ltd, Exeter

Contents

vi *Contents*

Foreword

The aim of the *Studies in the Early History of Britain* is to promote works of the highest scholarship which open up virgin fields of study or which surmount the barriers of traditional academic disciplines. As interest in the origins of our society and culture grows while scholarship becomes ever more specialized, inter-disciplinary studies are needed not only by scholars but also by students and laymen. This series will therefore include research monographs, works of synthesis and also collaborative studies of important themes by several scholars whose training and expertise has lain in different fields. Our knowledge of the early Middle Ages will always be limited and fragmentary, but progress can be made if the work of the historian embraces that of the philologist, the archaeologist, the geographer, the numismatist, the art historian and the liturgist – to name only the most obvious. The need to cross and to remove academic frontiers also explains the extension of the geographical range from that of the previous *Studies in Early English History* to include the whole island of Britain. The change would have been welcomed by the editor of the earlier series, the late Professor H.P.R. Finberg, whose pioneering work helped to inspire or to provoke, the interest of a new generation of early medievalists in the relations of Britons and Saxons. The approach of this series is therefore deliberately wide-ranging. Early medieval Britain can only be understood in the context of contemporary developments in Ireland and on the Continent.

In this volume Dr Barbara Crawford concerts a team of experts to study the Scandinavian place-names of the whole of Northern Britain and thus to contribute towards a better understanding of the impact of the Vikings. It has long been known that eastern and lowland Britain received mainly Danish settlers, while Norwegians predominated in the North and West. The division between the two groups was not absolute and did not correspond to the later boundaries which have largely determined the pattern of modern scholarship. Moreover the unevenness both of historical records and of modern philological expertise in different parts of Britain has meant that the Norse names of the Scottish islands and western seaboard have been very much less studied than the Danish names of the east midlands of England. Critical questions about the scale and chronology of the settlements, about the light that the names throw upon the relations of different ethnic groups, or upon internal colonization, estate fragmentation or feudal lordship remain controversial and have only been considered in relation to certain areas or classes of names. It is therefore a great pleasure to welcome to the series a volume which studies the whole of Britain north of the Humber and the Dee, sometimes with a sharply focused beam, sometimes with a broad overview. Here we can find both a rich mine of new interpretations and reassessments and a decisive step forward in our approach to the study of Scandinavian settlement.

N.P. Brooks
University of Birmingham
August 1994

List of contributors

Per Sveaas Andersen, Professor Emeritus, Historisk Institutt, University of Oslo.

Malcolm Bangor-Jones, Civil Servant, Arts and Cultural Heritage Division, The Scottish Office.

Barbara E. Crawford, Lecturer in Mediaeval History, University of St. Andrews.

Gillian Fellows-Jensen, Reader in Name Studies at the University of Copenhagen. *f. 179.*

Ian Fraser, Senior Lecturer, School of Scottish Studies, University of Edinburgh.

Margaret Gelling, Honorary Reader in Place Name Studies, University of Birmingham. President, English Place Name Society.

Mary C. Higham, part-time lecturer and researcher in the historical geography of north-west England.

Anne Johnston, Assistant Keeper (research), City of Aberdeen District Council, Art Gallery and Museum.

Richard D. Oram, Honorary Lecturer in History, University of Aberdeen.

Brian Smith, Shetland Archivist.

Simon Taylor, Place-name researcher and writer.

William P.L. Thomson, former Rector, Kirkwall Grammar School.

Victor Watts, Master of Grey College, University of Durham.

Doreen Waugh, Assistant Head, The Mary Erskine School, Edinburgh, and Place-name researcher.

List of plates

List of figures

Preface

'What's in a name?' I hope that these chapters will show that a very great deal lies in a name, and more particularly in those names given to numberless farms and features of the inhabited landscape of Scotland and Northern England by the invaders and settlers of Scandinavian speech who moved into these areas in the ninth and tenth centuries AD. The twelve contributors to this volume are all researchers – some of them historians and geographers, as well as

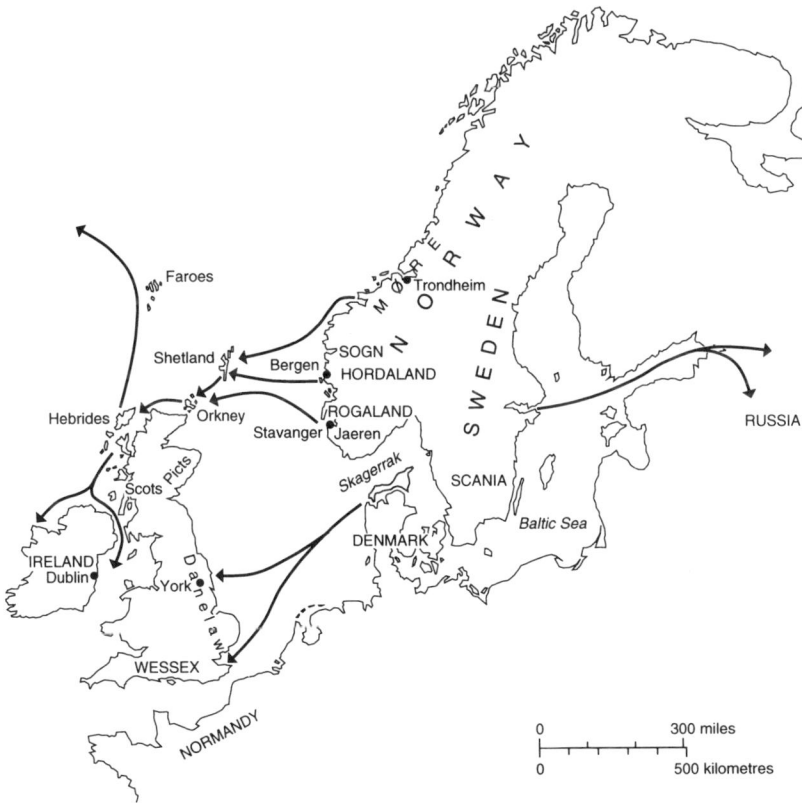

Figure 1 North Europe in the Viking Age.

linguists and place-name experts – who have worked on different aspects of Scandinavian settlement in widely scattered areas. They were invited by me to contribute a study of their research area, looking both at the wider settlement frame and, if possible, focusing more narrowly on one settlement locality in order to increase our understanding of the historical processes involved in that settlement. We will of course only understand those processes if we understand the linguistic principles involved in name formation and the application of names to the landscape. Linguists may feel that, all too often, historical interpretations are a smoke screen which mask inadequate knowledge of linguistic development and misunderstanding of place-name elements. Historians may feel that the linguists' specialized interest in the meaning and development of words lacks the broader understanding of the historical processes which lie behind the introduction of new peoples and new names. I have tried to encourage a meeting of these two viewpoints and thereby to create a volume which takes our understanding of the impact of Scandinavian settlement a step further. Towards that end I have inserted six link passages between some of the chapters which attempt to delineate the historical background to Scandinavian settlement or influence in that particular part of Scotland or north England. This will hopefully provide the broader canvas against which the more detailed studies have been set.

This volume is dedicated to Professor W.F.H. (Bill) Nicolaisen, who has done so much in a lifetime of study of names to show us what we can learn from the toponymy of our countryside, and particularly what we can learn about the process of settlement of Northern, Western and Southern Scotland by those Norwegians and Danes who made the islands and dales their new homeland in a remarkable colonial movement which is one of the most enduring features of the Viking Age. It is hoped that this volume will help to further the study of Norse and Danish names which he has pioneered, and contribute towards a better understanding of the place of Scandinavian settlers in northern Britain in the early Middle Ages.

Acknowledgements are due to the many people who have been involved in the production of this volume, not least the twelve contributors who responded so positively to my initial invitation, and who have equally endured many editorial interventions in their chapters. The success of a book devoted to settlement studies rests with the quality of the cartographic illustrations and for this Harry Buglass has been responsible, and is due many thanks for his professional productions. The cost involved has been very generously met by a grant from the Marc Fitch Fund. The visual pleasure and illumination which good photography adds to a book of this kind cannot be quantified, and I am lucky to have a good photographer in the house who emerges from evenings in the dark room with offerings from his photographic record of our northern sojourns and journeys. The difficulty of acquiring good photographs for publication is only appreciated by those who have tried to acquire them, and I am very aware of my good fortune in being able to profit from my husband's hobby. As regards the colour jacket photograph I have to thank an anonymous donor for covering the costs of its printing, and indeed for many other contributions to publications in the world of northern studies. But however good the maps and photographs, their reproduction rests with the skills of the printers, and my acknowledgement of the skills of the production team at Leicester University Press is borne out by the quality of the end product. I am very proud to be associated with a second volume in their Studies in The Early History of Britain Series, and for this I would like to thank the General Editor, who as usual has been a good mentor and friend in helping this volume through the tricky procedures of editing and publishing.

Barbara E. Crawford
Dept. of Mediaeval History
University of St. Andrews

Introduction – the study of place-names

BARBARA E. CRAWFORD

A book which attempts to draw together the areas of Scandinavian settlement in North England and the many different areas of Scandinavian settlement in Scotland is blazing a new trail. It is not absolutely clear where this trail is going to lead, for the *differences* between Danish-settled territory, areas of Norwegian settlement and those localities where Gaelic influence is relevant are perhaps more important than any postulated similarities. However, between the 'pure' Danish settlement of the Danelaw of eastern England and the 'pure' Norwegian settlement in the Northern Isles of Scotland it is now appreciated that there are many diverse pockets with mixed linguistic and ethnic components – as several of the contributions to this book make quite clear. It seemed therefore an appropriate time to try and draw together the results of research work which has been pursued in many different parts of Scotland and North England, in a novel attempt to set a boundary from Dee to Humber, rather than from Solway to Tweed, which is the more usual line of demarcation.

One of the main purposes of producing this volume has been to encourage contributors to present the results of small-scale studies of toponymic evidence in conjunction with other source material in an attempt to increase our understanding of settlement on the ground. Only then 'will conclusions of a more widespread nature' about Scandinavian settlement in general be justified, as I said in *Scandinavian Scotland* (1987, 114).

Despite the need for small-scale studies of the toponymic evidence, there is at the same time a requirement to be non-parochial where the Vikings are concerned. There can be few historical subjects which require a greater need to be comprehensive – comprehensive in one's awareness of the impact of the Vikings on society in all corners of the British Isles. The great growth in Viking studies in the past twenty years has helped to raise the consciousness of all historians, archaeologists and linguists that there is a vital need to understand the evidence for the

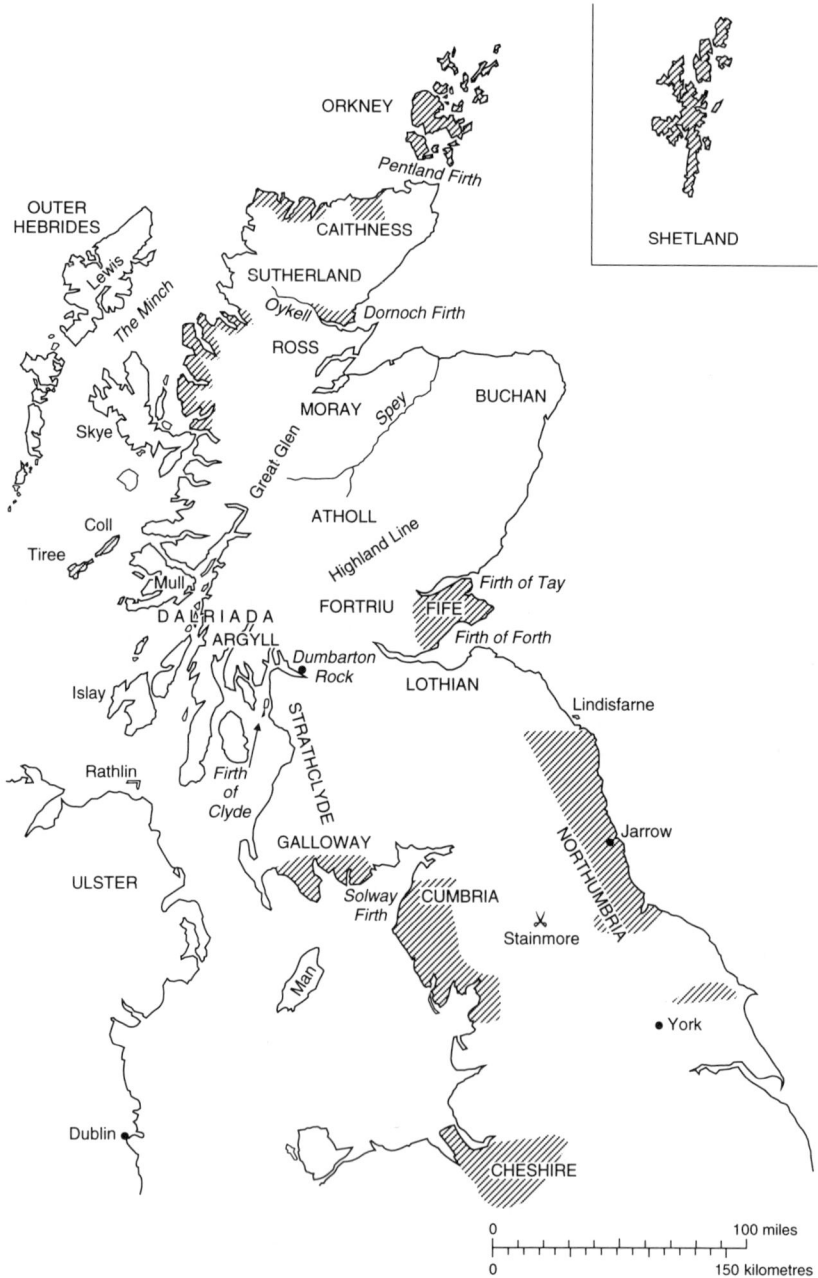

Figure 2   Scotland and north England showing areas of study (hatched).

Scandinavian presence in other areas of study (whether in Scotland, England, Ireland or Wales, as well as in the Scandinavian home-land and on the continent of Europe). In this process the regular meetings of scholars at the Viking Congresses and the publications of the papers delivered at them has helped to maintain awareness of research being pursued in so many disciplines in every country of Europe. One of the most important areas to be opened up has been the field of place-names, and there have been many studies of the Danish place-names in England which have shown how important this body of evidence is for our understanding of the impact of the Vikings on Anglo-Saxon England (for example, Fellows-Jensen 1981 and Lund 1981), although there have been far fewer concerning the Scandinavian place-names of Scotland.

The two fields of Scandinavian settlement – Norwegian and Danish – have always been treated entirely separately, for the very good reason that the nomenclature of each was rather different, being the result of distinct population movements. In England the main impact of the Danish settlement was in East Anglia, the eastern midlands (particularly Lincolnshire), and Yorkshire. As a result of the violent shake-up which resulted from the totally new assessment of the scale and extent of Danish settlement in England presented by Peter Sawyer in his book *The Age of the Vikings* in 1962, much research was focused on the village names of these areas, most notably by Kenneth Cameron and Gillian Fellows-Jensen.[1] Many settlements were studied in their geographical context, which included the underlying geology of the different localities. The process of settlement by sections of the Danish army in the late 870s is now better understood as a result of these detailed studies, as is the relationship of these Scandinavian incomers with the native Anglo-Saxon population. Gillian Fellows-Jensen's contri-bution to this volume (Chap. 10) is a retrospective assessment of her original work on the settlement of Yorkshire by Halfdan's army in 876, and the adjustments that have been made to her interpretation of that process of settlement in the years since she first studied it.

The intense debate about Scandinavian settlement in midland and northern England, and the fundamental questions raised by this debate are justification enough for including a discussion of the Danish settlement of northern England in a volume primarily con-cerned with the impact of the Scandinavian settlers in Scotland. Many of the issues raised about the nature of settlement and of integration, of the replacement of some place-names by those of a different language, of internal colonization and changing patterns of lordship, and especially of the problems of chronology, are pertinent to other areas of Scandinavian settlement, and some of these issues are raised by contributors who are focusing on areas far removed from the English Danelaw.

---

1. See Fellows-Jensen, Chap. 10 below.

Moreover the fluidity of the political situation in North Britain in the ninth and tenth centuries makes the concept of 'Scotland' quite irrelevant to the period with which most of these studies are concerned. The Scots had only moved out of their homeland in Argyll in the ninth century to make their successful takeover bid for the large and wealthy Kingdom of the Picts: a kingdom which stretched from the Forth north to the Moray Firth (with influence at times over the north Mainland and the Orkneys). The different tribal branches of the Scots moved eastwards and north-eastwards: the Cenél nGabrain into the Forth-Tay basin, and the Cenél Loairn through the Great Glen to Moray and the firthlands of Easter Ross. This move east and the Scots' remarkable success in dominating the Picts may both have been influenced by the impact of the Viking raids and settlement in the western Scottish homelands of Argyll as well as around the eastern waterways of Pictland (Broun 1994, 28–9).

South of the Forth and Clyde, the whole area of what is now southern Scotland, was at this time under the domination of the British Kings of Strathclyde, based at Dumbarton on the Clyde, and of the rulers of English Northumbria, based on a similar rock-fort at Bamburgh south of Berwick-on-Tweed. This block of territory, south of the Scotto-Pictish Kingdom and north of the Danish Kingdom of York, was therefore under the control of British and English warlords whose power fluctuated with the fortunes of war. The difficult geographical situation of this territorial region which includes the north Pennine range, the Lakeland hills and the southern Uplands was not suited to the establishment of political authority exercised by one dynasty or power centre. It was an area where Scandinavian raiders on the look-out for useful maritime bases, or even pockets of agricultural land worth exploiting, might successfully establish themselves without too much opposition from tribal leaders – who might indeed invite them to settle. It was a frontier land which Danes settled in the Kingdom of York might regard as a zone for colonial endeavour, and the place-name evidence has been interpreted as showing that they moved north-westwards through the Pennine valleys into what was in theory the Kingdom of Strathclyde (Fellows-Jensen 1985a and 1991). Some of the more 'typical' Viking element are recorded as moving south-east and seizing lands from the Community of St. Cuthbert between the Tees and Wear in the early tenth century. However, the scarcity of proven Scandinavian names north of the Tees, as shown by Victor Watts (see Chap. 13), suggests that these Irish-Norse warriors did not bring large numbers of settlers with them.

In north-west England we touch on the Celtic zone, and in all the regions bordering the Irish Sea we are in a very mixed Celtic-Scandinavian environment. The settlement of Ingimund and other Irish-Norse in the Wirral after 902 is supported by some place-name elements, and the *Ireby* names in particular are evidence for this component in Lancashire, Cheshire and Cumbria as Mary

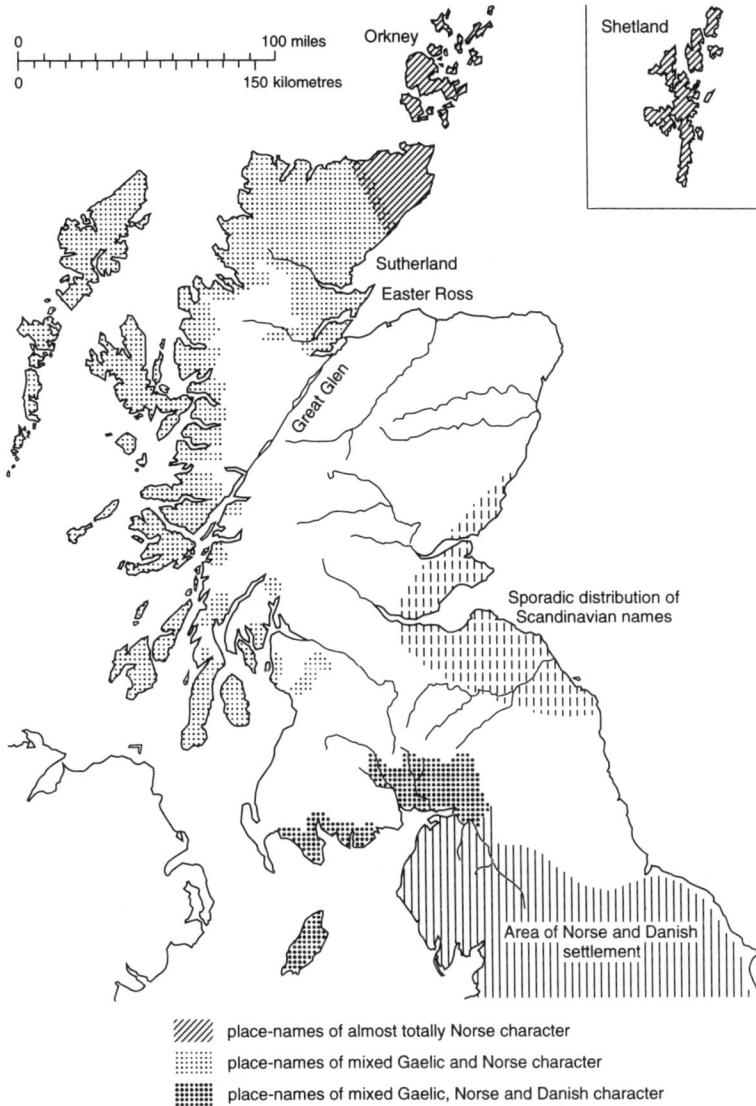

Figure 3 Areas of Scandinavian settlement in northern Britain.

Higham shows (see Chap. 12). In looking at the part of Cheshire south and east of the Wirral, Margaret Gelling (Chap. 11) suggests that a Scandinavian element in that place nomenclature may however be a result of settlement rather later than the tenth century.

This problem of dating raises an important issue regarding Scandinavian place-names in southern Scotland, and one which Bill Nicolaisen himself raised in his seminal distribution maps which were first published together in *Scottish Historical Atlas* (1975) – the *þveit, bekkr*, and *fell* names of southern Scotland. These abound in the western border counties, with *fell* names particularly thick on the ground throughout south-west Scotland. Despite the certain Scandinavian provenance of these elements, Nicolaisen argued that very few such place-names can have been given by settlers speaking a Scandinavian language, with *fell* in particular having to be regarded 'as an English dialect word borrowed from Scandinavian' (1976b, 108). They are thus evidence of a *later* move of colonists into south-west Scotland from northern England, bringing dialect words with them of Scandinavian provenance. The same is probably true of the hybrid names in *-tun*, or what are sometimes called 'Grimston' hybrids: farm-names with an English generic but a Scandinavian personal name as the first element. Nicolaisen examined such names in southern Scotland as long ago as 1967 and argued that they were 'late coinages by English speakers' (see Fellows-Jensen, below); but along with the *by* names of southern Scotland it is not clear yet exactly how late these names are, whether dating from the tenth, eleventh or twelfth century. The line of thinking would seem at present to link them with a movement north from the English Danelaw rather than south from the Norwegian settlements of north Scotland, but the very mixed societies that developed, as Simon Taylor shows in his study of the place-names of Fife (see Chap. 9), make it exceedingly difficult to pin the Scandinavian place-name elements down to any one particular century. There is some tangible evidence for such a movement in the 'hogback' monuments which are scattered throughout southern Scotland (Crawford, 1994), and which similarly span the period from the late tenth to the twelfth century.

SCANDINAVIAN STUDIES IN SCOTLAND

As the above discussion shows, there had been much thought, study and argument devoted to the study of the place-name evidence for Danish settlement in northern and eastern England, and the extension of settlement to southern Scotland by peoples who gave Danish place-names to their farms. At just about the same time as *The Age of the Vikings* was stimulating a whole research pro-gramme into Danish settlement in England, Bill Nicolaisen's seminal article 'Norse Settlement in the Northern and Western Isles – Some Place-Name Evidence' was similarly setting in train a new approach to the study of the chronology of the Norwegian place-names of Scotland (1969). This study was Bill's contribution to the Conference which had taken place in Kirkwall in 1968 to mark the five-hundredth anniversary of the pledging of the islands of Orkney to Scotland. It is conferences such as this – a previous one had been held in 1963 to mark the seven-hundredth anniversary of the Battle of Largs (*Orkney Misc.*, vol. 5), and another was held in 1987 to commemorate the eight-hundred and fiftieth anniversary of the building of St. Magnus Cathedral (Crawford, 1988) – which have done so much to help create an awareness of the Scandinavian heritage of Scotland among historians and university teachers of language and literature.

In 1969 the oil era was still over the horizon and the islands of Orkney and Shetland were little-known, far-away places, whose strong Scandinavian character was unrecognized by the majority of Scottish historians. The Western Isles were of course the last stronghold of that other ingredient of the Scottish ethnic 'cake', the Gaels, so that their Norse history was also unappreciated and their Scandinavian culture buried under centuries of Celticization. Bill Nicolaisen's article on the place-names of Scandinavian character in the Northern and the Western Isles was the first attempt to bring together these two very different parts of Scotland by focusing on several place-name elements which showed that they had both once been subject to exactly the same process of settlement by peoples of Norwegian origin.

Although there had been earlier pioneers in the study of place-names in Scotland (W.J. Watson being perhaps the most notable), publications had consisted primarily of lists giving explanations of place-name meanings or etymologies. Alexander MacBain had written on 'The Norse Element in the Topography of the Highlands and Islands' in 1893–4, and George Henderson on *The Norse Influence on Celtic Scotland* in 1910, much of which was devoted to linguistic elements. In the Northern Isles the ancient connections with Norway had never been entirely severed, and island historians and antiquarians have been well aware of the more advanced nature of place-name research in Norway which was so important for their understanding of the toponymical heritage in their own colonial Scandinavian outpost. The place-names of Norway had provided a marvellous resource record since the publication of Oluf Rygh's *Norske Gaardnavne* in eighteen volumes plus an intro-duction, between 1897 and 1936. This study of every Norwegian farm-name, with old written forms and present pronunciation as well as commentaries on the meaning, is still the main reference work for place-name research in Norway, although many other publications have followed it, particularly *Norsk Stadnamnleksikon*, edited by J. Sandnes and O. Stemshaug in 1976 (3rd edn. 1990). A brief summary of the study of place-names dating from the Viking period in Norway by Professor Per Sveaas Andersen is included below (Chap. 1), as a necessary preliminary for our understanding of the Norse toponymy of Scandinavian Scotland.[2]

Despite the hope expressed by Magnus Olsen in the introduction to his *Farms and Fanes of Ancient Norway* (1928, XII) that 'We must now expect every civilised country to give to the world its

---

2. This is reprinted from *Vikings of the West*, 1971, 1985 with permission of the author.

place-name material ... in a work paid for by grants from governments, academic institutions, or private associations', there has been little progress in Britain with the publication of the Scottish nomenclature. The Place-Name Survey of the School of Scottish Studies in the University of Edinburgh has built up an excellent archive over the years, a work which Bill Nicolaisen himself furthered when Director of the School, but the systematic publication of this material has not yet begun. The inability to acquire the basic source material makes study of the place-names of Scotland so much more difficult than equivalent work in those parts of England where the English Place-Name Society has published its lists and interpretations of names in county volumes. The difference in this respect (of obtaining access to the place-name record of the Norse-settled areas of Scotland) is reflected in the Scottish essays of this volume, where the authors have all had to acquire the earliest forms of names through their own researches.

The complexity of the linguistic patterns of Scotland's past is of course a main reason why the place-names have not been systematically studied. The breadth of the erudition of Watson's *The History of the Celtic Place-Names of Scotland* (1926) has not yet been matched, and he was also fully conversant with the Scandinavian place-names of the north which he covers admirably in his *The Place-Names of Ross and Cromarty* (1904). In the spanning of both Celtic and Germanic languages, Bill Nicolaisen is Watson's heir. But he has gone much further, and particularly in his study of the farm-name elements of the Scandinavian settlers he established a model which has been very closely followed by other researchers in the field of Viking studies; this is because his analysis sets out a chronology of these elements which gives insight into the pattern and growth of Scandinavian settlement in the Northern and Western Isles. The idea of a chronology of Scandinavian names was not new; both Rygh and Olsen had 'introduced important principles of chronological and social classification' into the study of farm names (Andersen, below, p. 17). This classification covered a much longer time-span than was relevant to the student of Scandinavian place-names in Scotland, for these only arrived here with the Viking Age. But the principles were adopted and applied to Orkney by Hugh Marwick, the teacher who studied the farm-names of Orkney with the personal knowledge that is essential for a correct understanding of the meaning of place-names in the landscape. He learned from Norwegian place-name scholars what the significance was of the different categories of names and particularly of those *habitative* names which signified a place of habitation or a farm established by Norse speakers. The *kvi, setr, land, gardr, bólstaðr, staðir, skali, bu, býr* endings (or *generics*, as they are known) all meant something special to the name-givers, although we struggle to understand exactly what that significance was; as a broad generality we can translate them as 'farm' although we must never forget that they all had shades of meaning. William

Thomson's chapter (Chap. 3) examines some of these meanings within the Orkney context, and shows the need for sensitivity in the translation of such terms.

Marwick limited his studies to Orkney, and published many papers on the names of different localities or islands, as well as his invaluable reference work *Orkney Farm-Names* (1952). He worked within an area which had its own geographical coherence, as well as its own political coherence, for most of the Viking period – once the earldom of Orkney had come into existence in the late ninth century. Bill Nicolaisen was bold enough to take Marwick's scheme and apply it outside the Orkney microcosm – to Shetland, Caithness and the North Mainland of Scotland and to the Western Isles – and within that wider geographical zone to establish his model of Norse settlement chronology. That model used three of Marwick's elements only, *setr, bólstaðr, staðir*, with the addition of *dalr*, a topographical name meaning 'valley' – 'in order', as he said, 'to gain some kind of perspective' (1969, 9). Immediately, a system which had been studied in a particular geographical and socio-economic location was made to stretch to archipelagos of very different kinds and, in the case of the Hebrides, to a world where the Celtic language had totally dominated the Norse speech of the Viking settlers and altered – and in some places superseded – their place-nomenclature (see Fig. 3). It was therefore risky to draw conclusions about this whole area, where a bi-lingual situation had subtly altered the Norse place-names and created a rather different basal pattern from that of the Orkneys. Nonetheless these same Norse generics were there in the landscape, sometimes unrecognizable except to the initiated (the *bólstaðr* element in particular suffering many changes through usage by Celtic speakers), but usable for someone like Nicolaisen who understood the linguistic changes that had taken place.

The distribution maps of the four names *staðir, setr, bólstaðr*, and *dalr* which resulted from his plotting of these elements throughout the Scandinavianized parts of Scotland became justly famous, and have been reprinted many times.[3] They have formed the stimulus to a lot of further research into the impact of the Vikings on Scotland, and particularly into their place in the cultural legacy of the Gaelic-speaking parts of Scotland. They have therefore served a very important purpose, which is to increase our understanding of the complexity of the settlement process, the expansion of the settlements established by Norse speakers, and the limitations of

---

3. His article 'Norse Settlement in the Northern and Western Isles – Some Place-Name Evidence' (Nicolaisen 1969, 6–17) was included virtually unchanged in Chap. 6 of his *Scottish Place-Names* (1976); the same material is included in the section and maps on 'Scandinavian place-names', in *An Historical Atlas of Scotland*, eds P. MacNeill and R. Nicholson (1975) and was re-used in 'The Viking Settlement of Scotland: the evidence of place-names' in *The Vikings*, ed. R.T. Farrell (1982), 95–115.

that settlement in the Gaelic west. But there are some respects in which these maps are now recognized to be somewhat misleading as a record of the total extent of Norse settlement in the Scottish islands: in the first place they are drawn from the 1" OS maps and are therefore by no means a comprehensive record of all place-names, or even settlement names. The more work that is being done, in the Western Isles in particular, the more it is realized that many Norse farm-names have passed out of the regular nomen-clature of a Gaelic-speaking population and may survive only in names of nearby natural features, such as hills or bays. Or they can be found by searching historical records and older maps; they are certainly not all to be found on the OS 1" maps. Second, these elements are, of course, only a selection of Norse farm-names, and were chosen for their particular suitability; and Nicolaisen justified his selection on grounds of permanence and the problems associated with other elements. So, for these reasons the topographical names are totally omitted (except for *dalr*), with the result that some very early and important farms are missing from the overall pattern, for it is now fully realized that some of the first settlements established were named after a dominant natural feature (Crawford 1987, 111).

Third, the conclusions drawn from the spatial pattern of the four elements have been queried by several commentators. Nicolaisen's 'theory of chronological sequence' argued that the most limited of the distributions of the place-name elements − the *staðir* farm-name − indicated that it was the earliest name to be used by Viking settlers, and that the widest distribution − that of *bólstaðr* − must be the latest. Questions have been asked of this system, such as, 'Do we have to assume expansion to be constant? . . . is it possible that the elements may refer to different types of settlement and therefore not be successive but contemporary?' (Morris 1985, 231). From wider evidence in the North Atlantic it was pointed out that *staðir* farms were still being created in the late ninth century and that the element was therefore in use after the date assigned to it in Nicolaisen's scheme (Fellows-Jensen 1984, 158). Further, the evidence of the *staðir* names in the Isle of Man, which were not included in these distribution maps, shows that it was in fact more widespread as a name in the Western Isles than was allowed (Crawford 1987, 108); therefore the conclusions drawn from the apparently restricted distribution of the *staðir* names were invalid. As regards the whole sequence, it has been suggested that the *setr* and *staðir* names should represent 'subsequent peasant consoli-dation' within the area delimited by the *bólstaðr* names and where there was room for expansion of population (Thomson 1987, 32). It was the recognition of infilling of colonized areas which was perhaps not sufficiently allowed for in the original scheme.

There remains still the problem of the topographical names which all are agreed were used for some of the earliest and most important farms, but which are very difficult to represent on a small-scale map; and such a map would never be a proper representation of

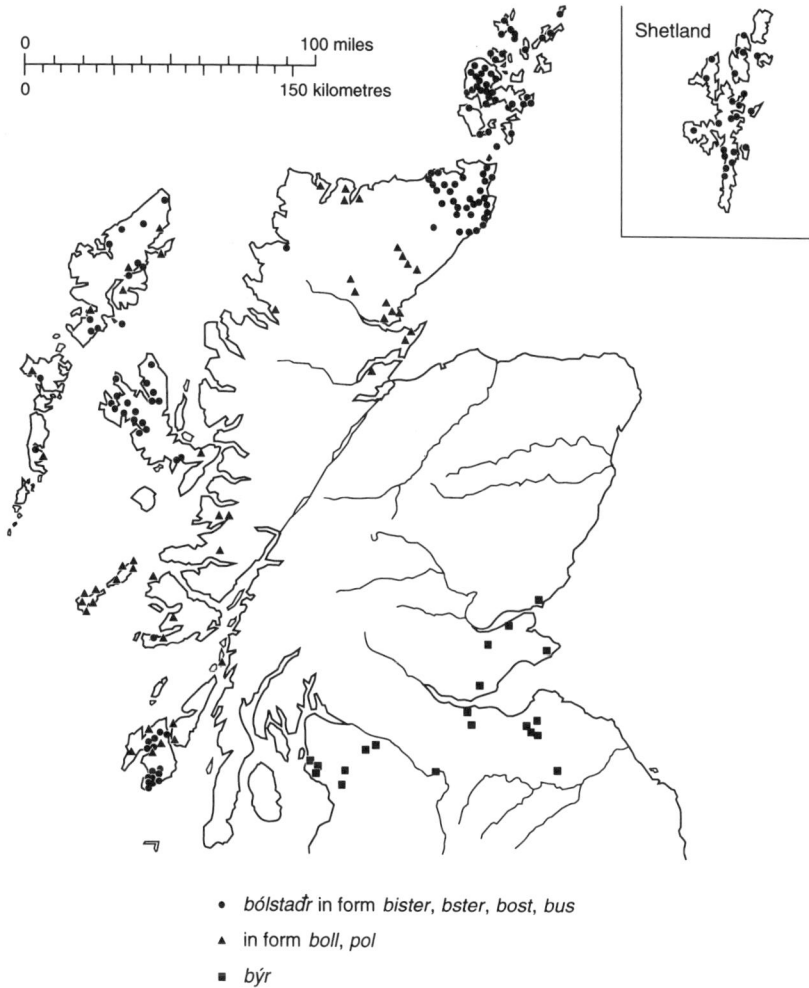

- • *bólstaðr* in form *bister, bster, bost, bus*
- ▲ in form *boll, pol*
- ■ *býr*

Figure 4 *Bólstaðr* and *býr* in central, north and west Scotland. (Adapted from Fig. 27 *Scandinavian Scotland* by Barbara E. Crawford, Leicester, 1987)

these early settlements as in many cases topographical names gave way at a later date to the habitative type, as the settlement expanded, and the original settlement name was superseded. Many of these points were later acknowledged by Nicolaisen in his article 'Place-Name Maps – How Reliable are They?', where he admits that he had not heeded his own warning that such a sequence of place-name maps should not be pressed for information which they cannot give (1989, 265).

In this more recent article the question of the topographical name is raised again: it is crucial for understanding the extent of

Scandinavian settlement down the west coast of the Scottish mainland. The statement in Nicolaisen's original article that the distribution map of *dalr* was not a map of permanent Norse settlement 'but rather of a sphere of Norse influence' was one of the most controversial conclusions which he drew from his analysis. His maps showed up the lack of habitative names, for there are very few true habitative names in this coastal zone, and the *dalr* names were therefore understood by him to indicate something other than true Norse settlement. (See Figs 3 and 4 for contrast.) This meant, in effect, that the Vikings' control of territory was limited to the islands except for a few pockets on the west mainland. Historians were thus deprived of a shaded littoral to add to their maps of Scandinavian Scotland – a limitation which was hard to accept by those who like to see Scandinavian influence on the increase, not decrease! In his original analysis Nicolaisen suggested that the *dalr* zone might be where the Norse carried out seasonal exploits like hunting, fishing and summer grazing, as well as military raids and friendly visits. In his more recent discussion he maintains his argument, although more guardedly, that the absence of habitative – particularly *bólstaðr* – names reflects, 'on the whole, less permanency of occupation, or at least a very different attitude towards the land' (1989, 266). As regards permanency it is undoubtedly true to say that a Norse-speaking population was not in control along the west coastal zone for as long as in the islands. It may be that settlement was curtailed because of the survival of the native Celtic-speaking population, or that the initial land-taking was never sufficiently firmly established for later generations to divide farms and give habitative names to the various portions. 'A very different attitude towards the land' may suggest some form of exploitation other than arable farming, the opportunities for which are very limited along wide stretches of the west mainland (but see Fraser Chap. 6). Hunting, fishing, and summer grazing are possible activities; so is timber-felling, a vitally important resource for the Vikings which has been rarely – if ever – mentioned as a very basic necessity in their Scottish colonies. The requirements which the Vikings had for oak and pine for the building and repair of their ships would have been very well served among the natural oak and pine forests of western Scotland, virtually absent as they were from the treeless Scottish islands.[4] These are all the factors relevant to the Norse economy which may have a bearing on the question of the nature of the west coast settlement and which need greater thought. First and foremost must be the collection and linguistic analysis of the *dalr* names themselves. Only once that has been

4. This factor is discussed in relation to the Norse settlement of Easter Ross in the forthcoming publication of my lecture to the Groam House Museum, Rosemarkie; *Earl and Mormaer: Norse-Pictish Relationships in Northern Scotland.*

done will historians have a better appreciation of the extent and nature of Scandinavian control of western Scotland. In this respect, as with his initial study of the habitative names, Bill Nicolaisen has set out the nature of the problem, provided the questions and set us thinking. Scottish historians and linguists can perhaps use the analysis which has been applied to the settlement of Danish colonists in England and see whether it can help to elucidate the circumstances of Norwegian settlement in Scotland.

The collection of the linguistic data is only the first step towards a better historical understanding of the Scandinavian settlement of Scotland. The major research which then has to be pursued is to place the names in their topographical context and to study their location within the human geographical environment. This was the way that Marwick worked, and his method is being followed and refined in Orkney by William Thomson and in Shetland by Brian Smith (see Chaps 2 and 3). Without the resources of a research team, such work is best done in small-scale studies, in an island or related group of islands, such as Anne Johnston's examination of the Hebridean islands of Coll and Tiree (see Chap. 7); or a geographically-defined location which probably underlies later medieval administrative or ecclesiastical units, as with Doreen Waugh's study of Reay parish on the north coast of Caithness, (see Chap. 4). It requires a familiarity with the landscape and an understanding of agricultural requirements which is not easy to acquire for those not born or living in the localities, and this approach has been followed admirably by Margaret Gelling in her book *Place-Names in the Landscape* (1984). In writing about the remote coastal areas of Durness and Wester Ross on the north-west extremities of the British mainland, Ian Fraser (Chap. 6) has the inestimable advantage of having a command of the Gaelic language acquired during his upbringing in the locality, as well as a familiarity with the terrain. Only close local knowledge can give the insight which enables the nature of a name to be fully understood in its environment, and the relationship of names with natural and man-made features to be correlated correctly, with the risk of mistakes minimized. A good geographical sense is vital, something not possessed by all historians or linguists and which Malcolm Bangor-Jones has from his specialized knowledge of the later historical geography of Sutherland, the south-east portion of which he examines in Chapter 5. There must be good cross-disciplinary relationships between researchers, and one of the aims of this book is to bring together the work of scholars trained in different disciplines, and to show that very interesting research has been carried out in many different locations in the past two decades. These studies are taking the question of Scandinavian settlement in Scotland onto a new plane, and linked with the work of place-name scholars in northern England they will help us to gain a better perception of the contribution made by Danish and Norwegian Vikings to early medieval society in northern Britain.

Plate 1 The limited nature of the cultivable land available in parts of western Norway is dramatically illustrated by this farm in south Møre, with its hay-fields squeezed between the edge of the fjord and the steep scree slopes above. (Copyright: R.M.M. Crawford)

The western fjords of Norway form one of the most magnificent stretches of European coastal scenery, and still today would be recognizable to the Vikings of the ninth century in a way that few other parts of the European countryside would. They form the backdrop to the maritime adventure and give some physical reality to the achievement of those sea-rovers who moved to and fro across the North Sea between Norway and Scotland. But, however much this scenery adds to our appreciation of the dramatic quality of the Viking achievement, it provided poor returns to those who farmed the steep slopes and thin soils of the settlements clinging to the fjord-sides and at the gravel outwash of the glacier rivers (see Plate 1). The comparative ease of raiding the monasteries of the Christian church which lay, exposed and defenceless, just a few days sailing away around the shores of the British Isles must have provided returns that years of farming the fjord-side settlements would never have provided. This basic economic situation lies behind the bleak entries in the Annals of Ulster:

795. Devastation of Iona of Columcille, and of Inishmurray and of Inishboffin.

798. Patrick's Island was burned by the gentiles; and they took away tribute from the provinces, and Dochonna's shrine was broken by them, and other great incursions were made by them, both in Ireland and Scotland

(ES I, 256–7)

These are the only facts of the new Viking phenomenon thought worthy of recording by contemporaries in Ireland or Scotland; the pagan state of the raiders was of more significance than where they came from or where they were going to. We assume that by this date raiding bases, which eventually led to permanent settlement, had been established in the islands; these provided highly convenient springboards for the launching of raiding and trading exploits around north-west Europe. But the historical record,[1] and even saga literature,[2] is very uninformative about the process of conquest of the islands, of the establishment of raiding bases, or of the development of permanent colonial communities. The archaeological record is also scattered, often poorly recorded and in some cases not fully published,[3] although the graves which have been found in the Northern and Western Isles, and which are unmistakably Viking from the artefacts buried with the dead, provide tangible evidence of the movement of men, women and children from their Norwegian homeland to new homes across the North Sea. The looted products of the raids on the wealthy monasteries of the Irish and Pictish churches are found in the graves of these pagans, both in the islands and back home: they clearly treasured the beautiful objects which had once adorned the altars and shrines of the holy places in the islands west-over-sea. The easy acquisition of this wealth must have ameliorated the economic situation of the Scandinavian raiders, and their control of the seaways gave them the power to dominate the native communities of the islands around the Scottish coasts – to stamp their culture on the social structures as well as their place-names on the landscape.

1. See Crawford (1987, 3–4) for consideration of the documentary sources for the Vikings in Scotland, most of which are conveniently edited and translated in Anderson's *Early Sources* (ES). Smyth assesses the Viking impact in his study of Dark Age Scotland (1984, Chap. 5).
2. Extracts from the sagas relevant to Scotland are incorporated in Anderson's *Early Sources* (ES); see Crawford (1987, 7–9) for an assessment of the value of saga information in relation to the Vikings in Scotland.
3. See Crawford (1987, 4–5) for a discussion of the archaeological evidence in general, and chaps 5 and 6 for the settlement and grave evidence. See also Ritchie, 1993.

1 The Norwegian background

PER SVEAAS ANDERSEN

It has been a main question in earlier Norwegian (and Scandinavian) research whether the Viking expansion overseas was due to overpopulation at home. The explanations given had more or less the character of guesswork, and quite naturally so. The sagas and skaldic poems were insufficient sources for estimating the growth of population during the Viking age and the preceding centuries. Between the two World Wars and especially after 1945 the study of the Viking period has gradually attracted a considerable body of scholars from the fields of archaeology, place-name studies and history, and their interest is not directed towards the sagas and the skaldic poems in the first place, but towards quantitative material such as farm-names and archaeological finds. Local historians have been able to give more penetrating accounts of the local prehistoric and Viking development of a region, partly by a recording of all the settlement names in their topographical situation and partly by distributing these names, and especially farm-names, among such chronological periods as the *Roman period* (first four centuries AD), the *Migration period* (400–600), the *Merovingian period* (600–800), the *Viking Age*, and the *Christian Middle Ages*. Then the results of these investigations are compared with recorded archaeological finds from the same region. The correlation between these two groups of source material may, as a rule, give some indication of the population development and expansion or contraction of settlement in the locality in question.

On the basis of recent farm-name research in Norway it is permissible to propound as a thesis that Norway had a growing population in the Merovingian and Viking periods. We are interested in the causes of this growth and shall return to it below. But contemporary with the population growth there seems to have been constantly expanding commerce between Norway (Scandinavia) and Europe. At the same time a brisk local trade was going on between the interior districts and the coastal areas.

The interior expansion in Norway therefore has two important aspects: a population growth with a resulting extension of the settled area, and an increase in domestic and foreign trade with such evident results as the formation of the first known markets and town-type centres at different places along the coast and in the interior. How did these two activities affect the Viking expeditions to the west?

Whereas Swedish and some Danish scholars studying the Viking period have been mainly concerned with the commercial expansion of Scandinavia, Norwegian historians have turned their attention chiefly to the problems of expanding settlement and overpopulation. This interest seems to have its roots in a strong Norwegian tradition of place-name research going back to the mid-nineteenth-century. The pioneers of the study of Norwegian place-names, P.A. Munch, Olaf Rygh and Magnus Olsen, introduced important principles of chronological and social classification of *farm-names*.

In giving a brief survey of classes of farm-names according to the system formulated primarily by Rygh and Olsen, we shall be concerned especially with compound names ending in *-vin, -heimr, -land, setr, býr (-boer)* and *staðir*. In addition to these there is a big group of farm-names consisting of monosyllabic words taken from physical features like *nes, as, aker* (i.e. naze, hill, field). According to Rygh and Olsen, farm-names from this group may be the oldest, possibly going back to the centuries before Christ's nativity – to the Celtic Iron Age or even to the Bronze Age. The next group with names ending in *-vin* and *-heimr* may be dated back to the Roman period (defined above). During the Migration period new groups of compound names became popular in namegiving: *-land* and *-setr* names. Finally we may mention three groups of farm-names which occur with marked frequency during the Merovingian and Viking periods, viz. those ending in *-staðir, -býr(-boer), -bólstaðr* and *-þveit*.

In the modern study of the growth of settlement in Norway during the Viking age it is primarily the *-staðir* group of farm-names, with supporting archaeological material, which forms the basis for a general assumption that there was a considerable expansion of settlement and growth of population. The historian usually distinguishes between *-staðir* names with a first element which is either obscure or connected with topography (such as *Blesa-staðir, Flagarstaðir,* and *Bliustaðir*) and compounds in which the first element is a personal name (as for instance, *Rolfstaðir, Herleifstaðir* and *Ulfstaðir*). It is also usual to associate the latter group with the Viking period, while the former is regarded as older. In quite recent place-name research, however, new views have been propounded as to the absolute and relative chronology of the farm-names. Scholars have become more hesitant in ascribing the different farm-name groups to definite periods. With regard to the *-staðir* group it is a tendency to look upon a proportion of the compounds, among others those with rare personal names, as pre-Viking.

In the region of Trøndelag it is quite safe to assume, on the basis of recent research, that most of the *-staðir* farms were settled during the Merovingian period. In the Viking period the less numerous *-setr* names predominated there. In the Sognefjord area we find a similar development during these two periods. But as full studies of the farm-name material in this region are lacking, we can only base this assumption on a general impression of the *-staðir* and *-setre* farms as being relatively old dwellings from the pre-Viking period.

A great many *-land* and *-boer* farms may also be dated to the Merovingian period, although the majority of the *-land* farms were evidently taken up in the Migration period, while the great mass of *-boer* or *-býr* farms seems to have been settled in the Viking Age.

The chief method employed in dating the *-staðir* farm-names as well as the other groups is archaeological, although the topographical approach which takes into account the situation and position of a farm in relation to the other farms of a certain district is just as essential. It goes without saying, however, that a student of farm-names feels rather reassured when he is able to date a certain farm by grave finds from the holding. But an archaeological find cannot automatically be connected with the farm where the find has been made: the question always arises as to whether the find belonged to the same farm in the prehistoric periods. A few cautious conclusions may perhaps be drawn from recent farm-name research. On the basis of farm-name and archaeological material it must be correct to say that a strong growth of population and expansion of settlement began in the region of Trøndelag, parts of western Norway (especially the Møre, Sognefjord and Rogaland areas), and in south-eastern Norway at the beginning of the eighth century. It probably reached a climax towards the end of the century. Then *c.* AD 900 there seems to have been a temporary contraction of settlement in Norway and possibly also a decline of population.

How shall we explain this course of events? One method of exploring it may be, or rather should be, to see the development of settlement in relation to the Norse expansion overseas. Do we find the same farm-name groups in such settlements as Orkney and Iceland? And if so, is there any correlation between the farm-names of the same classes?

In Orkney 23 *-staðir* names have been identified, 26 *-boer* names, 50 *-bólstaðr* names, 35 *-land* names, and 25 *-setr* names; in Iceland the corresponding figures are 1165 *-staðir* farms, 174 *-boer* farms, 11 *-bólstaðr* farms, 77 *-land* farms, whereas no old *-setr* names are found. It is unimportant in this connection to go into the moot question of the social stratification of the various name-groups. It must be sufficient to say that the majority of the *-land* and *-setr* farms of Norway are considered secondary in relation to the *-staðir*, *-vin* and *-heimr* farms. It is fairly certain that the *-setr* farms in

north-western Norway, Trøndelag, and the upper parts of Gud-
brandsdalen, Valdres, Hallingdal and Hedmark, and a great many
of the *-land* farms of south-western Norway reflect a settlement
extension farther into the hinterland and also towards the outer
coastal area. These farms, mostly on marginal land and much
exposed to crop failure, would soon be deserted when better
opportunities became available. The propitious time came in the
ninth century.

The first waves of Viking emigration from Norway must
undoubtedly be seen as an overpopulation phenomenon in the *-land*
and *-setr* regions: i.e. primarily in the fjord regions of north-western
and south-western Norway, where tillable soil and pasture land
were scarce. The settlement of Orkney and Shetland, as the later
settlement of Iceland, should therefore be looked upon as a
continuation of a settlement movement which had begun inside
Norway in the Merovingian period.

We have established population growth as one of the social forces
explaining the Viking expeditions to the west. But why did this
expansion overseas occur precisely in the ninth and tenth centuries?
It is quite evident that population growth by itself only gives part of
the background. A highly significant question is: how did the
Norsemen go out? We know that they sailed to their new homes in
quite large ships, capable of holding a fair number of men, domestic
animals and personal equipment. It does not matter whether we
call the ships of the emigrants 'knorrs' or longships, but it is
essential to bear in mind two important factors about the 'Viking
ship': it was technically on a high level, and it was quite expensive
to build. Who had the technical know-how to construct such a ship;[1]
and above all, who had the means for fitting it out? Continued
research on the Viking ship and on Norwegian commerce with other
parts of Europe may throw further light on the background of the
Norse expeditions to the west.

There is a long ship-building tradition behind the Viking ships of
the ninth century. We can well understand this when we look at the
Oseberg, Tune and Gokstad ships, now in the Viking Ship Museum
at Bygdøy, Oslo. Here it is possible to observe the technical improvements in ship-building within a relatively short period by
comparing the Oseberg ship built at the beginning of the ninth
century with the Gokstad ship dating from more than 50 years
later. The general impression we get of the latter is that it is more
solidly constructed, as may easily be seen in many details. The keel
of the Gokstad ship has a pointed transverse section, and it is cut
out in one piece from a choice, straight-grown oak. The same is the
case with the Oseberg ship except that its keel does not protrude so
much from the hull. Another detail worth noting is the gunwale. It

---

1. The reader interested in Viking ship-building should consult T. Sjovold: *The
   Vikings Ships* (Oslo 1954), or A.E. Christensen: *Boats of the North* (Oslo 1968).

Plate 2 This photo of the excavation of a Viking boat burial at Scar, Sanday, Orkney shows how half of the boat had been destroyed by erosion. Very little wood had survived, but the rivets have been marked by pegs and the structure and dimensions of the boat can be satisfactorily reconstructed. (see Fig. 5). This was a small vessel and could only have been used in coastal waters, but it had probably been brought over from Norway by the Viking settlers who were buried within it in the ninth century. The group comprised a mature male, an old woman and a child of ten, whose possessions had been buried with them, many of which survived the erosion to be excavated. (Owen and Dalland, 1994.) (Copyright: Historic Scotland)

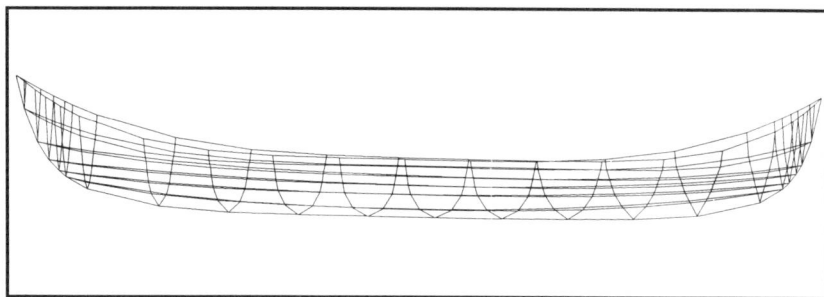

Figure 5 Reconstruction of the boat excavated at Scar, Orkney. (Reconstruction drawing by Anne Allen.) *Dimensions*: length 7.15m; height from stem to keel 1.06m; depth amidships 0.45m; beam 1.60m

is higher above the water level in the Gokstad than in the Oseberg ship. But both these ships are definitely superior to their predecessors of the eighth and seventh centuries: for instance the Kvalsund ship of north-western Norway and the bigger Nydam ship of south Jutland. Unlike the Viking ships, these older vessels have no real keel. Finally we should mention the most important innovation of all: the mast, sail and rigging. In this special field, however, the historian is faced with considerable problems as no sails and very little of the rigging of the Viking ships have been preserved. Nevertheless it is probably in the sailing ability of the Viking ship that we find one of the main clues to the large-scale maritime invasion of western Europe and the North Atlantic islands. Another important asset of these ships is their shallow draught. The Gokstad ship, for instance, draws only 33.5 inches. Although modern historians hesitate to connect any of the three excavated ships with certain historical individuals in Norwegian history, there can be no doubt as to the place and rank in society of the persons buried in them. The ship-mounds of Gokstad, Tune and Oseberg have been constructed over members of royal or chieftain families.

To what extent did *trade* in general contribute to the prosperity of Norway in the Viking period, and in particular to the economic resources of the shipbuilding aristocracy?

We have already dealt with such sources as the sagas, Ottar's account, and the merchant and market laws, all of which substantiate the existence of Norwegian domestic and foreign trade during the Viking age. We have also accepted the *coin material* as an indication of trade. In the final pages of this chapter we shall return to this important group of sources and consider the Norwegian coin material in its Scandinavian and European context, mapping the chronological trends in the circulation of coins.

The late Danish historian Aksel E. Christensen has given the following approximate figure of Viking-age coins found in Scandinavia (1969, 196):

Sweden: 100,000 Arabic or Kufic coins, 60,000 of which have been
found in Gotland
35,000 Anglo-Saxon coins (25,000 in Gotland)
75,000 German coins (40,000 in Gotland)
420 Byzantine coins (400 in Gotland)

Denmark: 4,000 Kufic coins, 800 of which have been found in
Bornholm
4,000 Anglo-Saxon coins (3,600 in Bornholm)
9,000 German coins (500 in Bornholm)
46 Byzantine coins (13 in Bornholm)

125,000 of Sweden's foreign coins and 5,000 of Denmark's have been
found in the relatively isolated islands of Gotland and Bornholm.

If we turn now to the *Norwegian material* we find that the coin
groups are composed as follows: 400 Kufic, 3,000 Anglo-Saxon, 3,500
German and 26 Byzantine coins. The important question then is:
What can the dates of the coins and the dates of the deposits tell us
about the direction of the flow of coins and about the chronological
trends in the material? In Norway it is quite evident that the Kufic
coins predominate in the period anterior to 950, while the Anglo-
Saxon and German coins have almost a complete monopoly between
950 and 1050. Then at the end of the Viking period the national
coinage begins in Norway and the other Scandinavian countries,
excluding foreign coins from circulation.

In order to decide the importance of the Oriental silver to the
trade of the ninth century, it is also necessary to establish the
chronological composition of the ninth- and tenth-century hoards
and finds, both as to dates of issue of the coins and the dates of
laying down the deposits. We then get a fairly simple picture for
Norway. About two-thirds of the Kufic coins found in Norway were
issued by the Samanid dynasty of Transoxania in Central Asia
between 895 and 925. A similar concentration is to be found in
Sweden and Denmark. In Norway most of the remaining one-third,
however, belong to earlier issues by the Abbasids of Baghdad. The
greater part of the deposits were made during the eleventh century,
especially its first half. Thus the flow of Kufic coins was streaming
westward in the ninth century, starting like a brook, expanding into
a river in the late ninth and the very early tenth century, then
drying up in the middle of that century. It was followed by a stream
of Anglo-Saxon and German coins in the opposite direction. Trade
and war accompanied the diffusion of the Kufic coins in Europe
from the Russian plains through Scandinavia to the British Isles
(where 135 Kufic coins have so far been found, mostly within the
Norse sphere of influence). War, Christianization, and the
unification of Norway followed in the wake of the Anglo-Saxon
pennies.

It does not seem possible at the present stage of research to
decide which of these main causes of the Viking expeditions from

Norway is the more important. And we should not forget other explanatory elements in the general background, such as improvements in iron and steel production, which possibly converted it into an industry taking place in certain mountain areas of southern Norway at almost every farm; a political unrest in Norway at the end of the ninth and the first half of the tenth centuries, causing a certain emigration to Iceland and other islands in the west; an expanding domestic trade, feeding the coastal markets with the commodities of the hinterland; the Viking greed for booty, causing scores of young men to join their chieftains in daring raids against western Europe; the spirit of adventure, probably nourished by the preference for death in battle rather than in bed – an important element in the old pagan religion; and the weakened royal and princely authority in some states of western Europe plus the non-existent authority of the state in parts of eastern Europe.

In his book *Ancient Emigrants* (1929), the Norwegian archaeologist A.W. Brøgger emphasized two important aspects of the Norse Viking expansion: the exodus as a drain on the population of Norway and the unparalleled cultural effort of the Norsemen during the Viking centuries. It is Brøgger's grand idea that the emigration from Norway in the Viking age might be comparable to that taking place in the nineteenth and twentieth centuries to America. In the course of a century, 800,000 persons emigrated out of a population which in 1825 counted one million and in 1929 2.8 millions. It is no doubt a realistic comparison when we take into account the territories settled by the Norsemen in the Viking period: parts of Normandy, Ireland, the Isle of Man, and north-western England, the Hebrides, Sutherland, Caithness, the Orkneys, Shetland, the Faroes, Iceland and Greenland. Of course, we do not possess any figures, either of the population in Norway in the Viking period or of the number of people in the Norse colonies in the eleventh century but, when we bear in mind the relatively dense Norse population in some of these areas (Iceland, the Orkneys, the Isle of Man), Brøgger's comparison seems tenable.

His thesis of the early Viking period as a time of cultural splendour, 'a golden age', has gained ascendancy in modern historical writing. The 'Viking achievement' is in the limelight of modern interest. And it seems as if the culture of Scandinavia, not only in the Viking centuries proper (800–1050), but also in the Middle Ages in general, has received the label 'Viking'.

It is essential to bear in mind what changes were caused by internal Norwegian development, and what were the influences from the outside world which would have had some impact on Norse society. Although Norway of the Viking age probably left an important oral literature (later to be recorded in writing), produced such monuments of ship-building technique as the Gokstad, Tune and Oseberg ships, and such social institutions as the *things*, Norway remained a barbarous country until the introduction of Christian and Latin culture. With Christianity came a certain knowledge of classical culture, of writing and of social organization based on a centralized pattern. With Christianity came a new ethical code and a new spirit, which dealt a death blow to the warlike ideals of the Vikings of the ninth and tenth centuries.

But certain ideals of the Viking Age never died and were carried on by later generations of Christianized Norsemen. One of these should not be left unmentioned:

> Wealth dies,
> kinsmen die,
> a man dies likewise himself;
> I know one thing
> that never dies,
> the verdict on each man dead.
>   (Hávamál*)

The Vikings did not settle in empty lands when they came to Orkney and Shetland. Both groups of islands provide abundant archaeological evidence of flourishing Celtic societies which had been converted to Christianity in the preceding centuries (Ritchie 1993, Chap. 2). The well-preserved brochs (of earlier date) and associated settlements (from the period preceding the Viking Age) which are visible in the landscape and appear in excavations tell of a well-organized and structured community. The historical record hints at links with the Pictish Kingdom, which the carved stones also demonstrate. The effects on this society of Viking raids and ensuing settlement is difficult to trace in the archaeological record, which does however clearly show Norse houses succeeding to native structures in the long term. The place-names give a picture of blanket replacement of the existing toponymy by Norse names and surely demonstrate the replacement of the previous culture (if not the previous population) by a new one. This linguistic evidence provides us with a model of Viking settlement and colonization apparently uninfluenced by the existing social structures – a situation quite different from the situation in the Western Isles (where the Gaelic language and population survived to a greater or lesser degree to influence the newcomers); different from the situation in Ireland (where the urban settlements were alien groupings in a Celtic land); and different from the English Danelaw

---

* Translation by P. Foote and D.M. Wilson: *The Viking Achievement*, 1970, p. 432.

(where the Danish armies settled within the framework of surviving Anglo-Saxon villages). We do not know how the original settlement of the Northern Isles was accomplished and the only reference to it comes from a later chronicle (Historia Norvegiae)[1] which believed that:

> Certain pirates, of the family of the most vigorous prince Ronald, set out with a great fleet, and crossed the Solundic sea; and stripped these races (the Picts and the Papae) of their ancient settlements, destroyed them wholly, and subdued the islands to themselves.
>
> (Trans. by Anderson, Early Sources, I, 331)

As far as the medieval Norwegian and Icelandic writers were concerned, the founding of the earldom of Orkney by the sons of Earl Ronald (Rognvald of Møre) was all that needed to be known about the origins of the Norwegian settlement of Orkney and Shetland. The role of powerful chieftains and warlords was indeed probably integral to the whole initiation of the movement overseas and the settlement of the islands in the west. The families who followed in the wake of the raiders were probably relatives and dependants of individual hersir ('warlords') from Rogaland, Jaeren and Møre – which is where Rognvald Mørejarl himself ruled.[2]

The apparent 'peasant' quality of the Norse settlement of Orkney and Shetland is an impression which results from the continuity of landholding which followed the generations of descendants of the original land-takers who farmed the rich arable lands of the Orkney islands and the lush pastures of Shetland; they gave their names to the ensuing farm-divisions and subdivisions. As is stressed by both the writers on Shetland and Orkney in Chapters 2 and 3, the settlement names of the islands were laid down throughout the Middle Ages and beyond, and are witness to the long-term success of the initial colonial venture of the ninth century.

1. See consideration of this source and what it says about Picts and Papae in Crawford (1987), 3, 34, 56, 166, 168, 211.
2. Archaeological evidence points also towards close connections with more northern parts of the Norwegian west coast.

2 Scandinavian place-names in Shetland with a study of the district of Whiteness*

BRIAN SMITH

> Though Shakespeare asks us, what's in a name
> (As if cognomens were much the same),
> There's really a very great scope in it.
>> Thomas Hood, 'Miss Kilmansegg and
>> her precious leg' (1840)

INTRODUCTION

Shetland, colonized from Norway – so comprehensively that not one name used by the colonizers' predecessors can be proved to have survived – is full of Scandinavian place-names. 'In names', John Stewart wrote in 1965, 'Shetland is in fact a province of Norway' (1987, 36).

Scholars of place-names should aim to do more than collect names (or celebrate the 'nation' which coined them). They should attempt to reconstruct, or at least probe into, the societies where the names came to life. Jakob Jakobsen's work (1936) on Shetland place-names (constructed around Old Norse nouns), and to some extent Stewart's, which resembles Jakobsen's, have a more restricted purpose. They merely assembled evidence to show that Shetland names were paralleled by names in Norway: that Shetland names, in Stewart's phrase, were a provincial shadow of those in the motherland. But what we need, as Magnus Olsen urged in 1931, is 'the systematic working-out of [Shetland's] place-name

---

* I am grateful to Alistair and Florence Grains for information about Hoove, and for a guided tour of Unaberries and environs; to Barbara Crawford for helping me to clarify my ideas; to Val Turner for information concerning the castle of Strom; and to George Jacobson for details concerning the Brig of Baccasetter in Dunrossness.

material in its geographical order' – 'from the standpoint of settlement history' (1931–2, 138n.).

Before this project is even remotely feasible, scholars have to find the names – and that is more problematic than it sounds. There is a difference in availability between hill- and shore-names, usually not recorded before the arrival of the Ordnance Survey's sappers in the late 1870s, and farm-names of all kinds, sometimes available in relatively old forms (but even then almost always after the Reformation). In most areas there is a dearth of names. There are two places in Shetland – the large townships of Funzie in the island of Fetlar, and Laxobigging, in North Delting – where an inspired land surveyor of the 1820s recorded and mapped hundreds of names, probably the bulk of names then known there, at the tail-end of those townships' existence *qua* townships. In these cases, for all I know the most numerously named places in the Scandinavian west, we have material for detailed reconstructions of the township economies – at least in their later forms – and their histories. But such cases are rare.

Even at Funzie and Laxobigging it would be rash indeed to assume that the names of 1820 are the names of the Scandinavian settlement. A moment's thought will show that they are the result of a thousand years' settlement, and may or may not reflect change and crisis in their local society during that period. But attempts to plot the change are fraught with danger – and the task, in the last analysis, probably impossible.

A glance at the hill- and shore-names on the Ordnance Survey maps of Shetland proves the point even more spectacularly. Many names on these maps look 'modern'. They are names which could well have been bestowed during the past few hundred years or so: Muckle Leog, Da Waari Geo, Tansie Knowes, and so on. Often they incorporate words from the modern Shetland dialect. It is no use blaming the Ordnance Survey for 'corrupting' these names. The meticulously-kept name books of the survey show that, more often than not, male Shetlanders themselves – close neighbours of the places in question – were the sources of the names and their spellings. Another tack, employed by Jakobsen and more recently by Stewart, is to argue that the modern names are literal translations of Old Norse originals which linger tantalizingly in the background. This argument fails to give credit to the ingenuity of modern Shetlanders in naming their own localities. The Jakobsen-Stewart thesis might lead us to suppose that Clickhimin Loch, outside Lerwick, is a translation of an (inexplicable) Old Norse name with *vatn* attached to it – until we notice that 'Clickemin' is an inn-name common on the Scottish mainland, and that the loch in question was known as the Picts' Loch, after the famous broch there, in the early eighteenth century. The scholars might go on to suggest that Picts' Loch was a translation of something like *péttavatn*, but I think the point is made.

From the 1920s onwards the Orcadian scholar Hugh Marwick, using (as Jakobsen had not been able to do) the copious material in Oluf Rygh's *Norske Gaardnavne* (1897–1936), formulated a theory about the chronology of and relationship between farm-names in Orkney. His work has been enormously influential. Marwick deployed fifteenth-century and later documents (and his unrivalled knowledge of the islands' topography), to outline how the (Scandinavian) settlement of the islands had developed in its earlier stages. We can criticize Marwick's tendency to exaggerate the age of the settlements (see W.P.L. Thomson, Chap. 3 this volume), and disciples have sometimes used his methods in an over-schematic way. However, Marwick's contribution is crucial and, as an account of township morphology in a northern community, unsurpassed (and, to date, relatively undeveloped).

There is very little in Shetland farm-name studies to contradict Marwick's schema. (And, as can be seen from Nicolaisen's work, all the four elements *staðir, setr, bolstaðr* and *dalr* are well represented in Shetland – in fact so well represented that *-setr* and *-dalr* names swamp his maps.) There are few Shetland names ending in -by, from ON *boer* or *býr*. Marwick regarded -by farms as seminal and prestigious; when they do appear in Shetland, however, they are often poverty-stricken and late. (William Balfour wrote of Touby in Weisdale that it was 'the worst [farm] in Shetland' [Shetland Archives, Hay & Co. papers].) On the other hand, there is some evidence that the forms of Shetland farm-names we possess may date from a period of reformed taxation, around 1300, a time when original -by farms may have been split up (and the original names discarded). The other main difference between Shetland names and those in Orkney is the way that Shetland's numerous 'setter' farms (ON s[a]etr) replace Orkney 'quoy' farms (ON *kví*).

In this paper I consider the small Shetland district of Whiteness (see Fig. 6), at first sight an unpromising case for place-name studies. In Whiteness we can see the principles hinted at above – negative and positive – in practice. Whiteness is an area which saw rapid, although not ruthless, 'modernization' in the nineteenth century, and has seen depopulation and population change in the twentieth century. As a result, records of Whiteness names are relatively meagre. There is no trace, in documents or folk memory, of more than a few field-names in Whiteness, which is surprising because there are, as we shall see, large farms in the parish. Records of hill- and shore-names are, by and large, confined to the Ordnance Survey map. In the following, therefore, I concentrate on farm-names. In doing so I keep Marwick's schema in mind, but use documentary, topographical and oral material – and some imagination – to suggest that things may not always have been as they seem today.

N

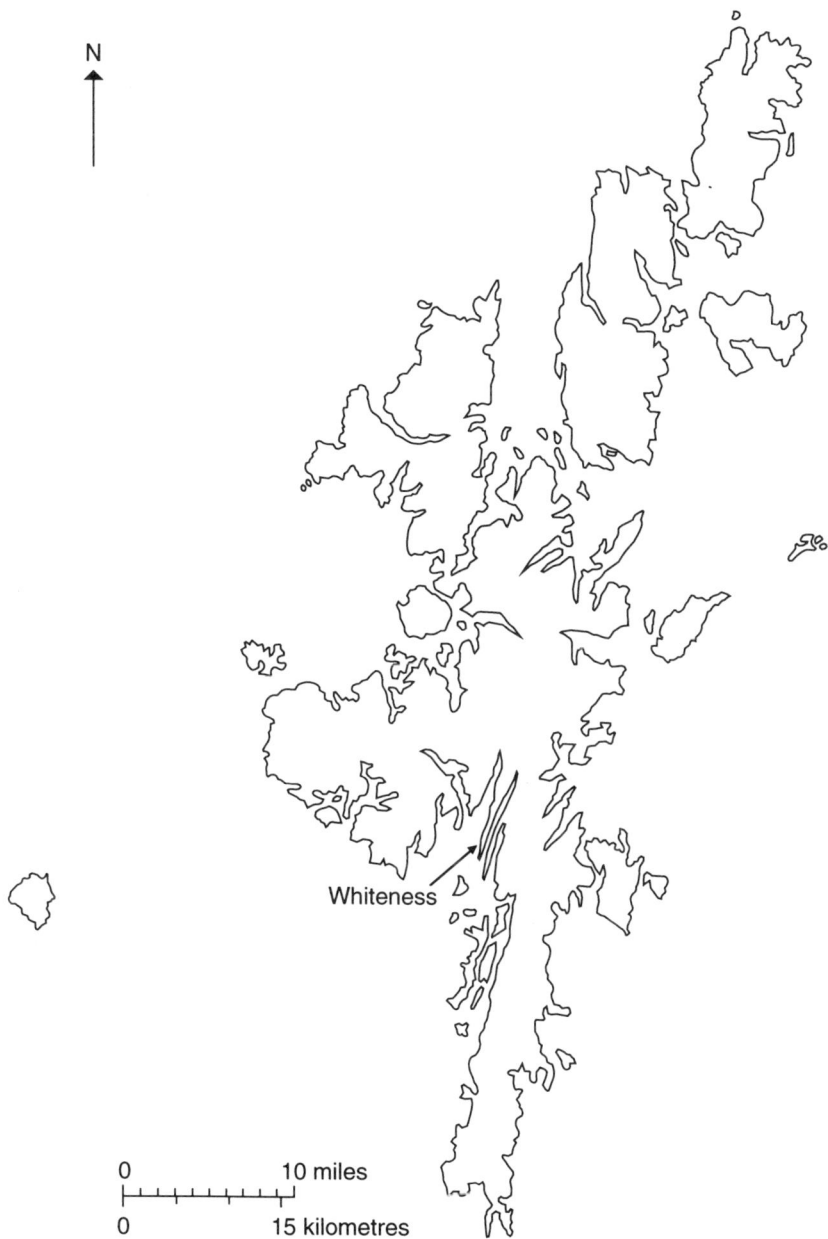

Whiteness

0   10 miles

0   15 kilometres

Figure 6   Shetland, showing location of Whiteness.

WHITENESS AND STROM

Whiteness is the southern part of the post-Reformation parish of
Whiteness and Weisdale. The modern district of Whiteness is
divided into two parts: North Whiteness and South Whiteness.
These divisions do not appear in documents until the late nineteenth century, when they were made the basis for divisions of
commonty, and there is no knowing how old they are. As will
be seen from the map (Fig. 7), North Whiteness and South
Whiteness are parallel – running NE–SW – with each other: both
terminate on the south in a substantial ness or promontory. The
district, especially its southern part, is fertile. As William Balfour
wrote in the 1770s, 'the grounds . . . are of small extent, but for
goodness of soil and rich pasture, superior to any in Shetland,
part of the island of Fetlar excepted' (Shetland Archives, Hay &
Co. papers).

Whiteness as a whole is a land of nesses. The district takes its
own name from the longest of these promontories, which is
presumably so-called because it looks 'white' or fertile from a
vantage point on the east side of the district, several hundred feet
above. Whiteness itself terminates in Ustaness, the 'outmost ness';
nearby are Stromness, the 'stream ness', and Binnaness, perhaps
named after a man Beini (cf. Beinnes in Nordre Bergenhus in
Norway, spelled 'i Beinanese' in 1340 [Rygh 1919, 493]). The
northernmost arable part of the farm of Strom (of which much more
later), jutting into the loch of Strom, is called Quoyness, from *kví*,
'enclosure'. There is even a bizarre case of a farm on a hilltop, a
quarter of a mile from the sea, called Breckness.[1]

Inland the farm-names of Whiteness pose few problems, at least
with regard to etymology. There are no forms of these names
extant earlier than *c.* 1500. This is normal for Shetland. Our source
of that date is a text entitled 'The skat of Yetland', a copy made
about 1540 of an older original (SRO, GD.1/366/1). As its title
suggests, it is a list of scats or taxes exigible from named taxable
lands in Shetland (or rather from the Mainland and its adjacent
isles), and also of rents collected from royal estates. Unfortunately,
it is an extremely poor copy. The copyist, who apologizes for his
lack of knowledge of the 'strange leid and termis' in the original,
distorts many of the farm-names out of recognition, and we have to
turn to later, similar documents to find out precisely what he
meant to render.

These sixteenth-century and later documents show that the farms
of Whiteness, like farms elsewhere in Shetland, were grouped

---

1. The name does not appear in documents earlier than the nineteenth century. I
   suspect this is the farm originally called Dossabrek, a name now not known in
   the parish (perhaps from *dysjar*, referring to cairns in the vicinity: cf. Dysjeland
   in Norway, spelled Døsseland in 1608 [Rygh 1919, 299]).

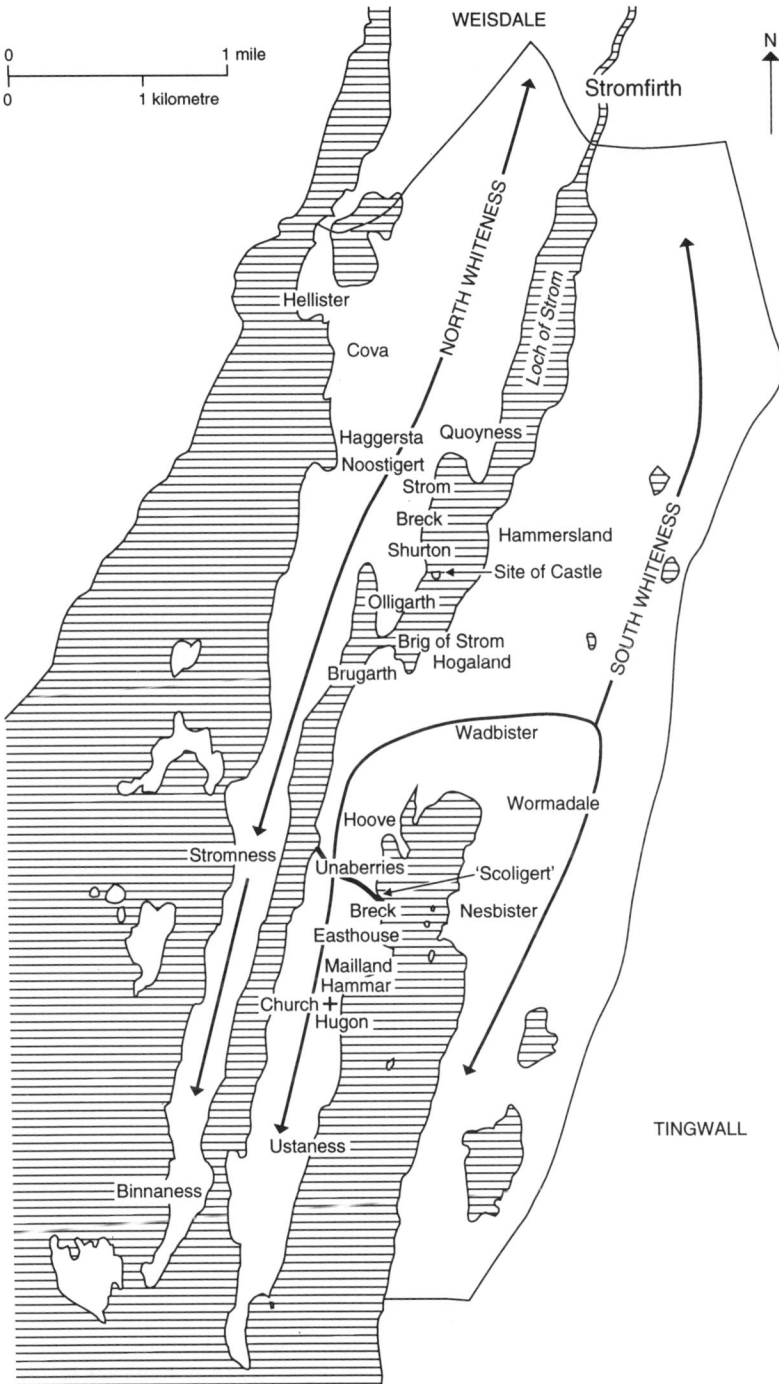

Figure 7 Whiteness, with places mentioned in the text.

together in scat-paying districts, as follows, with the number of 'pennies' of cloth scat that each paid.[2]

> **Strom** (including Quoyness, Breck, Shurton, Olligarth and perhaps Unaberries): 72
> **Haggersta and Hellister** (and Cova): 24
> **Wormadale, Nesbister and Stromness** (and perhaps Binnaness): 24
> **Ustaness**: 72
> **Midstrand** (comprising Hugon, Hammer, Mailland, Easthouse, Breck): 72
> **Hoove**: 72
> **Hogaland, Hammersland and Wadbister** (and perhaps Brugarth): 40

These district-names and farm-names, all of them clearly very old, do not contradict Marwick's famous hierarchical schema; in some ways they are a remarkable confirmation of it in a tiny area. (Note, however, that there are few s[a]etr names in Whiteness, suggesting that the original settlement had been so comprehensive that there was not much room for expansion.) Many of the names are from topographical features: nes itself; strandr, a 'strand'; haugr, 'mound' or 'cairn'; brekkr, 'slope'; hamarr, a 'rocky outcrop' on a hillside; straumr, 'stream'; berg, a 'rock'; and dalr, 'dale'. We also have bólstaðr, staðir, s[a]etr, land, garðr, hús and tún, words meaning 'farm', 'enclosure', 'house', etc. There is nothing unusual about the farm-names of Whiteness, other than the appearance of such a comprehensive collection in a small area.

What is problematical is the districts themselves: the snapshot they provide of settlement in Whiteness. These districts look primordial. Shetlanders have assumed that they are ancient settlements of, presumably, free peasants, proudly separate from each other, whose inhabitants 'scatted' together (as 'scat-brethren': these concepts are invariably patriarchal) and pastured their animals in common, from time immemorial. Just as Orkney historians like Marwick considered that rentals from the late

---

2. The sources for these lists are: (1) the *c.* 1500 document already discussed; (2) a rental of Shetland written down *c.* 1640 (SRO, E.41/7); (3) Thomas Gifford's rental of Shetland of 1716–17 (SRO, RH.9/15/176); and (4) a valuation roll of Shetland of 1825 (Shetland Archives, CO.1/3/1). The names in bold are the scat-paying districts, listed in *c.* 1500 and *c.* 1640; additional names are taken from the rental of 1716–17 and the valuation roll of 1825. The spellings of all names are the modern spellings, which in most cases are a fairly accurate reflection of present-date pronunciation (except in the cases of Unaberries [pronounced 'Winnabers'], and Hugon [pronounced something like 'Heon']). All these farms paid scat in 1716–17, with the possible exception of Binnaness, and can be assumed to be early. (Binnaness appears as inhabited in a document of 1602 [Donaldson 1954, 118].) A 'penny' of cloth-scat in Shetland was half a Shetland ell, or about a foot of cloth.

fifteenth and sixteenth centuries recorded the layout of settlement in the ninth century, Shetlanders assume, rather more vaguely, that our 'townships' and their relationships with each other are old and 'Norse'.

There is another, more technical danger in the Marwick proposals. If we take it for granted that the 'districts' delimited in late early–modern taxation lists are original, this has implications for the way we read the development of settlement. Thus Hellister, a late s[a]etr, is an offshoot of the 'parent' farm Haggersta, an earlier staðir. Haggersta becomes an original settlement, or at least an early moment in the process of settlement. Some archaeologists and historians have taken this argument to grotesque conclusions by drawing schemas of individual small settlements which develop inexorably, in an almost biological way, from original nucleus to larger complexity – but still isolated from their neighbours. These highly theoretical diagrams automatically prevent us from reconstructing larger settlements, more extensive and complex in origin, and different from the tiny peasant idylls of the theoreticians.

This is not to say that there were no isolated settlements – far from it (although none, to the best of my knowledge, developed in precisely the way proposed by the 'biologists'). But we should pause before we assume that such settlements were universal. An historical monument in North Whiteness which may make us pause is the little castle in the loch of Strom, perched on a holm and attached by an impressive causeway to the 'mainland'.[3] Small as it is, it seems to emerge from a different kind of society from the peasant idyll just described. Little or nothing has been written about the castle of Strom; there is no tradition concerning it in Whiteness, and archaeologists have been chary about commenting on it. A Royal Commission leaflet concerning Scalloway Castle suggests that Earl Patrick Stewart (*fl.* 1600) lived there. There can be little doubt, however, that the building is a typical, albeit tiny, castle of the high or late Middle Ages. There are cognate, more elaborate versions in Orkney (personal communication, Dr Raymond Lamb). When we encounter a building like this we should at least contemplate the existence of an estate rather than a township. The importance of the castle in the ancient landscape can be gauged from the fact that its name frequently appears in documents as 'Stroholm' or 'Strotholm', suggesting a folk-etymology where the holm was regarded as the most important feature of the landscape there.

---

3. The ruins are about 18ft × 21ft, with walls about 4ft thick; at the north-west corner these walls are about 10ft high. The holm seems to have been enclosed by a wall. Access to it is often possible via the causeway. What is mysterious is the precise *purpose* of a building on such a strange site. W. Douglas Simpson remarked that 'no medieval site in Shetland would better repay investigation' (1954, 176).

Plate 3 Whiteness, Shetland (looking south). Strom lies in the foreground, the remains of the castle are visible on the holm in the loch near the (modern) church of Shurton. Stromness and Binnaness are on the far right of the picture and Hoove and the old church of Whiteness (St. Ola's) lie on the south side of the Loch of Strom in the centre of the picture. (Photo taken by Jack Peterson in the autumn of 1935.) (Copyright: Shetland Museum and Library)

The oldest forms of the name, however, are Strom (1510, *REO*, 84) and Strome (1539 [Low 1879, 208]). Strom is from ON *straumr*, a 'stream' (Rygh *passim*). The stream in question is probably the large one at the north end of the loch of Strom, now invariably called 'Da Burn'. (Or perhaps it may be the tidal 'stream' of water at the brig of Strom: a similar feature seems to be the origin of the name at Stromness in Orkney, Strome Ferry in Wester Ross and Streymoy in Faroe [ed.].) Strom is not a common name in the north, presumably because of a lack of large streams; according to Stewart the only example in Orkney is Stromness. The only instances in Shetland are the series of names in and just outside Whiteness: Strom itself, a large farm, two miles south of the stream which gives it its name; Stromness, a long promontory with a small farm about a mile to the south, and the oddly named Stromfirth,[4] right

---

4. I am inclined to think that Stromfirth is so called because the loch has been regarded as a 'firth'.

at the north end of the large loch of Strom, beside the putative *straumr* itself. These names suggest an old Strom estate, centred on the castle (or with a castle later built at the centre). It is notable that the *straumr*-names cover the whole of North Whiteness, and indeed breach its boundaries at the north: Stromfirth is actually part of the adjacent district of Weisdale.[5]

Where do we look for more clues about this putative estate? In the absence of older documents or archaeological material, we must concentrate on names. Next to Strom lies the farm of Haggersta, perhaps – since *staðir*-names normally derive from a personal name – called after someone called Hallgeir or Hallgerðr (Stewart 1987, 256), or Haki (cf. Rygh viii, 43). By the sixteenth century, Haggersta and Hellister were a snug pair of townships which paid scat together, with a small croft, Cova – apparently derived from *kofi*, a chamber (cf. Koven in Søndre Bergenshus Amt in Norway [Rygh xi, 85]), in between. In later years satellite crofts appeared at the shore and on the hills below Haggersta: the tiny farm of Noostigarth, for instance, and Moor of Haggersta. Other sources, however, suggest that the nomenclature of this area is rather more complex. Noostigarth appears in various sources as the Airs of Strom[6] – named after the 'ayre' or small beach there – and Moor of Haggersta features as Moors of Strom in the 1871 and 1881 censuses. In other words, the relationship of these (apparently separate) communities with Strom seems to be closer than might be imagined. This seems to be confirmed by the fact that the ness where some of these crofts are situated is referred to as the 'Ness of Haggersta and Stroholm' in 1827 (Shetland Archives SC.12/6/1827/77).

It is worth looking more closely at the farm of Strom itself, and trying to establish precisely where its own boundaries lay. Its constituent parts were, as stated above, Strom itself, lying just east of Haggersta, and Quoyness, Breck, Shurton and Olligarth – all south of Strom. The whole township was valued at 72 merks of land;[7] it was thus a relatively large Shetland farm. The division of the merks of land among these parts seems to have taken place at a relatively late date, because the resultant quotas look 'artificial': Strom 'proper' 28, Shurton 15, Quoyness 8, Olligarth 6, Breck 12. The allocations for Strom itself and Shurton do not conform to the normal Shetland duodecimal kind of allocation. In addition, as will be apparent, they add up to 69 rather than 72. When the

---

5. If my argument is correct, the 'scat-paying district' in Weisdale which contains Stromfirth – presumably for geographical convenience – must have been created *later* than the Strom estate.

6. A gold ring with a talismanic inscription, perhaps from the fourteenth century, was found on the beach at Noostigarth sometime before 1914 (Maxwell 1957–8, 193–4).

7. All old Shetland farms were valued in merks of land. The valuation, first referred to in a document of 1299, was of arable land (a merk of land was about an acre), and facilitated division, allocation, sale and inheritance of property.

Commissioners of Supply of Shetland drew up their great valuation roll in 1825 (Shetland Archives CO.1/3/1) they cast around for the missing 3 merks of land, and concluded that they were at Unaberries. Unaberries – pronounced 'Winnabers' by those who remember it – did indeed consist of 3 merks of land, but it was about a mile south of Strom. It is a tiny croft whose ruins are still visible on a steep, rocky outcrop just opposite Stromness, on the east shore of Stromness voe. In later years Unaberries was considered part of Hoove (see below) but in our scenario it seems – like Stromness, its neighbour across the water – to have been part of an early Strom estate. From place-name evidence we seem to have constructed an old settlement, with its castle (contemporary or later), which incorporated more or less the whole of North Whiteness – and, as stated above, part of the adjacent district of Weisdale.

What we have, then, may well be a much larger original settlement in this area than sixteenth-century documents would lead us to believe. Instead of micro-settlements splitting up into more complex ones, we have a large estate with individual farms planted throughout it – and that original estate subsequently fragmented into its component parts.

This situation, unexpected in Shetland, is not entirely unparalleled (and there might be further examples, if we had the documents or wit to see them). There is a similar situation at Broo in Dunrossness, a large farm which was the home of the chief magistrate of the islands in the 1560s. That name indicates a bridge (ON *brú* – as in Brugarth in Whiteness, and Brouster and Brouland in Sandsting, at the modern Brig o' Waas), but it is not clear at first sight where the bridge is. It turns out to be more than a mile north of the farm, amidst entirely different farms, and had actually given its name to a large district. In 1700 the baillie court of the parish appointed two men 'to be informers of cursing, swearing etc. within the parochen of Dunrosenes within the bridge': i.e., as appears from the context, within an extensive area incorporating most of the south half of the parish. The bridge in question is the land-bridge between the lochs of Spiggie and Broo – people in the vicinity still say that they are going to shoot ducks 'at da Brig'. The situation at Strom in north Whiteness, where we have a district far bigger than the modern farm, is similar.

TOWNSHIP IN SOUTH WHITENESS

It would be unwise, however, to stop our investigation there, or to imagine that the castle of Strom and its associated place-names have provided us with a comprehensive theory of Shetland settlement. Strom was clearly important in olden times, although we have no idea who owned it, or built a castle there. It was still important in the early sixteenth century, when the parish 'lawrightman' lived there (*Orkney Recs.*, 86). In 1525 the archdeacon of Shetland bought a chunk of Strom, and later still Edward Sinclair, chief magistrate of Shetland (and probably a relative of the archdeacon) had his Shetland seat there (Smith 1989, 101–2). The 'second mansion' of the Sinclairs of Brough was there in 1608 (Ballantyne and Smith 1994, no. 467). But there were other spheres of influence in the district, in South Whiteness, and very different kinds of settlement. Place-names, used tentatively, may help us investigate these as well.

There were two scat-paying districts in the territory adjacent to Strom: Hogaland, Hammersland and Wadbister, with Brugarth attached, and Wormadale and Nesbister. Even these districts have faint connexions with Strom. Brugarth takes its name from the bridge (*brú*), of Strom, a hoary construction, mentioned in a document of 1603 (Donaldson 1954, 91). Wormadaill and Nesbister paid scat together with Stromness – a surprising situation, since Stromness is separated from the other two townships by a mile of land and water.

On the other hand, the townships in the long promontory of Whiteness – Hoove, Midstrand and Ustaness – fall into an entirely different category. These are the townships that make up the district now commonly known as South Whiteness. As in the case of Strom we know nothing about these districts prior to 1500. On the other hand two of them, Hoove and Ustaness, were important estates, in different ways, in the sixteenth century.

The name Hoove derives from the ON *hof*, which originally meant a heathen temple, although it eventually meant simply a farm. There are few *hof* farms in Shetland: the only other examples in Shetland which appear in older documents are Howff in Skerries – now lost – and another Hoove, just north of Whiteness, in Weisdale. Hoove in Whiteness was a large farm, valued at 48 merks of land; the soil, said Balfour in the 1770s, was 'exceeding good, so that there are few if any so good lands in Shetland'.[8] It was the home of Magnus of Hoove, a member of the Shetland assize in the late sixteenth century, and later of his son Paul Manson, baillie of Whiteness and Weisdale in the early 1600s. Magnus had an impressive establishment at Hoove: a document of 1577 describes his prestigious 'lugeing' there, with houses grouped around a courtyard (Balfour 1859, 79–80). One historian conjectured from this description that Magnus's 'lugeing' must have resembled 'a Norse chieftain's house of the tenth century' (*Orkney Recs.*, lxvii).

Perhaps the most telling piece of information about the township and its history, however, concerns its name – or rather names.

---

8. In the modern period Hoove successfully encroached on the lands of Wadbister, to the north. Balfour remarked in the 1770s that Wadbister was 'entered in the rentals as a distinct town, but in fact [was] one and the same toun, and the lands lying runrig with those of Hoove'. In 1808 the runrig of Wadbister was divided with that of Hoove.

When the runrig of Hoove was divided, in 1808, the surveyors drew a massive boundary dyke on their map, delineating the southern boundary of the settlement. This structure was obviously impressive, and is still visible; it was so notable in 1808 that the cartographers preserved its name: Scoligerth (Shetland Archives, SC.12/6/1808/59). This name, not now remembered, irresistibly suggests Old Norse *skáli*, used in Orkney (and no doubt Shetland) of imposing halls, and thought to date from the first centuries of Scandinavian settlement of the islands.

No document concerning Hoove mentions a *skáli* farm-name, or any other farm-name except Hoove itself and Northerhouse; but people in the township today speak fluently of Norderhoose, Sudderhoose, Mews (*miðhús*, middle house), Nusterhoose, and, right at the middle of the township, Skollen. Obviously Skollen, whose site is now a hen-house, was in origin something far more imposing. Thomson argues (1987, 33) that *skáli*-houses may have been public meeting-places, at a relatively early date, rather than farms – something, he suggests, like a *hof*. It is thus fascinating to find a *skáli* right at the centre of a *hof*-farm. Thomson's theory is intriguing but, in the present case, if we consider the dyke-name, I think we simply have a pair of alternative names for the whole township: a settlement originally called Hoove, later called Skollen, which subsequently reverted to Hoove.[9] It is sobering to think that this crucial piece of information about one of Shetland's *skáli*-names appears in no known document, other than as an enigmatic dyke-name on a map of 1808. In a few decades the name of that hen-house will probably fade from local memory. Historians no less than place-name scholars should be wary about assuming that all evidence about all farm-names is enshrined in the available documents,[10] or that folk memory is infallible.

Midstrand, the district south of Skoligert, is another matter entirely. The name appears in no document prior to, or after, the seventeenth century. It is obsolete today, and has probably been so for centuries: there is now no collective name for the farms in the centre of the South Whiteness peninsula. It is difficult to look at Midstrand's constituent parts – Hugon, Hammer, Mailland, Easthouse, Breck (three topographical names, a *land*-name and one of the ubiquitous Shetland *hús*-names (as at Hoove) – and see any pattern or structure in their distribution. As Midstrand's bland positional name suggests, it is a sort of no-man's land between

---

9. Another Shetland example is Broo in Dunrossness (mentioned above). It became known as Quindista for a while, a name now forgotten.
10. Barbara Crawford warns us about names which will never 'make the place-name statistics' (1987, 111). There are several examples of Shetland *skáli*-names which do appear in documents, but infrequently, because they denote small fractions of a divided township. Two examples are Scollatoft, part of the large farm of Muness in Unst, and Uthascoll, part of the farm called Uphoose at the Biggins in Papa Stour.

Plate 4 This iron axe-head of Viking type was found in 1938 in the graveyard of St. Ola's Church, Whiteness, along with some bones, in a stone-lined grave (RCAHMS, Twelfth report, vol. iii. Inventory of Shetland, no. 1527). It dates from the second half of the ninth or early tenth century (Petersen type E), and appears to be from a pagan burial within a Christian cemetery (Crawford 1987, 163). As it is the only evidence for a male pagan burial in Shetland it is extremely important, although the significance of such burials in churchyards is not fully understood. (Acknowledgement for information to Steffen Stumman Hansen.) (Copyright: Shetland Museum and Library)

Hoove and Ustaness. Place-name studies cannot reconstruct the relationship, if any, between an area like this and its neighbours, or any other settlement; nor can historical research, if the documents are absent, or archaeology. Having said that, we come up against the uncomfortable fact that the pre-reformation kirk of Whiteness – St Ola's – was in this district, just south of Hammer. No doubt the boundaries between the scat-paying districts of South Whiteness were more fluid when that church was first established, and a pre-Norse date for the kirkyard would seem to be indicated by the discovery of a Viking axe there (see Plate 4) (Crawford 1987, 163–4).[11]

Our last Whiteness settlement is Ustaness, another 72-merk township, right at the end of South Whiteness. Here we have a different kind of establishment from Hoove. In *c.* 1500 someone called Effe was responsible for (and had withheld) most of the scat of the township. We do not know who Effe was; perhaps (although there is not a scrap of evidence for this) she was Euphemia Sinclair, sister of David Sinclair of Sumburgh, the probable compiler of the *c.* 1500 scat book. Certainly Ustaness later became the main seat of a key member of the Sinclair family in Shetland: William Sinclair of Ustaness, who flourished in the late sixteenth and early seventeenth centuries. Once again, however, the place-names tell us nothing about the township's original relationship (if any) with its neighbours – or, of course, about other possessions that its owners may have had elsewhere.

I warned that my putative Strom estate does not amount to a new theory of Shetland settlement. It may well be that, in the cases of Hoove and Ustaness, and the townships which make up 'Midstrand', the traditional theory about Orkney and Shetland farm-names is apposite. Perhaps these scat-paying districts were discrete settlements, planted by chieftains, or even by 'not particularly aristocratic' peasants, to use Knut Helle's epithet (1993, 13), at an earlyish date in the Scandinavian settlement of Shetland. It may be that they did develop in a predictable way – if not a biological way – within their ancient boundaries: boundaries like Scoligert, the massive dyke which separates Hoove from its neighbours to the south.

CONCLUSION

Magnus Olsen concluded his great study of *Farms and Fanes of Ancient Norway* by 'attempt[ing] to make the place-names reveal a poetry about the gods' (1928, 318). It would be unwise to attempt any such exciting experiment in Shetland toponymy. Our settlements are prosaic: the putative estates of Strom and Broo may be startling exceptions in the Shetland scheme of things. William Thomson has discovered traces of several such estates in Orkney, but there are grounds for assuming that society and polity in Viking Shetland was much less aristocratic than in Orkney.

On the other hand, it is important not to make confident assumptions about the organization of a society which are based on

---

11. That the kirk site was important appears from the fragments of carved stone discovered there. One of these includes part of a late (? tenth-century) ogam inscription, although the carving itself seems to have northern English connections (Stevenson 1981, 286–7): evidence for a very mixed cultural situation! (ed.)

documents written more than half a millennium later. And even though we have better records of farm-names than we have of any other type of name, we always have to keep in mind that this or that name, ancient as it may appear, may have replaced another at an early date. We may be seeing that in the case of Hoove/Skollen. The farm-names recorded in *c.* 1500, just as much as rig-names, are the product of many hundreds of years of settlement, and even the most conservative society can break out in exotic ways from time to time. We need to keep an eye open for exceptions.

3 Orkney farm-names: a re-assessment of their chronology

WILLIAM P.L. THOMSON

It is now over sixty years since Hugh Marwick first published his 'chronology' of Orkney farm-names (Marwick 1930/1). It proved to be a fruitful scheme, much used to shed light on Norse settlement in Orkney, and it also provided the starting point for W.F.H. Nicolaisen's wider study of Scandinavian naming. However, even in his *Orkney Farm-names* (1952) which set out his chronology in its final form, Marwick described it as 'a rough blazing of the trail . . . subject to amendment or correction in the light of later research' (Marwick 1952, 227). Yet his chronology has been remarkably durable and, despite studies which have suggested various amendments and sometimes expressed a certain unease at the whole concept of a chronology (Wainwright 1962; Nicolaisen 1976 and 1989, Fellows-Jensen 1984; Crawford 1987, Waugh 1991), it has proved difficult to undertake a revision. As F.T. Wainwright remarked, the chronology was based on a familiarity with Orkney's topography and history, and so people who lacked Marwick's local knowledge had largely to take his conclusions on trust (Wainwright 1962, 139). It may therefore be timely to take a fresh look at the chronology from an Orcadian perspective, and to do so with the aid of case studies which provide concrete examples of how names were actually used.

Between 1922 and 1927 Marwick contributed a series of 'Antiquarian Notes' for the newly formed Orkney Antiquarian Society of which he was secretary (Marwick 1922/3a, 1922/3b, 1923/4, 1924/5, 1926/7). These papers are a rich hotchpotch of place-names, saga, folk-lore, history and archaeology. Already Marwick was combining place-names with the kind of material needed to put them into their context. In the last of the series, his 'Antiquarian Notes on Stronsay' (1926/7), he went a stage farther. He identified four large settlement-units associated with *boer*-names (Everbay, Housebay, the Bay and Erraby) which he described as 'great

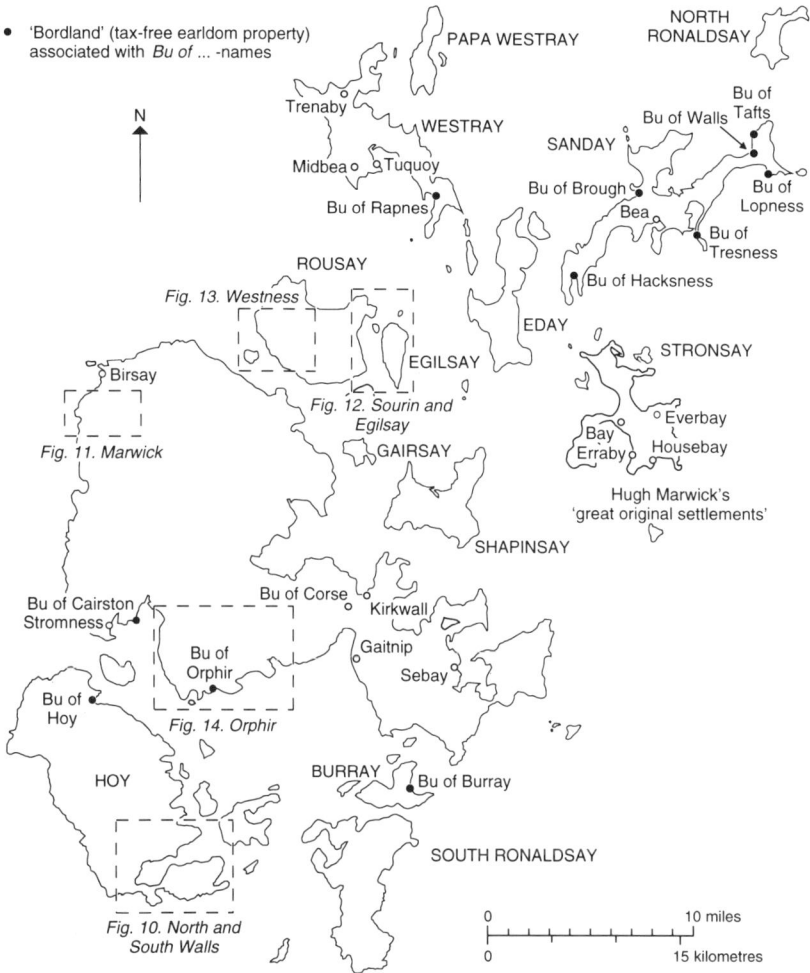

Figure 8 Orkney, showing areas of local studies.

original settlements', and he discussed similar places in other islands. In some cases these *'boers'* had been 'replaced and overlaid', and were now preserved only in vestigial names such as 'the Noust of Erraby' (the boat-place of the beach *boer*). Marwick looked at farms with *bólstaðr*-names, now identifiable by their *bister*-termination (Grobister, Kirbister), and he showed how in relation to the *boers*, they were 'secondary and derivative'. Implicit was the idea that they were secondary in two ways – in geographical location and in chronological sequence.

The appearance of Magnus Olsen's *Farms and Fanes of Ancient Norway* (1928) and A.W. Brøgger's *Ancient Emigrants* (1929) encouraged Marwick in the idea that a fuller chronology might be

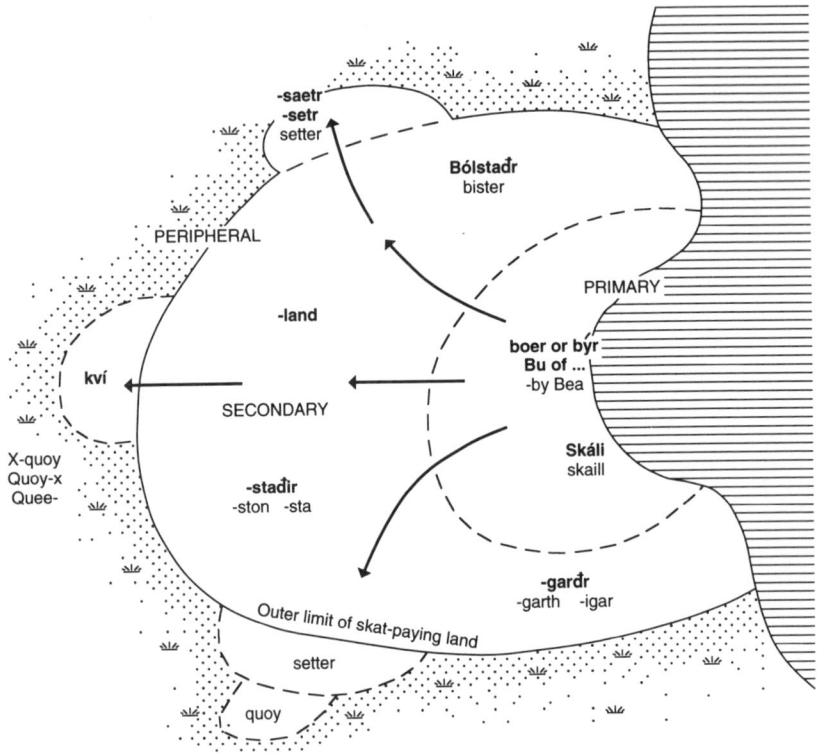

Figure 9   Marwick's 'Chronology' of Settlement. (After Bailey 1971, 76)

discovered, although he disagreed with most of the actual details of Brøgger's scheme, particularly the proposition that *setr*-names were early, and that *land*-names represented a 'second great wave of emigration from Norway' (Brøgger 1929, 84–5). In 1931 Marwick's own ideas were set out in his key paper, 'Orkney Farm-name Studies' (Marwick 1930/1), much of which reappeared *verbatim* in the 'chronology' section of his *Orkney Farm-names* (1952). Marwick envisaged a zone of 'primary settlement' characterized by *boer*-names of the kind he had described in his Stronsay paper (Sebay, Trenaby, Bea) – these places were 'greatest in the scale of ancestral dignity'. In the same primary zone he placed *skáli*-names (Skaill, Langskaill) although he did not give them quite the status as was currently bestowed by Clouston, who believed that the skaills were the halls of the early ninth-century Viking chieftains (Clouston 1932, 14–18). In a surrounding zone of secondary settlement Marwick placed *land, garðr* and *bólstaðr*-names (Redland, Trumland; Bressigarth, Colligarth; Rennibister, Kirbister). The further class of *staðir*-names, older forms of which preserve a 'staith'-ending (Tormiston/Tormistaith, Tenston/Tenstaith, Costa/

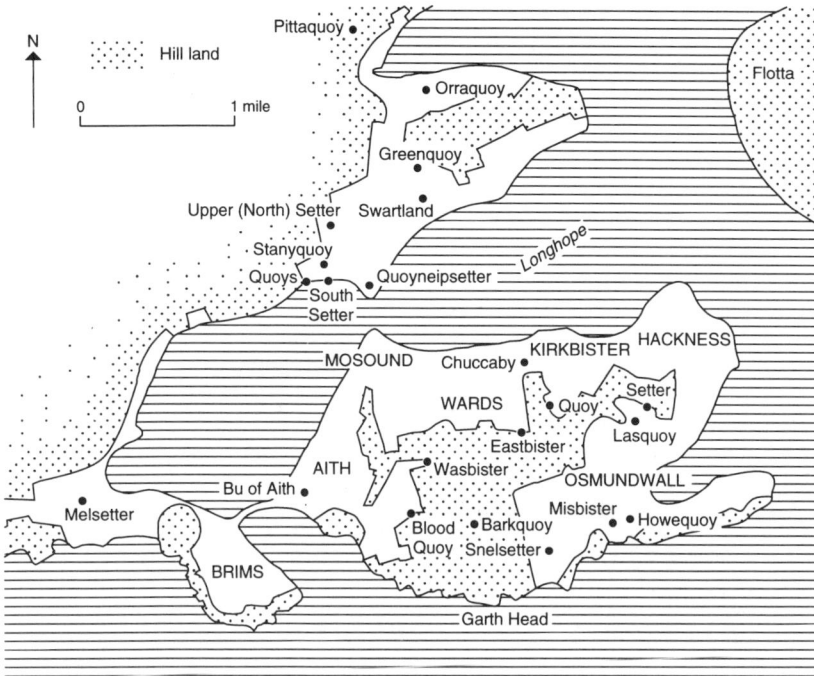

Figure 10 North and South Walls: compare this pattern of names to the theoretical model shown in Fig. 9.

Costaith), possibly represented new names on already-settled secondary land. A final peripheral zone was characterized by *setr* or *sætr*-names (Warsetter, Morsetter) and by the very numerous *kví*-names (Cumlaquoy, Quoybanks, Queenameikle). This chronology is summarized in Fig. 9.

In estimating the value of Marwick's scheme the first question to ask is how closely it corresponds to real patterns on the ground. North and South Walls (Fig. 10) have been selected as a case study because it comes as near as any part of Orkney to matching Marwick's theoretical model. The real map may come as a disappointment to those who expected a series of townships replicating the layout in Fig. 9, yet on closer examination many of the features which Marwick described are readily identifiable. The bulk of the population has always been in peninsular South Walls where the Bu of Aith occupies the prime site on good land commanding the *eið* (isthmus) from which it is named. Chuccaby is an example of an isolated *boer*-name in a somewhat less favourable position, although still on good land, but with nothing to suggest that it was 'a great original settlement'. Other South Walls names include four *bólstaðr*-names (including an east–west pair), two setters and numerous quoys, but *garth*-names are few, and *staðir* and *skáli*-names are absent – reminding us that we ought not to expect to find all

Plate 5 View looking south over Melsetter, towards Bu of Aith, South Walls, Orkney. The ideal quality of the location for Viking settlers, lying accessible to the sea and with excellent beaching facilities, is evident from this photograph. South Walls also has a strategic advantage controlling the entrance to the sheltered waters of Scapa Flow from the Pentland Firth. (Copyright: G. Moberg, Orkney)

generics within a single district. In North Walls (north of Longhope) many places have *kví* and *setter*-names, and from this distribution we can imagine permanent settlement developing from sheilings and stock enclosures. This suggests the outward spread which Marwick envisaged, but not many other parts of Orkney can demonstrate this sequence so clearly.

Although extensive reclamation has greatly reduced the heather-covered moorland, the formerly self-contained South Walls town-ships are still recognizable in Fig. 10, and it is within each of these that we might expect to find Marwick's sequence of names. Osmundwall provides the best example. The prime site is at the head of the inlet and, as is often the case, it has a topographic generic (*Ásmundar-vágr*, Asmund's Inlet) rather than a *boer, Bu of* . . . or *skáli*-name. In relation to this focus, Misbister is in a secondary position, and Setter, Lasquoy and Snelsetter (but not Howequoy) are in marginal locations.

Historical records do not always confirm the status implied by the generics. Despite the prestigious name and prime location of the Bu of Aith, it is not mentioned in the *Orkneyinga Saga*, nor is it ever recorded as being the leading place in the district. Latterly the Bu was uncharacteristically divided into the Mickle Boe and the Little Boe. Conversely, two important places developed from low-status *setter*-names – by the sixteenth century, Snelsetter had become the 'Castle' or 'Manor Place' of Snelsetter and, in the nineteenth century, the landlord lived in the elegant Lethaby-designed mansion house of Melsetter. Names which begin as low-status do not necessarily stay that way.

In developing his chronology Marwick relied instinctively on his detailed knowledge of the location, status and history of Orkney farms, but he also attached a great deal of importance (indeed overmuch importance) to whether or not a place paid *skat*, the Norse land-tax (Marwick 1930/1, 26; 1952, 211). He believed that skat dated from King Harald Fairhair's ninth-century expedition which established the Orkney earldom and, although it was possible that the system had subsequently been modified, 'there were difficulties in accepting such a view'. He also believed that places with the generics, *boer, skáli, bólstaðr, staðir, garðr* and *land* generally paid skat and so he attributed places with these names to a pre-AD 900 date. Half the 'setters' and many of the 'quoys' were skat-free and so must be later. The existence of a dozen or so places named Kirbister (church farm) caused some heart-searching. The Kirbisters paid skat, so Marwick's reasoning placed them earlier than Earl Sigurd's conversion to Christianity in AD 995. Perhaps, he argued, they could have been founded by Viking-Age Christians comparable to the Christian settlers which *Landnámabók* recorded in Iceland. Skat-paying was an argument which Marwick considered crucial to his chronology; if any of the skat-paying bisters could be as late as the official conversion to Christianity then 'the whole argument must go by the board' (Marwick 1930/1, 30–1).

However, more than sixty years later, much of this argument has indeed 'gone by the board'. Most fundamentally, Marwick's model was explicitly based on Icelandic land-taking as recorded in *Landnámabók*, whereas there is a growing realization that the settlement of Orkney – with its Pictish population – must have been a quite different process from the colonization of a large and empty land. It seems unlikely that the first Norse settlers marked out large blocks of territory on prime sites from which new settlement spread outwards without reference to the farms and fields already created by the native population.

Second, the way Marwick used tax-paying to date settlement is suspect. It would not now be thought possible that a system of taxation based on land assessment could have been imposed during Harald Fairhair's ninth-century expedition, or indeed at anything like so early a date (Andersen 1991). If skat was not imposed by King Harold Fairhair, it no longer need be assumed that skat-paying farms were all in existence in the ninth century. This

actually makes the whole time-scale of farm-naming more accept-
able. Marwick's chronology distorted the historian's understanding
of Norse settlement by implying that the settlement pattern as we
know it was essentially in place by AD 900. We can now recognize
that development was over a much longer time-scale, probably with
a particular need for new names in the eleventh, twelfth and
thirteenth centuries as population increased and settlement
intensified. Outward expansion on to common land did occur in
times of population pressure both in medieval and modern times
but, in islands of no great land mass, internal division was usually
more important. This intensification generated a whole host of
names such as Everbay, Midland, Nears, Nistigar, Uttesgarth,
North Setter, Symbister and Isbister (respectively upper, middle,
lower, lowest, outermost, north, south and east). The growth of
settlement strained the language of subdivision to its absolute limit,
resulting in such peculiar names as 'Upper Nisthouse' ('the upper-
lowest house'). At the same time, fields with generics such as *garth,*
akr and *kví* were turned into farms, and outlying grazing places
(setters) became permanent settlements. Even in central places,
important new classes of names could appear such as the *skaill*-
names and, much later, the *stove*-names which are 'primary' in
terms of their location, but not in terms of their age.

The third and most compelling reason for questioning Marwick's
scheme as a chronology is that there can be no doubt that the
generics were active simultaneously rather than consecutively. His
scheme leads us to expect that many generics had largely ceased to
form new names at an early date, even before AD 900, but there is
a great deal of direct evidence that this was not the case. New
names continued to be formed as late as the nineteenth century
when *kví* (field), *garth* (enclosure) and *bu* (big farm) remained in
use as common nouns. The essential meaning of *skáli* (hall) was
also still understood – the relatively modern 'Windy Skaill',
Deerness, is one of those fun names like Tarry Ha', Crab Ha' and
Sparrow Ha' where the meanest of hovels were described as 'halls',
but it shows that it was possible to substitute 'skaill' for 'hall' in a
name of this type. Shetland provides evidence of the continuing use
of other generics. The term *setter-land* was commonly used in the
eighteenth century for land reclaimed from the hill (moorland). The
word bü or bö also appears in Shetland fishermen's tabu language
so that, not only would Bö be used instead of Kirkaby with its
unlucky 'kirk'-element, but the noun could be attached to farm-
names, hence Harrier in Foula could be termed Harrier-bö (Stewart
1987, 68). Shetland and Orkney usage might be quite different, but
it seems dangerous to suggest that a termination recently capable
of being attached to farm-names in Shetland could really have
become obsolete in Orkney in the very early stages of Viking-Age
settlement. Although the generics, *bólstaðr* and *staðir*, generally
fell into disuse, information supplied by Brian Smith, Shetland
Archivist, suggests that a new *bólstaðr*-name, Lunabister in

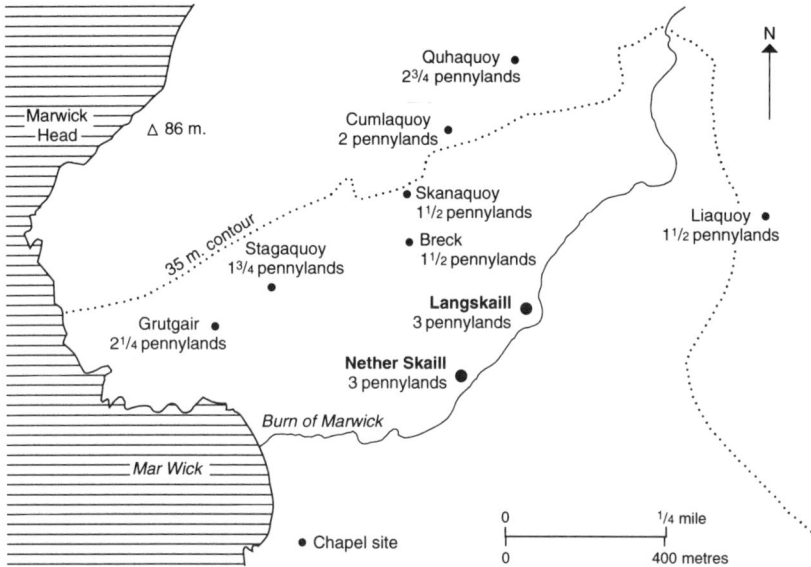

Figure 11 Marwick. (Place-names and pennylands after Peterkin 1820, II, 50–4)

Dunrossness, was created as late as *c.* 1570, and so, of all the generics, it seems that only *staðir* has not formed new place-names in the post-medieval period.

If all or most generics continued simultaneously to form names over a long period, Marwick's scheme cannot strictly speaking be described as a chronology, yet clearly it reflects some kind of reality. At the beginning of his 'Orkney Farm-name Studies' he based his case on Marwick, the district which gave rise to his own surname (Fig. 11 and Plate 6). At the centre, near the sea and standing on good land, are the two farms of Langskaill and Nether Skaill, situated close together and obviously representing a divided high-status settlement with a *skáli*-name. Then in a semi-circle around the northern margin and at a rather higher altitude, there is a whole series of small places characteristically with *kví* (*quoy*)-names such as Steadaquoy (Stagaquoy), Cumlaquoy, Quaquoy and Leaquoy. He commented that 'there can indeed be no doubt at all as to the general chronological sequence of these names from the original skaill settlement to the series of quoys along the hill-dike' (Marwick 1930/1, 25). That argument was crucial to Marwick's reasoning, but there are other ways of looking at it. In this instance he was arguing, not from known historical facts of which there are none, but simply from a distribution, in which case there is an obligation to consider all possible interpretations. It may be that the pattern indeed reflects the chronological outward spread of settlement, but we should remember that the *skáli*-name could be,

Plate 6 View of the north side of Marwick, Orkney, looking towards Marwick Head and the Kitchener Memorial. The remarkable quality of the arable land in this part of the West Mainland of Orkney can be appreciated from the field of barley in the foreground. The farms of Langskaill and Nether Skaill lie in the middle distance. (Copyright: R.M.M. Crawford)

and probably is, a new name developing in a central place replacing the original farm of 'Marwick' (which is now found only as the name of the district) and so theoretically the *skáli*-name could be newer than some or all of the *quoy*-names. Nor is it necessary to think in terms of chronology – the skaill was a high status place because its occupant commanded the labour of his poorer neighbours. The skaill and the quoys may have been bound together in a single social unit which, from its inception, required both high and low status names. Hugh Marwick never quite came to grips with the fact that 'secondary' in terms of location, size and status need not automatically imply a secondary date although, of course, that is often a strong possibility. His so-called 'chronology' is essentially a hierarchy based on size, location and status – whether the relationship is also chronological is usually more debatable.

To summarize: names primarily describe the nature of the farm, and it is only by inference that these characteristics can be translated into chronology. Farms which are large, central and high status will often but by no means invariably be oldest, and small, marginal, low-status places will frequently but not always be recent. It is not safe to use generics as an automatic mechanism for putting names into sequence, and even less safe to try to assign dates on the basis of tax-paying. Instead of thinking in terms of chronology, it is useful to think of the Norse generics as forming a group not unlike a collection of English-language names which might be applied to farms. When you consider a list such as ranch, croft, homestead, home-farm, plantation, manor, small-holding, township, mains, kibbutz and grange, it can be seen that it might often be possible to guess the date of their creation, yet it would not occur to us to describe the list as a 'chronology'. We recognize that, first and foremost, names describe different kinds of farms and only by inference are they farms of different dates. Norse names no doubt had a rather narrower range of meanings, but they too are primarily concerned with the nature of the farm rather than its age. It seems likely that the Norse arrived in Orkney with a whole range of names for farms, some old and some not so old in a Norwegian context, but all capable of being applied from the first in Orkney – in whatever were appropriate circumstances.

Common usage, even at a late date, continued to be remarkably sensitive to the appropriateness of names, so much so that if the nature of the farm changed the generic might also change in a way which reflected the farm's new circumstances. When in the sixteenth century Earl Robert Stewart created a single farm on the outskirts of Kirkwall from the former townships of Newbigging, Foreland, Corse and Archdeaconsquoy, his new farm was described as being 'labowrt in ane bow' (cultivated as a *bu*) and was renamed the Bu of Corse (Peterkin 1820, No. II, 118; Clouston 1926/7, 41, 46). This is a good example of how names carry a sense of their own appropriateness. The place lost a *land*-name (Foreland) and a *kví*-name (Archdeaconsquoy) and it acquired a *Bu of* . . . -name which signalled that it was now the dominant farm in the district, and was worked as a single unit in contrast to the more common multi-tenanted runrig townships.

As a means of exploring the characteristics of Marwick's generics, Table 1 analyses one thousand place-names (not all habitative) from such sources as early rentals, maps and published collections. The list is not exhaustive. It is likely to omit only a few of the *skáli* and *Bu of* . . . -names, and no doubt it includes the majority of places for which pennyland values can be discovered, but a thorough search might produce several hundred additional *kví* and *garth*-names and, even among the more prestigious generics, more examples of bisters, lands and vestigial *boer*-names could fairly readily be found. The table gives the average size based on the number of places for which the value in pennylands is known. The height and the median distance from the sea and 'hill' (moorland) have also been measured for this sample.

Another measure which this table seeks to explore is the relationship between place-names and *urislands* (ouncelands), the 18-pennyland districts on which skat (tax) was paid. Places with *Bu*

Table 1 Measurable characteristics of Orkney place-names

	Boer	Bu of	Skáli	Bólstaðr	Staðir	Land	Garth	Saetr	Kví	All
Total number	41	35	42	83	31	109	161	60	438	1000
Number with known pennyland value	14	22	15	52	22	47	54	26	73	325
Percent with known pennyland value	34.1%	62.9%	35.7%	62.7%	71.0%	43.1%	33.5%	43.3%	16.7%	32.5%
Average size (in pennylands)	14.4	13.2	5.1	8.2	8.0	7.0	5.9	2.5	2.0	6.2
Whole urislands (=18 pennylands)	4.9%	28.6%	2.4%	9.6%	9.7%	5.5%	5.0%	0.0%	0.2%	3.9%
Whole urislands plus regular fractions	29.3%	48.6%	11.9%	48.2%	54.8%	28.4%	18.0%	16.7%	3.7%	17.7%
Division and directional names	22.0%	14.3%	7.1%	19.3%	3.2%	3.7%	9.5%	10.3%	4.0%	7.7%
Average height above sea level	69 ft	38 ft	55 ft	68 ft	84 ft	107 ft	80 ft	112 ft	112 ft	87 ft
Median distance from the sea (yards)	500 yds	75 yds	300 yds	500 yds	900 yds	700 yds	400 yds	1000 yds	500 yds	600 yds
Median distance from the 'hill' (yards)	350 yds	775 yds	700 yds	500 yds	650 yds	400 yds	500 yds	200 yds	400 yds	450 yds
Pastoral or marginal specifics	0.0%	0.0%	9.5%	7.2%	0.0%	13.8%	8.7%	38.3%	18.0%	14.1%

of . . ., bólstaðr and *staðir*-names must have been readily visible
when skat (tax) was imposed since they were often assessed as
whole urislands or regular fractions such as a half, quarter, two-
thirds, one-third and one-sixth (i.e. 9, 4½, 12, 6 and 3 pennylands).
Less important names have a much weaker relationship to
assessment, often because these places had then not been farms but
merely a field (*kví, akr*), an enclosure (*garth*) or a grazing place
(*sætr*). In other cases the minor name, although habitative, was
subsidiary to the main farm which paid skat on its behalf. It follows
that the proportion of names with independent values in pennylands, and the proportion which are whole or even fractions of
ouncelands, are measures of the status of place-names.

Although Table 1 in many respects confirms Marwick's model,
there are a number of ways in which our mental map requires
adjustment. For example, Fig. 15 (p. 61) shows how most generics
cluster around the average location, including the supposedly
marginal but in fact ubiquitous *quoy*-names, so that it is only *Bu
of . . ., skáli, staðir* and *setter*-names which can really be described
as having well-defined locational characteristics. The sections which
follow re-examine each of the generics, making use of these
measurable characteristics.

Boer-names

Table 1 shows that there is only a small number of *boer*-names for
which pennyland values are known. However, these indicate that
'boers' were large and valuable, and the high proportion of division-
names suggests that they had once been even larger. However, the
majority of 'boers' are known only by minor names without
pennyland values, some of which form clusters, but others are found
in isolation in circumstances where there is nothing to suggest large
size, great age or high status. The typical location is hardly so
favourable as Marwick suggested, although it should be noted that
boer-names never have pastoral or marginal specifics. In the cases
of Bea (Sanday), Midbea (Westray), Husabae (Rousay) and possibly
others, it does appear that the name was associated with very
large Norse or pre-Norse farms which subsequently disintegrated
(Thomson 1990 and 1993). Gillian Fellows-Jensen has suggested
that *boer*-names perhaps came into existence when a big unit with
a topographic name was divided (Fellows-Jensen 1984, 156–7). In
that case, as indeed with some of the other names, we may need to
make a distinction between settlement units which are genuinely of
great antiquity and their names which may not be so old.

The vanished farm of Husabae, Rousay, (Fig. 12) provides a case
study which illustrates the characteristics of *boer*-names. The
huseby-names, of which Orkney has four, are a special case. They
have been interpreted as royal or comital administrative farms,
dating from a period before the Earls of Orkney had a fixed

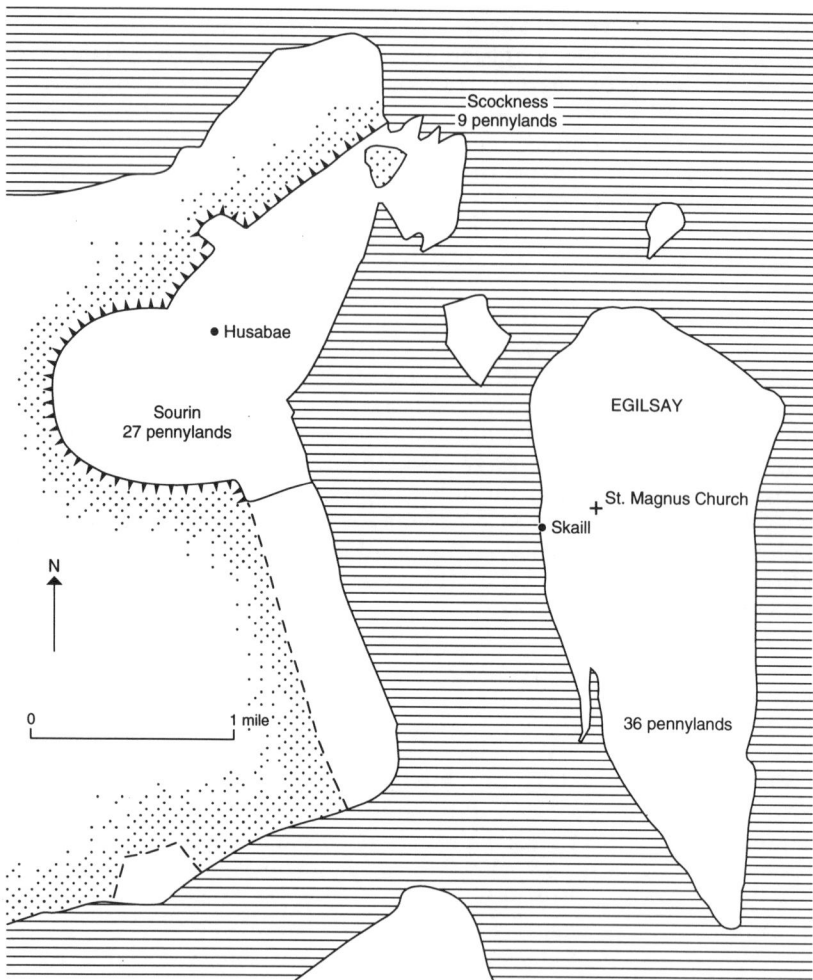

Figure 12   Sourin and Egilsay. (After OA map E.29)

residence (Steinnes 1969). Whatever the truth of this controversial theory, the area associated with this *boer*-name was certainly an important block of territory. Orkney estates were exceptionally fragmented, and so large property blocks of this kind were unusual. Note the symmetrical arrangement whereby the two sides of the Sound were each assessed at 36 pennylands, 72 pennylands or four ouncelands in total. All of this became bishopric property, so it does seem possible that an earldom estate was used to provide part of the original endowment of the bishopric (Thomson 1993, 341–2). Like much of the bishopric property, Sourin seems to have been thoroughly reorganized at an unknown date and laid out for renting purposes in 3-pennyland units, some with names such as Brendale and Overdale which incorporate, not 'dale' but 'deild', a portion (Marwick 1947, 37–8). Hence both the settlement-unit and the *boer*-name were 'replaced and overlaid' in the way which Marwick suggested.

Bu of . . . names

These places are much more visible since they mostly still exist as large farms. They occupy prime sites, and have a tendency to be located at low-altitude in the arable heartland in very markedly coastal positions. The term 'bu' continued to be explicitly under-stood as meaning a large farm worked as a single unit, and frequently 'Bu' was translated as 'Manor' or 'Mains'. *Bu of . . .* names were used for the principal properties of the Earls of Orkney (Bu of Rapness, Hackness, Brough, Tresness, Tafts, Walls, Lopness, Cairston, Orphir, Hoy, Burray).

Despite the status and undoubted antiquity of these places, the names reach us only in a form which has been subject to Scottish influence. The *Orkneyinga Saga* refers to the earl's residence at Orphir as a *bú* but, as a place-name, it occurs simply as 'Orphir'. Similarly the saga in 1155 records Earl Rognvald as staying 'at Rapness' rather than at the Bu of Rapness. Of the twenty or so places to which the *Orkneyinga Saga* applied the common noun, *bú*, not all developed *Bu of . . .* -names. Some have names with *skáli* and *staðir*-elements, which suggests that these generics shared certain characteristics with the high status, single-farm *Bu of . . .* -places (Taylor 1938, 372–4).

Skáli-names

These also occupy high status coastal sites in arable districts, but it is instructive to contrast their characteristics as shown in Table 1 with those of the *Bu of . . .* -names. Only one *skáli*-name was a whole ounceland, Backaskaill in Sanday, and even that had an alternative *boer*-name, Southerbie. 'Skaills' often have surprisingly low pennyland values, or else do not appear in skat-rentals although there is no doubt that they stood on skat-paying land. It seems that 'skaills' were not particularly visible when assessment was imposed – perhaps 'skaills' did not then exist, or else the name may at that time have been applied to a specific building (the hall) rather than to the land. These features are consistent with a special type of high status hall appearing on already settled prime sites (exactly like the later *Stove*-names). 'Skaills' are often found in unmistakable close association with a church or district chapel, suggesting that they flourished at a time when church organization was being consolidated, perhaps in the eleventh and twelfth centuries. Around that date we also find the term *skáli* used as a

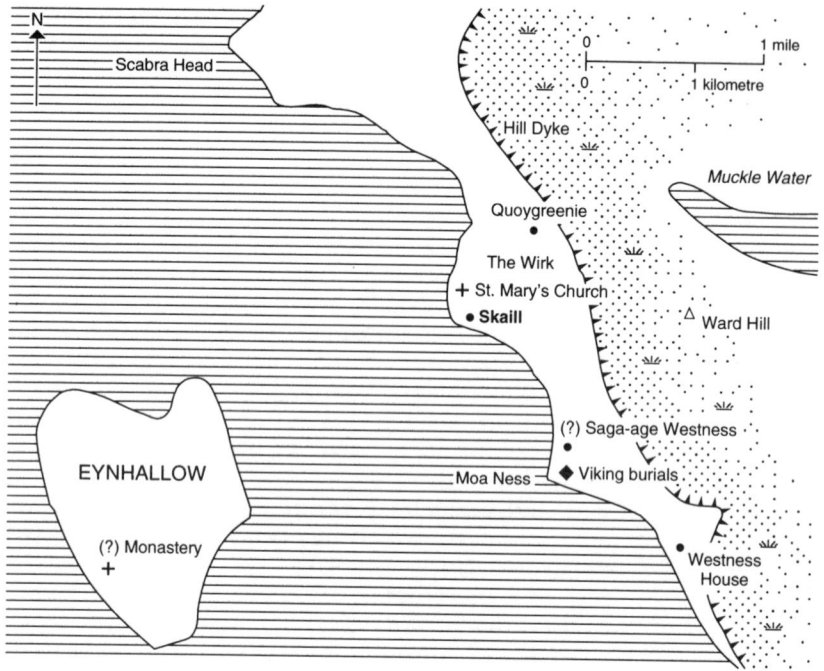

Figure 13   Skaill, Westness, Rousay.

common noun in the *Orkneyinga Saga* (written *c.* 1200) and applied
to the halls at Orphir, Gairsay, the unidentified 'Hlaupandanes',
and Freswick in Caithness. One might expect that *skáli* would
combine with a personal specific to commemorate the builder or
owner of such a prestigious hall, but names of this kind are never
found. The place-name usually appears in either of two standard
and apparently interchangeable forms – there are more than a
dozen Skaills and a similar number of Langskaills. Orkney 'skaills'
are often found at the rate of one per parish and, while that might
have some kind of organizational significance, it more probably
simply reflects the fact that each district was likely to have only one
'skaill'-owning family.
   Whereas Huseby in Rousay is a very shadowy unit about which
we know next to nothing, as are most of the *boer*-names, it is often
possible to put *skáli* into a clearer context. Skaill, Rousay, is a good
example (Fig. 13). It lies on the opposite side of Rousay from
Husabae, and is located in a district the importance of which is
attested by saga and archaeology, and which is still part of the
biggest farm on the island. The present Westness House is some
distance from the 'west ness' of Rousay and, in the last two
thousand years, the chief farm has occupied various sites along
about a mile of coast. Westness figures in the *Orkneyinga Saga* as
the home of Sigurd of Westness, a leading supporter of Paul

Hakonsson (Earl of Orkney *c.* 1128 × *c.* 1136), and it was while staying at Westness that Earl Paul was abducted by Sweyn Asleifsson. Earl Paul was described as *a veizlu* when he was staying with Sigurd, *veizla* being the obligation to accommodate, feed and entertain the lord when he was travelling around his possessions (Taylor, 1938, 191, 215, 217, 237, 241, 250, 254, 255, 258–60). The remains of a house 35m. long, with two adjacent buildings which were possibly byres, has been interpreted as the home of Sigurd of Westness, and this stands at no great distance from a spectacular cemetery containing pagan boat-burials, as well as other graves with and without grave goods, and which appears to bridge the transition between the Pictish and Norse periods (Lamb 1982, 23; Kaland 1993).

It seems that soon after the time of Sigurd of Westness the nucleus migrated westwards to Skaill. This site is closely associated with the now-abandoned parish church. At the corner of the churchyard stand the remains of a well-constructed stone tower known as the Wirk for which a twelfth-century date has been suggested. It was described in a document of 1556 as 'a fortalice', and Dietrichson discussed parallels with the detached fortified bell-towers of some Scandinavian churches (Dietrichson 1906; 29, 105–9; Marwick 1923/4, 17; Lamb 1982, 10–11, 27). On the neighbouring island of Eynhallow are the remains of a church and associated buildings which have been interpreted as a Benedictine monastery of similar date (Lamb 1982, 10, 30), which probably ought to be seen as associated with the Skaill power-centre. The twelfth-century date of Skaill, its high status, and its location within an important settlement unit which is much older than the name, forms part of the evidence that *skáli*-names were relatively late and took their names from halls which were built in central places on already-settled land.

As an active name-forming element *skáli* may not have survived much beyond the saga period, perhaps because changing social conditions no longer required open halls and the feasting of a military retinue. The *Orkneyinga Saga* describes how, after Sweyn Asleifsson's death (*c.* 1171), his sons built a partition across his great drinking-hall in Gairsay, and the dividing of the *skáli* was used by the saga to symbolize the end of the Viking way of life (Taylor 1938, 342).

Bólstaðr-names

Table 1 shows that 'bisters' are large and often fairly low-lying places, but with no particular siting characteristics in relation to hill or coast. The first element, *ból*, is an allocation or portion, and in Norway *bólstaðr* was frequently used when the home-fields were divided (Olsen 1928; Crawford 1987, 110). Similarly Orkney *bólstaðr*-names often come in pairs or groups such as Easterbister

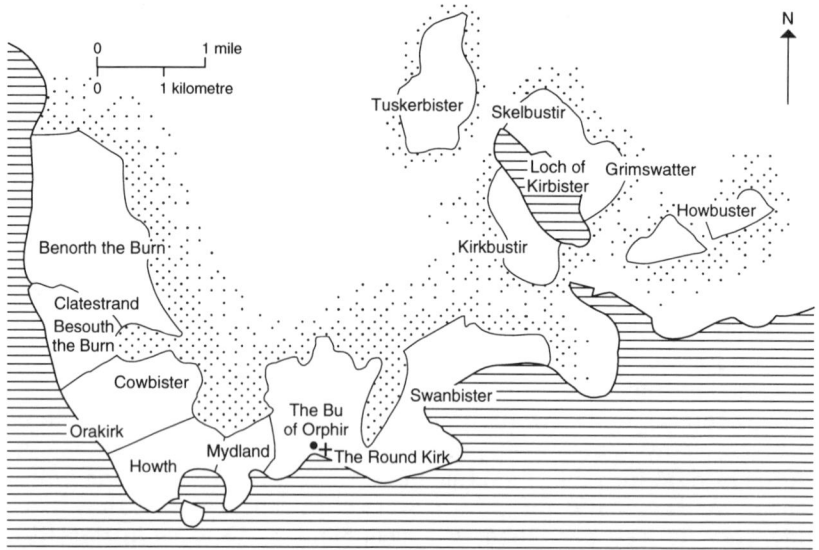

Figure 14 Orphir, the Bu and *Bólstaðr*-names. (After OA map W.15; Johnston, 1903, 174–214)

and Westerbister in Holm, Wasbister, Midbister and Isbister in South Ronaldsay, and the South Walls Wasbister and Eastbister which are shown in Fig. 10. Apparently the name was particularly appropriate for district divisions and so *bólstaðr* was one of the most frequent generics for urislands (ouncelands). In parts of Scotland where Norse and Gaelic names are found side by side, *bólstaðr* was often equivalent to *baile*, the township or extended farm, and in Orkney it is very often used in the same sense. The example of Orphir (Fig. 14) shows how a *Bu of . . .* -name was used for the central place, the earl's hall, and *bólstaðr*-names were used for many of the surrounding multi-tenanted townships. New 'bisters' were not usually created in the post-medieval period – at a guess one might suggest that late medieval climatic deterioration combined with more difficult economic and political conditions may have brought a temporary halt to the process of township-splitting which generated many of the *bólstaðr*-names.

Staðir-names

It is difficult to understand the circumstances in which *staðir*-names were applied. Part of the problem is that nearly all have a personal specific, so we do not have the pastoral, marginal, directional and divisional components which help us to understand certain other classes of names. Places with *staðir*-names tend to be located in inland arable districts at a comparatively low altitude, and are mainly concentrated in the interior lowlands of the West Mainland. In Shetland, Iceland and Norway *staðir*-names are also found in secondary locations, and in the Isle of Man they have a localized distribution as in Orkney (Fellows-Jensen 1983b, 41).

The generic *staðir* is plural but the frequency with which it was joined to a personal name suggests that the significance of the plural was lost. On the other hand, the personal name perhaps tells us something important about the nature of the farm. It would hardly have been possible to attach a personal name to the townships found at the close of the Middle Ages, with their highly dispersed and fragmented runrig and complex intermixture of owner-occupied and rented properties. It is unclear whether we ought to envisage similar field systems in the eleventh and twelfth centuries but, if they existed even in a simpler form, the distinction between *staðir* and *bólstaðr* (which seldom has a personal specific) might broadly be the difference between a farm and a township. It is possibly significant that the *Orkneyinga Saga* applied the common noun *bú* ('a large single farm') to places with *staðir*-names (Cairston and Knarston), but never to *bólstaðr*-names. In one instance, the farm of Jaddvararstaðir, the *staðir*-name can be linked to its eleventh-century owner, Jaddvor, illegitimate daughter of Earl Erlend – a person important enough to be described as 'unpopular' (Taylor 1938, 218; Marwick 1952, 236–7). It may be that, if *bu* was an appropriate name for the earl's great farms, a *staðir*-name was suitable for a more modest but similarly self-contained farm belonging to a person of Jaddvor's standing. A high proportion of *staðir* remained udal property, presumably often held by descendants and successors of the eponymous founder although, by the time we meet these places in fifteenth-century rentals, most were no longer under single ownership but had split into townships as a result of udal inheritance among co-heirs. Several of the *staðir* mentioned in the *Orkneyinga Saga* were subsequently renamed, or perhaps reverted to a previous name, suggesting that the name did not always survive the name-giver. Jaddvararstaðir, for example, became the farm of Gaitnip, just south of Kirkwall (Marwick 1952, 97, 237).

Land-names

There is a tendency for 'lands' to occupy rather less advantageous sites than the 'bisters'. A greater proportion are names which do not appear in early rentals and they are, on average, rather smaller. However, this is probably because 'land' was a very general term which could be applied in a wide variety of circumstances varying from district-names to quite minor non-habitative features. It is a name element which continued to be understood in Norn, Scots and English, and so it is a generic which has had a particularly long life.

Garth-names

Table 1 suggests that the 'garths' (*garðr*, enclosure) were of about average size but, because so many are from Sanday where pennylands were unusually small, they were not really as valuable as the average indicates. While some 'garths' were extensive hill-margin enclosures possibly associated with medieval sheep management, others, like those in the flat Sanday landscape, were townships enclosed within earthen dykes. Non-rental garth-names are very common, and many were minor enclosures where a *kví*-name might have been an alternative. 'Garth' continued to be used, possibly into the twentieth century, as a common noun, meaning an enclosure. The 1329 form of Thurrigar, *i þordar eckru*, 'Thord's *akr*' (cultivated field), raises the possibility that some names generally supposed to derive from *garðr* may in fact contain other generics (Marwick 1957, 50).

Setter-names

Early forms of Shetland names such as Brekka Saetr, recorded in 1299, suggest a *sætr*, sheiling, root rather than *setr*, farm (Crawford 1987, 109; Fellows-Jensen 1984, 161). The *sætr* root in Orkney setter-names is confirmed by their very clearly defined charac-teristics. Table 1 shows that 'setters' tend to be small, high and, of all generics, definitely the most marginal – more marginal than 'quoys'. Of all names, 'setters' have a much higher proportion of specifics which indicate a pastoral land-use or a marginal location (moor, moss, cow, meadow, stony, headland, ward-hill etc.). Many seem to have developed from 'home-sæters' or milking places at no great distance from the parent farm. Often 'setters' do not appear in early rentals and, of those which do, a significant number were genuinely skat-free.

Quoy-names

'Quoy' was the standard Orkney term for 'field', hence *quoy*-names are very numerous, and most were fields rather than farms. Of all farm-names they are smallest in size. The great majority were too small and unimportant to appear in rentals and, of those which do, such a high proportion paid no skat that 'quoyland' was used as a technical term for skat-free land. Quoys often originated from little hill-margin enclosures where cattle could be 'quoyed' at night, and this is reflected in their altitude, and by the quite high proportion which have pastoral or marginal specifics (Grassquoy, Gossaquoy, Heathery Quoy). However, quoys were also formed by dyking-off headlands and coastal grazing spots (Sponessquoy, Quoyneipsetter, Backaquoy), while others were simply fields, or in exceptional cases

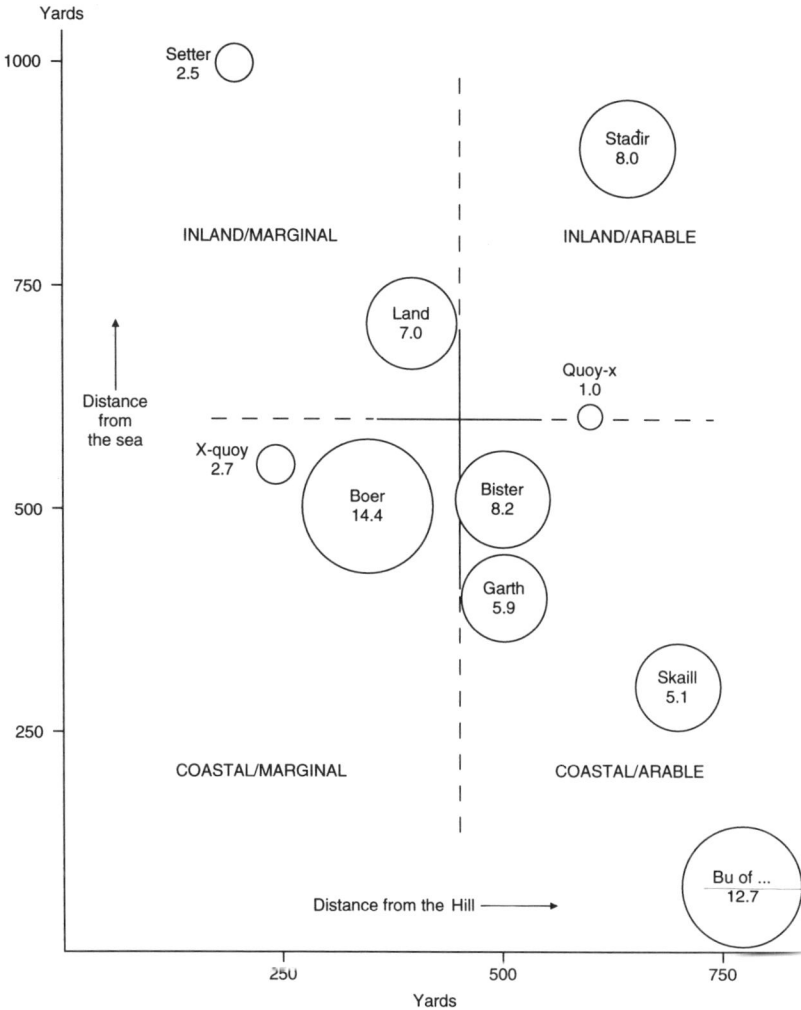

Figure 15 Size and location of Orkney place-names. The graph shows the average size in pennylands, median distance from the sea, and median distance from the 'hill' of each of the generics. 'X-quoy' names are those where the generic comes second (Hussaquoy) while 'Quoy-x' names are the inversion compounds (Quoyhokka).

quite large enclosures in the arable heartland, sometimes with specifics denoting arable use. One such is Buckquoy (*bygg*, bere or barley-quoy), a 6-pennyland farm in Birsay, centrally situated within the 'capital' of Earl Thorfinn's eleventh-century earldom. *Quoy*-names continued to be coined until the landscape was squared in the mid-nineteenth century. They were often transient names with specifics which indicate comparatively recent origin (Fieldquoy, Smithquoy). Tuquoy in Westray is the only early example of a *kví*-name which was applied to a high status farm and a whole urisland, but in that instance there is archaeological evidence that the original Norse hall was elsewhere and was probably abandoned because of coastal erosion, with the result that the principal settlement was relocated and acquired what had hitherto been a minor name (Owen 1993, 318–39; Thomson 1990, 40). *Quoy*-names come in two forms, either with the *quoy*-element second (Gloupquoy, Pickaquoy) or else as 'inversion-compounds' (Quoygreenie, Quoy-dandy). The average size of the inversion-compounds (1 pennyland) is a good deal smaller than those with the *quoy*-element second (2.7 pennylands), and their location is less marginal (see Fig. 15). However, most *quoy*-names are non-rental places and so we ought to be careful about drawing conclusions from the minority which have values in pennylands.

Orkney farm-name chronology is one of those frustrating areas of study where further research has produced, not greater certainty, but less. Although farm-names are of different dates, they originated over a greater time-span than Marwick envisaged, and we have less confidence in our ability to assign dates and put names into a chronological sequence. On the other hand, we are gradually building up a better understanding of the meaning of farm-names and the circumstances in which they were applied. The way forward is probably through detailed local investigations in which sets of place-names are considered in their geographical setting and in relation to saga references, early rentals and estate maps. Perhaps it is safe to speak about 'chronology' only when supported by that kind of evidence.

The position of the Orkney and Shetland Islands at the northern apex of the British Isles was strategically most important for the development of the Norse earldom (see Fig. 2). The earls of Orkney controlled the sea routes between Ireland and Norway; they also controlled the routes down the east and west sides of Scotland. With the extension of their power to Caithness on the Scottish mainland, they controlled the stormy waters of the Pentland Firth and the passage around the north of Britain. The Scandinavian place-names of the north coast of Caithness give the impression of total domination (see Chap. 4 below), but the earls' power in Caithness must have been tempered by some sort of accommodation with the native Celtic aristocracy; the stories recorded in the Icelandic Sagas suggest that there was intermarriage between the earls and native Caithness dynasties, as well as clashes with the rulers of the province of Moray over possession of the northern Scottish territory. That the title of 'earl' over Caithness was understood to be a Scottish title is indicated by the statement in Orkneyinga Saga that Skuli Thorfinsson was given the title by the 'king of Scots' in the late tenth century;[1] although which Scottish dynasty is meant, whether the MacAlpin kings of south Scotland or the rulers (mormaers) of Moray, is disputed (Crawford 1987, 64).

The earldom of Caithness covered the whole territory north of the River Oykell; but this included two provinces, Caithness proper (the north and east coasts) and Suðrland south of the Ord, facing south on Breiðafjord and looking across the Oykell to Ross (see Fig. 16). This southern, frontier territory is the true 'Sutherland'; the county today stretches north-west to Cape Wrath, but that only reflects the seventeenth-century territorial position of the earls of Sutherland (an earldom created in the twelfth century for the de Moravia family as part of the process of curbing the power of the earls of Caithness).

The Oykell was not, however, the extreme southerly limit of Norse settlement or influence on the east side of Scotland. The province of Ross is (or was) permeated with Norse place-names – habitative on the arable lands of the east coast and topographical (particularly dalr names) up the river valleys of both Wester and Easter Ross. These must all post-date the tenth century, for no pagan graves have been found in Ross at all. They probably relate to the hard-won campaigns of Earl Thorfinn the Mighty in the 1030s who fought the famous battle of Torfness against Karl Hundason in this locality (OS, Chap. 20). The earls' wish to control Ross may be connected with their strategic requirements for access to the Great Glen (Crawford 1986, 35); or it may be connected with their need for timber, an economic resource with which the valleys of Easter Ross were well supplied (Crawford 1995).

Whatever the reason for the earls' aggressive campaigns in northern Scotland the result meant involvement in the Celtic societies already established in that region, an involvement which took them into the heartland of 'Scotland' and meant that they became inextricably part of the obscure and complex political history of the MacAlpin dynasty's domination of Scotland both south and north of the Mounth. A more lasting result, as seen in the Norse place-names which are an integral part of the toponymy of north Scotland, was their settlement of the land. The earls also established political structures in Caithness and Sutherland which tied these provinces into the Scandinavian world of the Orkney earldom for some centuries, until the medieval Scottish kings managed to break the grip of the earls in the late twelfth and thirteenth centuries and bring this area slowly under central royal control (Crawford 1985, 1986, 1994).

---

1. The Saga of the earls of Orkney was written down in Iceland c. 1200. The composite version known as *Orkneyinga Saga* is available in Penguin (trans. H. Pálsson and P. Edwards, 1986); also in the Hjaltalin and Goudie trans. with notes and an intro. by Joseph Anderson (1873, reprint 1973); trans. with notes on the text by A.B. Taylor (1938, now out of print); the definitive Icelandic edition is by Finnbogi Guðmundsson, *Islensk Fornrit, 34* (Reykjavik, 1965).

4 Settlement names in Caithness with particular reference to Reay Parish*

DOREEN WAUGH

The visitor coming from Orkney immediately perceives the similarity between the island topography and that of mainland Caithness and can appreciate the potential for settlement offered by the easily cultivated plains of eastern Caithness. The Scandinavians who came to the Northern Isles of Scotland c. AD 800 (Wainwright 1962, 140), and who then crossed the Pentland Firth, obviously found Caithness appealing and place-name evidence points to extensive settlement over a number of centuries, paralleling the Norse settlement of Orkney (Fig. 16). There are, however, some indications in the surviving place-names of Caithness that Norse settlement there was less dense than in neighbouring Orkney which, given that the administrative heart of the earldom was located in Orkney, is not surprising.

There is a lack of archaeological evidence for settlement in the early Viking period in Caithness but what evidence there is points to Norse settlement along the north and east coasts (Batey 1989, 67–77). Place-name evidence confirms the coastal habitation and points to a movement inland along the major waterways, the Wick and Thurso Rivers, where the land is also reasonably fertile (Waugh 1989, 142). Some place-names suggest Norse pastoral farming in the less fertile interior of Caithness, possibly on a seasonal basis. Expansion of settlement to the south and west, however, was limited, perhaps because the fact that the land was unattractive for

---

* The following unpublished records have been used in the preparation of this chapter:

SRO, GD 136	Sinclair (Freswick), estate papers.
SRO, GD 96	Sinclair (Mey), estate papers.
Thurso, Lord Thurso's estate office	Sinclair (Thurso), estate papers.
SRO, GD 139	Sutherland (Forse) estate papers.

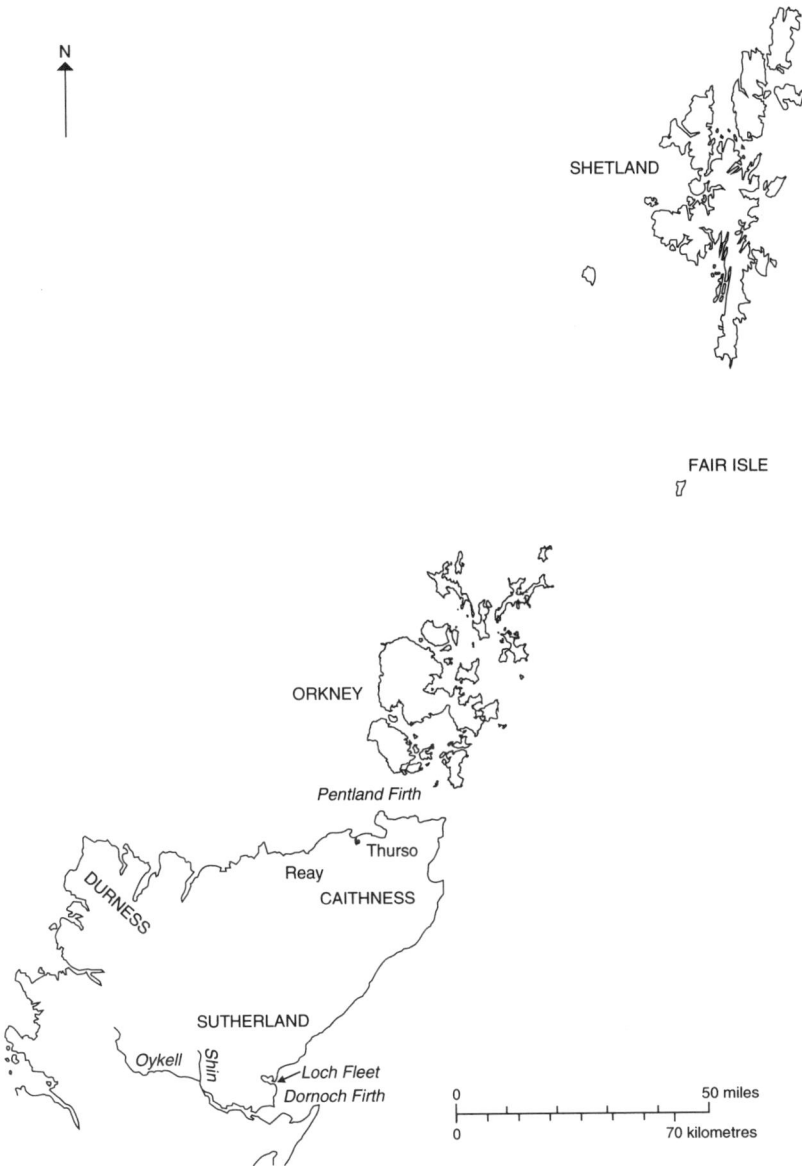

Figure 16 North Scotland, showing places mentioned in Chaps 4 and 5.

arable farming militated against the expenditure of effort required to oust the Gaelic-speaking people who, as W.F.H. Nicolaisen has argued, must have been in the area before the end of the ninth century (Nicolaisen 1982, 80).

It is the presence of Gaelic elements and the later slight advance of the language east and south into former Norse territory, which distinguishes the Norse place-names of Caithness from those of Orkney, and it is the meeting of the two languages which makes the place-names of Reay Parish particularly interesting. It is very difficult to say when this infiltration of Gaelic-speakers into Caithness took place and, in all probability, it was a gradual process, but Nicolaisen's suggestion of a twelfth/thirteenth century date is very reasonable and fits with what is known of the historical situation (Nicolaisen 1982, 80). Gaelic was the chief language spoken in Reay Parish for several centuries and it survived into the twentieth century; a few older people still have a passive Gaelic vocabulary of limited extent which they can use in the translation of place-name elements. The language now spoken in Reay, as in the rest of Caithness, is English and a local dialect of Scots is also spoken which has a great deal in common with Insular Scots.

Reay Parish is situated on the west side of modern Caithness (see Figs 17 and 18) but, although the area may appear marginal from a present-day point of view, it has many features which would have made it most attractive to Scandinavian settlers. The sheltered sandy beach, now known as Sandside Bay (see Plate 7), would have offered excellent harbourage for ships. Various streams reach the sea at Sandside Bay and fresh water would have been plentiful. In addition, these streams deposit sediments which, combined with the sand, produce the type of soil which the Norse favoured for its ease of cultivation. The land on which the present village of Reay is situated would certainly have been suitable for cultivation and the establishment of homesteads, although the more likely situation of the Norse settlement is under or near the area occupied by the medieval village of Reay, which is thought to have lain between present Reay and the sea at Sandside Bay (New Statistical Account 1845, 13). The higher land to the west and south of Reay village would have afforded opportunities for rough grazing and peat extraction, and the fertile valley of the Forss Water to the east (ON *fors* 'a waterfall') would have provided further arable farming. It is not altogether surprising that Gaelic-speaking people also saw the attraction and moved in when the opportunity offered.

As mentioned, archaeological evidence for the Viking period is sparse, but the finest collection of Viking pagan graves in Caithness was discovered in Reay (Batey 1989, 73; 1994, 152) (see Plate 8). The fact that people were buried in a place does not necessarily prove that they lived there but, combined with an equally fine collection of Norse place-names, the indications of habitation are conclusive. The graves were recovered as a result of weathering of sand dunes between the present village of Reay and Sandside Bay and it is quite probable that further organized excavation would produce more evidence of settlement.

It is typical of Norse settlement in Caithness, Orkney and Shetland that the nuclear habitation, situated in the prime position at the head of an inlet of the sea, should have a topographical

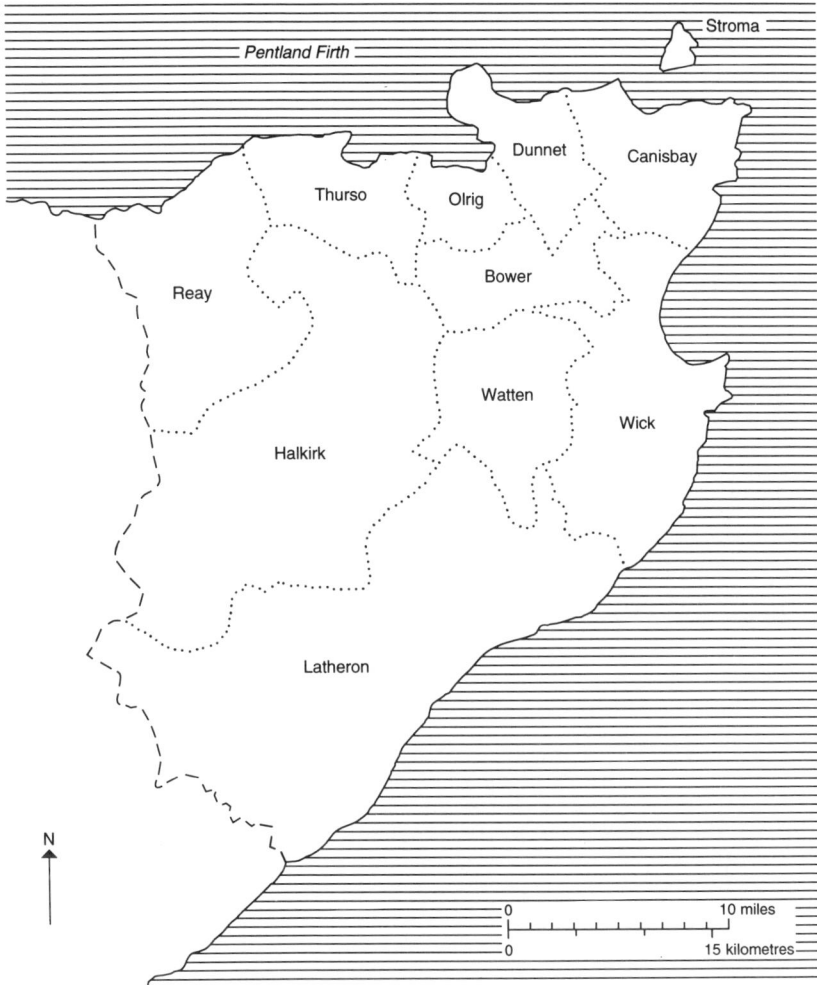

Figure 17 The Parishes of Caithness.

name, referring to some significant characteristic of the surrounding landscape, and Reay seems to fit this pattern although, as with many centuries-old names, there is room for debate. In this case, etymologizing is obstructed both by the age of the name and by the fact that subsequent Gaelic speakers have interpreted it as a lexical item in their own language and have created other names with it. In our search for the origin of the name, therefore, we should turn to the landscape which gave rise to it and to the earliest forms of the name which can be found on record. The Gaelic-speaking parishes of Caithness are generally very poorly served by early documentation but, in the case of a larger village such as Reay, early forms are reasonably frequent.

Plate 7 View over Sandside Bay, Reay, looking north towards
Orkney across the Pentland Firth (note the nuclear establishment of
Dounreay in the middle distance). Reay lies at the western edge of
the Old Red Sandstone plateau which forms the north-eastern corner
of Caithness, and is part of the same geological formation that makes
up the Orkney Islands. (Photo: Doreen Waugh)

If we turn first to the landscape we find that a substantial part of
Reay Parish, lying roughly west of a line from Shebster to Loch
Shurrery and south of the main A836, is underlain by old, hard,
resistant rocks such as granite, porphyrite and metamorphosed
rocks which have produced rising ground to the west and south of
Reay, noticeable due to the comparative flatness of the coastal plain
to the east. One Old Norse word which suggests itself – because it
fits both the situation and the early forms of the name listed below
– is *rá* which appears in Norwegian place-names in the sense of 'a
long stretched-out elevation'. But Old Norse *rá* (originally *vrá*) can
also have the meaning, 'corner, nook' (Rygh vol. 10, 140), and either
of these descriptions could be seen to fit the local topography,
depending – quite literally – on one's viewpoint. The low-lying ridge
of hills immediately to the west of Reay is a most noticeable
elevated feature in an otherwise flat landscape, while the ridge
forms shelter for the settlement sited in a corner, or nook, of flat
and fertile ground.

There is little variation in the early forms listed for Reay and the
following is a representative selection:

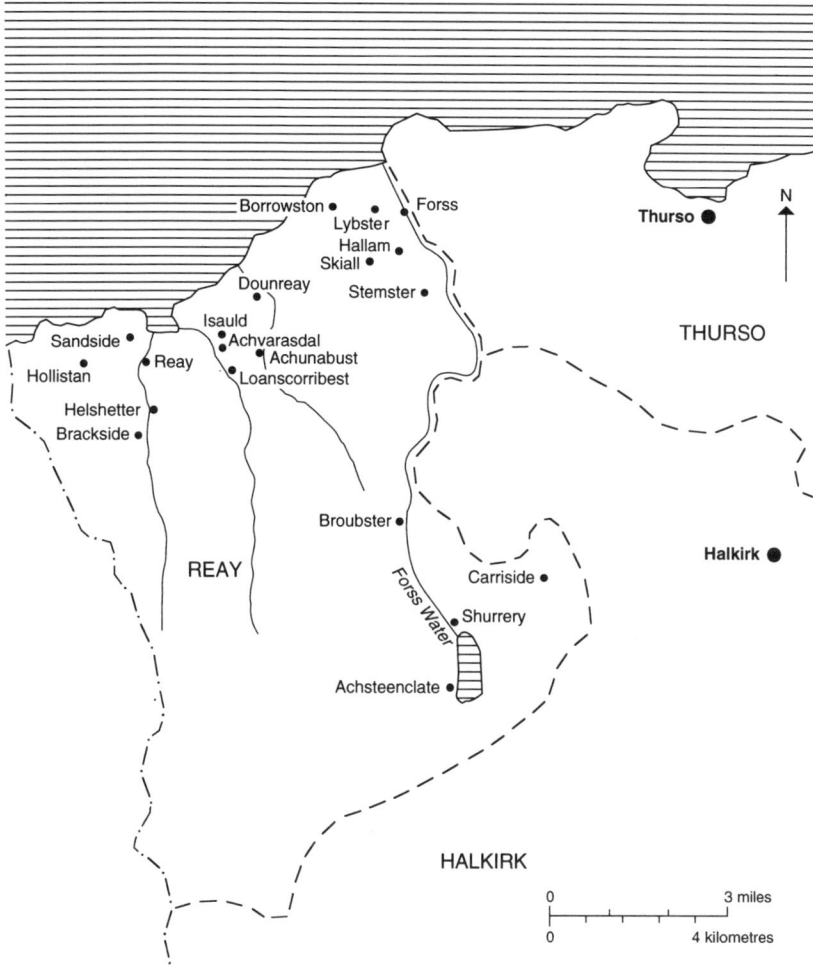

Figure 18 Reay Parish showing places mentioned in the text.

Ra	1222–45	Constitution of Bishopric (*CSR*, 14)
Ra	1439	Cawdor Charters (*CSR*, 225)
Raa	1507	*Register of the Privy Seal* (*RSS*)
Ray	1554	Sinclair (Mey)
Rhae	1640	*Retours*
Reay	1755	Roy Map (*Early Maps*)

There is also, however, the Gaelic dimension to consider. When Gaelic-speaking people became the dominant linguistic group in Reay they adopted the name and they derived other place-names from it, using their own language. It has been suggested by Gaelic scholars that Reay itself is of Gaelic origin and that it derives from

Plate 8 Grave-goods from a male pagan burial, Sandside Bay, Reay, Caithness. This is only one of the burials from a group of graves found at Reay, indicating the well-established nature of Norse settlement on the north coast of Caithness in the tenth century. The warrior's equipment includes an axe and shield boss, cloak pin and buckle, a small whetstone as well as a sickle (symbol of his farming and land-owning status). (*VA*, vol. ii, 19; Batey, i, 1987, 35–6. Batey, 1994, 152–4.) (Copyright: Trustees of the National Museums of Scotland)

the Gaelic word *ràth* 'a fortress, artificial mound' (Watson 1926, 117–18), but there is no trace of the final -th in the earliest written forms, which is strange, even though it may have been silent in speech (MacDonald 1981–82, 30–39). It seems more probable that the original place-name was of Norse origin and the Gaels used it because it was there, and they understood it as a reference to a place and had no need to understand its meaning. However, because it is human nature to wish to imbue a place with personal significance, they 'translated' the name homophonically into their own language and, when the need arose to create new place-names such as Beinn Ràtha, which lies to the south of Reay, it was the Gaelic element *ràth* which they aptly used.

This process of 'translation' of a name from one language to another is limited in practice because it depends on the existence in the translating language of a word roughly similar in sound to the original name and, simultaneously, meaningful as a referent to the place described. A more common type of borrowing from one language to another is the adding of an element in the new language to the original place-name as, for instance, in the name Dounreay. It appears that Gaelic *dùn* 'a hill or fort' has been added to the original Norse *rá* to form a composite word. Early forms of Dounreay are as follows:

Dunra	1542	*Register of the Great Seal (RMS)*
Downra	1562	Sinclair (Mey)
Dounrey	1567	*Origines Parochiales Scotiae (OPS)*

The name Dounreay has, incidentally, provided a most fascinating recent example of the process of 'translation' from one language to another. A local informant offered the comment that many people now interpret the initial Doun- as the Scots equivalent of English *down*, with reference to the position of Dounreay in relation to Reay, and have no inkling that it might be Gaelic in origin!

Some considerable time has been spent on what is a speculative reconstruction but it is the process rather than the specific example which is revealing. Many Norse names have been used in subsequent Gaelic names and the exercise of probing backwards in time to the original names is rather akin to unravelling a word puzzle. Except in the case of a very few names, none of them in Reay Parish, it is impossible to unravel further and to probe behind the Norse names because we do not know enough about the language situation in Caithness in the pre-Viking period.

Let us return, therefore, to our Scandinavian community in Reay Parish. In addition to topographical place-names such as Reay and Forss, it is typical of well-established Scandinavian communities in the north of Scotland and the Northern Isles that one finds place-names containing a variety of descriptive terms which refer to types of farm, although precise distinctions between the types are not always clear to us. There are, in addition, local differences in the application of the terms and it is clear that the Scandinavians enjoyed a degree of elasticity in the use of their place-name elements. Examples of these terms for 'farm' are *staðir*, *bólstaðr/ (bú-staðr)*, *setr* and *sætr*. In addition, there is *ærgi*, which the Scandinavians borrowed from Gaelic and which features quite prominently in Caithness.

It has been pointed out elsewhere (Waugh 1987, 61–74) that, although not particularly common in Caithness, *staðir* does occur more frequently than Nicolaisen suggested (1976, map. 5). There are two possible examples in Reay Parish: Borrowston and Drum/ Loch Hollistan, although there is no habitation at Hollistan now and the name only occurs in combination with the Gaelic topographical elements *druim* 'a ridge' and *loch* (which requires no translation). The Orkney historian, Storer Clouston, advanced a very convincing theory about the significance of the distribution of Orkney place-names containing *staðir*, suggesting that *staðir* was particularly appropriate for use when grants of land were being given as a reward for loyal service to an earl (Clouston 1932, 11). One can certainly envisage similar grants being equally appropriate across the Pentland Firth in the earls' mainland possessions. Clouston's explanation is one of the many attempts to account for the fact that *staðir* is compounded with Norse personal names much more frequently than any of the other Norse terms for farm. Even allowing for the fact that some of the suggested interpretations of specifics as personal names may be wrong – as a percentage almost inevitably will be at this distance in time and without written evidence in many cases – there does seem to be a preponderance of personal-name specifics with *staðir*.

In the case of Borrowston and Hollistan, the specifics could be *Borgarr* and any one of *Holfr*, *Hólmr* or *Holi* but, in the absence of early record, there can be no certainty. The names are recorded from the sixteenth century onwards and there is considerable influence from Scots:

Burrostoun	1549	*RSS*
Borrowstoun	1604	*Retours*
Drumhellesten	1662	Blaeu Map (*Early Maps*)
Drumhellesten	1745	Revised Mercator Map (*Early Maps*)

Indeed, it is only by turning to Orkney, where similar names occur and, in the case of Borrowston, an identical name which can be traced back to an earlier *staðir* form from a present -ston ending. (Waugh 1987, 68), that one can argue with any degree of conviction that one is dealing with a Norse *staðir* name. The change from earlier -sta endings to -ston probably came about due to confusion with Norse *tún* which was borrowed into Insular Scots as a description of enclosed land attached to farm buildings. In a Scots medium, it is very easy to read the initial s- of sta- as a possessive attaching to the end of the immediately preceding personal name and, having done that, to interpret the remaining -ta- as a 'mistake' and alter it to the more comprehensible *tún*.

Much more common than *staðir* in Caithness farm-names is *bólstaðr* (or *bú-staðr*?). In fact, *bólstaðr* is common in all parts of Scotland which were colonized by Scandinavians. In the Northern Isles it can generally be recognized as the modern ending -bister in names such as Brettabister, Norrabister and Wadbister in Shetland, and Aikerbister, Foubister and Musbister in Orkney, to name but a few. In Caithness, *bólstaðr* has been further telescoped and, on the east side of the county it appears as -bster in Ulbster, -mster in Stemster, and even -ster in Haster. Whether this further reduction of the element in Caithness is due to Gaelic, Scots or some other influence is a matter for debate. It has been quite convincingly argued that the term used in Caithness is often *bústaðr*, another Norse word for 'a farm' (Coates 1976, 188–90), which neatly accounts for the regular loss of the [l] of *bólstaðr*.

There are three examples of the -bster ending in Reay Parish in the names Broubster, Lybster and Shebster which are on record from the sixteenth century. Early forms of Broubster, and its situation, point to ON *brú* 'a bridge' as the specific in the name:

Browbstar	1562	Sinclair (Mey)
Broubuster	1662	Blaeu Map (*Early Maps*)
Brubist	1755	Roy Map

Lybster is a name which occurs elsewhere in Caithness and, although the early forms of the name are not particularly helpful, its situation in all cases would tend to support derivation of the specific from ON *hlíð* 'a slope'. Farms were very frequently situated on slopes because of drainage problems on flat ground. Examples of early forms are:

Lybuster	1549	*RSS*
Lybstar	1585	Sinclair (Mey)
Lybuster	1604	*Retours*

In the case of Shebster, the early forms give no clear indication of the identity of the specific in the name and it is wiser not to speculate. Examples of these early forms are:

Schabuster	1539	*RMS*
Shebster	1634	Sutherland (Forse)
Shabster	1755	Roy Map (*Early Maps*)

The -mster ending which was mentioned above also occurs in Reay Parish and, as in the case of Lybster, it occurs in a name which can be found elsewhere in Caithness. The Scandinavians did not hesitate to use names again and again if the situation fitted, and the repetitive habit is still with us today – we follow fashions in naming just as much as the Scandinavians used to do. Duplicate names seldom occur in close proximity, however, and it seems likely that each example of Stemster occurs in a clearly defined small local community within the larger Scandinavian world of Caithness. There are four further examples of Stemster; one each in Bower, Canisbay, Wick and Latheron Parishes on the east side of Caithness (see Fig. 17). Early examples of Stemster in Reay Parish are as follows:

Stamster	1529	*RMS*
Stambuster	1605	*Retours*
Stempster	1726	Macfarlane (vol. 1).

Old Norse *steinn* 'a stone' is the most likely source of the specific, with reference either to stony ground or to a neighbouring standing stone. The Stam- of the sixteenth- and seventeenth-century forms can be attributed to influence from Scots *stane*.

The final two examples of *bólstaðr* are Achunabust and Loanscorribest, in which the original Norse name forms the latter part of a Gaelic/Norse hybrid name. The Norse place-names must have been well known to the Gaels who moved in to Reay Parish and, in fact, the Gaelic elements with which the Norse names are compounded perhaps point to a period of coexistence when the Gaels farmed part of the original Norse holding in the period when Scandinavian power was dwindling. The prefixed Gaelic elements are *achadh* 'a field, farm' in Achunabust and *lón* 'a meadow' in Loanscorribest. The -bust and -best of the modern endings are parallel to the -bost ending of place-names in the Western Isles which may derive from an original ON *bólstaðr* (Nicolaisen 1976, 94), or possibly from *bú-staðr*.

Proposed etymologies for Norse place-names which have been part of Gaelic names for centuries are, at best, doubtful when no early spellings are available, but parallel names elsewhere can sometimes provide a clue. A.B. Taylor mentions a place-name, *Unustadir*, in Shetland, suggesting that the first element is a personal name (Taylor 1954, 125), and it is quite possible that the same female personal name – 'Una' – occurs in Achunabust. Scorribest, on the other hand, can be interpreted with a reasonable degree of certainty, even in the absence of early forms, because, like Lybster and Stemster, it is a commonly occurring name, although it is not immediately recognizable as such. The Caithness name which it duplicates, and with which most people will be familiar, is Scrabster, which is recorded as *Skarabólstaðr* (*Orkneyinga Saga* 1978, 196) in which the specific could be either *skári* 'a young sea-mew' or the related Norse personal name Skári. *Skári* was borrowed into Insular Scots in the form *skori* (Jakobsen 1932, vol. II, 801), and is still commonly used in Caithness to refer to the young gull.

Old Norse *setr* 'a pastoral farm' is very common in both Orkney and Shetland, particularly so in Shetland where the terrain is suited to pastoral rather than arable farming. The same may be said of the suitability of the Caithness terrain but *setr* is not a common element in Caithness place-names, although it does occur. In Reay Parish, the only surviving example is Helshetter in which one can see the palatalization of the initial s- of *setr* resulting from Gaelic influence. The earliest available recording of the name is from the eighteenth century, when it appears variously as *Helsettir* and *Helshitter* in the Sinclair (Freswick) estate papers. The most likely explanation of the specific is that it derives from Old Norse *hella* 'a flat stretch of rock'.

Pastoral farming would certainly have taken place in Reay Parish in the period of Scandinavian occupation and one assumes, therefore, that another element was playing the part of *setr* in the nomenclature. W.F.H. Nicolaisen has drawn attention to a group of names on the west side of Caithness and in Sutherland which now end in -side or -said and suggested that they may be derived from

ON *sætr* 'shieling', a word which is closely related to but distinct from ON *setr* (Nicolaisen 1976, 92). His argument is that where the original Old Norse form was *setr*, the initial s- should have been palatalized when subsequently used by Gaelic speakers. The fact that there is no palatalization in these place-names ending in -side, many of which are early names, suggests a non-palatal vowel in the final syllable, such as that in *sætr*. The argument is very convincing but, unfortunately, there is no proof in written record. One has to be particularly careful about suggesting that -side should derive from ON *sætr* when there is a common English place-name element -side which is also in use in Reay Parish, but English is a nineteenth-century arrival on the Reay place-name scene and when English -side does occur it is generally recognizable because of the English specific with which it is compounded, as in 'Quarry Side'.

Examples of place-names ending in -side are Brackside, Carriside, and Sandside. Unfortunately, shielings are not the material that written records are made of and there are few early references, except in the case of Sandside which has survived as a place-name throughout the post-Norse centuries because of its coastal position and its proximity to Reay. Suggestions regarding specifics must be very tentative in the case of Brackside and of Carriside, but there can be no doubt, at least regarding the meaning if not the language of origin, of the specific in Sandside. For Brackside (also recorded as Braxside on the 1876 OS map) one might propose ON *brekka* 'a slope', on the grounds that, while there is a descriptive element – *breac* 'variegated in colour' – which is popular in Gaelic toponymy, the word order in this compound favours an ON derivation. Carriside is recorded in the early nineteenth century as follows:

Carriside	1819	Sinclair (Thurso)
Caryside	1831	Thomson Map (*Early Maps*)

A tentative suggestion for the specific might be the ON personal name *Kári*.

Sandside, on the other hand, is frequently mentioned in records from the sixteenth century onwards – perhaps as it increased in importance as a settlement site. It is very aptly named, whether the language be English or Norse and, as mentioned earlier, it was the weathering of sand dunes in the vicinity of Sandside which led to the discovery of Viking graves. The following is a representative selection of early references:

Sandsid	1507	*RSS*
Sanstsyde	1558	*RSS*
Sandsyde	1640	*Retours*
Sandset	1662	Blaeu Map (*Early Maps*)

Blaeu's 1662 reference deserves special mention because Timothy Pont, who prepared the manuscript originals of the maps of Scottish counties which were published by Joannis Blaeu of Amsterdam, was minister in Dunnet Parish, Caithness, at the time when he was collecting his material. I have observed, from examples throughout Caithness, that he has attempted to make the spelling of the place-names which he records reflect local pronunciation. Many place-names can still be heard pronounced today as Blaeu recorded them and *Sandset* may be a case in point, taking us back aurally to the [t] of Old Norse *sætr*.

There is a further term for a hill farm which is quite common in inland areas of Caithness and which seems to occur in places which would have been marginal settlements of the shieling type during the period of Scandinavian occupation. The ON word is *ærgi*, which was borrowed by the Scandinavians from Gaelic *airigh* 'a shieling'. The element occurs most frequently in place-names in Latheron, Watten and Halkirk parishes, but there are also examples in Wick, Canisbay, Bower and Reay parishes, appearing variously in modern place-names as -ary, -ery, -ory. In distribution, *ærgi* appears to complement the distribution of the Norse *setr/sætr* type which suggests that the elements were meaningfully distinct in some respect, although all apply to hill farms of some sort. The *setr/sætr* type tends to be scattered along the north coast, where the Scandinavians may have established their initial habitation, whereas names containing *ærgi* lie to the south and may reflect Scandinavian contact with Gaelic speakers in the area leading to a definite preference for the Gaelic term. Gaelic *airigh* also occurs in Caithness place-names but one can generally distinguish between the two languages by the differing word order in the compounds. In Norse compounds, the normal order is specific followed by generic, whereas in Gaelic the reverse applies.

The single Reay example of ON *ærgi* is Shurrery. Some *ærgi* names are well-documented and, fortunately, Shurrery is one such. It occurs in the following forms:

Showrarne	1558	*RSS*
Schourari	1619	*RMS*
Schurarie	1640	*Retours*
Shureri	1662	Blaeu Map (*Early Maps*)

Many of the *ærgi* names appear to have Norse personal-name specifics and *Sióvarr* is the most likely in this instance. Sadly, the area round Loch Shurrery has now been virtually abandoned, with the exception of Shurrery Lodge which is used by shooting parties, but it was described in the eighteenth century as ' a tennent toun of about 21 families' (Macfarlane 1906, 184), and it was obviously inhabited before that date for so many references to the name to have survived.

A comment should be made regarding the variable survival rate of place-names that originally referred to shielings which, by defi-nition, are temporary dwellings. Some of these place-names have survived as the names of permanent habitation and others have either vanished off the modern map or now refer to topographical features where there must, at one point, have been habitation. There is, in fact, no clear pattern of survival but one feature of the landscape which does affect longevity of settlement is the presence of water in the form of loch, river or sea. Shielings, such as Shurrery, which had the advantage of being situated close to a large and productive expanse of water were more likely to survive as permanent settlements than those which were situated beside a minor stream.

In addition to the terms for farm and hill farm which have been discussed, there are some further Scandinavian names which survive in the modern nomenclature of Reay Parish: the name Skiall, for instance, which derives from ON *skáli*, an element which is quite common in Orkney place-names but which is rare in Caithness. The earliest Norse sense of the word *skáli* is 'a hut or shed put up for temporary use' (Icelandic-English Dictionary 1874, 541), but the Orkney examples indicate that it refers to a much more permanent and important residence, and the same appears to be true of the Reay example which was obviously an important settlement judging from the number of early references. The spelling Skiall first appears in 1876. Other references are:

Skaillye	1604	*Retours*
Skalie	1644	*Retours*
Skaill	1612	*RMS*

As in the earlier-mentioned case of Achunabust, Skiall became part of a later Gaelic place-name, Achiebraeskiall, which has, in turn, been Scotticized in spelling. Comment has already been made about Gaelic *achadh* which regularly appears in the form *Achie-* in word initial position, particularly in areas of later Scots influence. Gaelic *bràigh* 'a stretch of ground rising with a fairly steep slope' is well known in the form *brae* in which it was borrowed into Scots.

Another Norse name which has been compounded with *achadh* is Achsteenclate, although it is possible that it may be a later Scots coinage because both elements in the name were borrowed into the Caithness dialect of Scots and are used in the construction of place-names. There are no early references to prove the case. Arrowsmith records the name in 1807 as *Achna Steanclet* (*Early Maps of Scotland* 1973, 213). The Norse elements which could form the basis of the name are *steinn* 'a stone' and *klettr* 'a rock or crag'. Old Norse *klettr* was borrowed into Gaelic as *cleit* and into the Caithness dialect of Scots as *clett*. It is an extremely common place-name element in the Outer Hebrides, particularly Lewis and Harris, where it often applies to inland features; whereas in Shetland, where it is equally common, it generally refers to a rock in the sea. The modern spelling of the ON element in areas where there is Gaelic influence is usually -clate.

Achvarasdal may also be Norse in origin, with Gaelic *achadh* prefixed. The placing of the generic *-dal* at the end of the name indicates Norse *dalr* 'a valley' rather than Gaelic *dail* 'a meadow', but the specific is obscure. The name is recorded in the nineteenth century but neither of the references is particularly helpful in determining the nature and origin of the constituent parts:

Achavaristil	1831	Thomson Map (*Early Maps*)
Achrarasdal	1876	6" OS Map

In addition to these *achadh*-compounds, there are a few of uncertain origin which are most probably Norse, such as Isauld and Hallam. Isauld appears on record from the sixteenth century and Hallam from the seventeenth. The early forms of Isauld are very varied, indicating that the scribes were equally uncertain of the name:

Eishald	1573	Sinclair (Mey)
Isald	1573	Sinclair (Mey)
Easeald	1619	*RMS*
Isould	1667	*RMS*
Easthald	1662	Blaeu Map (*Early Maps*)
Easall	1750	Roy Map (*Early Maps*)
Isauld	1770	Sinclair (Freswick)

Norse *hald* 'a hold, fastening' or, as a law term, 'possession', does not occur in the sense of a landholding, although one suspects that the sixteenth- and seventeenth-century scribes were thinking of a landholding when they recorded the name. It is interesting that Blaeu should record it as *-hald* and it may be significant in conjunction with the directional specific *east*, which offers an easy interpretation of the name. In this instance, however, one suspects Timothy Pont of proposing his own English etymology after hearing the name in use. The Old Norse word for east is *austr*, which generally develops into the diphthong [ai], as in Isbister, not the monophthong [ʊ] as in Isald.

Hallam is recorded from the seventeenth century as follows:

Holme	1612	*RMS*
Holme	1630	*Retours*

This seems to point clearly to ON *hólmr* 'an islet' with reference to an island in the Hallam Burn or to dry land in a marsh.

The coastline, as one would expect, offers further evidence of Scandinavian presence, at least in boats, but most of the topographical names inland are of Gaelic origin and have the appearance of being comparatively recent in origin. In fact, even on the coast where the naming elements such as Scots *geo*/Gaelic *geòdha* 'a steep-sided inlet of the sea' and Scots *clett* 'a rock, crag' obviously derive ultimately from ON *gjá* and *klettr*, the compounds in which they occur sometimes suggest coinage by speakers of Gaelic or Scots rather than Norse.

In conclusion, therefore, Reay Parish presents a picture of an early Scandinavian settlement which only expanded to a limited extent in subsequent centuries. Gaelic speakers then moved in to areas which were formerly farmed by Scandinavians, using and adapting the Norse place-names with which they were already familiar. The Gaelic-speakers have, in turn, been replaced by the English or Scots speakers who now people Reay Parish and who have introduced their own place-names to mingle with and supersede those of earlier centuries and different tongues.

5 Norse settlement in south-east Sutherland*

MALCOLM BANGOR-JONES

From the ninth to the twelfth century south-east Sutherland was a part of Scandinavian Scotland. The Kyle of Sutherland/Dornoch Firth was an important political boundary, marking the furthest extent of *Suðrland*, the southern land beyond Caithness, although Norse control extended into Easter Ross. Indeed political control and settlement may well have fluctuated in this frontier region (Crawford 1985a).

There is a relative lack of documentary sources as well as a limited amount of archaeological evidence for Viking activity (see Plate 10: grave goods from a female grave near the house of Ospisdale) (Crawford 1975). This means that a great deal of emphasis is inevitably placed on the evidence of place-names in determining the extent and nature of Norse settlement in Sutherland. Recent work on Sutherland place-names includes: articles by Fraser on the Norse element in Sutherland place-names and on Norse and Celtic place-names in the Dornoch Firth area; a general survey by Macaulay of place-names in Sutherland as a whole and Mackenzie's account of the Vikings in east Sutherland which made considerable use of the place-name evidence (Fraser 1978b, 1986; Macaulay 1982; Mackenzie 1985). All of these studies owe a considerable debt to the pioneering work of MacBain and Watson (Watson 1906; MacBain 1922).[1]

There is as yet no systematic study of the place-names of any

---

* The following unpublished records have been used in the preparation of this chapter:

SRO, CS	Court of Session Records
Dep. 175	Edinburgh, National Library of Scotland, Deposit 175
Dep. 313	Edinburgh, National Library of Scotland, Deposit 313
SRO, GD 153	Gilchrist papers
SRO, SC	Dornoch Sheriff Court records
SRO, TE	Teind records

1. Watson's paper of 1906 is a critical reassessment of MacBain's original articles which appeared in the *Highland News* in 1898 and were reprinted in 1922.

Plate 9 View from Struie looking west over the Kyle of Sutherland up the River Oykell. This waterway and artery into the heart of the north-west Highlands was an important political boundary in Norse Scotland. The River Oykell (ON *Ekiallsbakki*) was known in Iceland as the traditional frontier between the southernmost province of the earldom of Caithness (*Suðrland*) and the Scottish province of Ross. The earls sometimes exercised control south of the Oykell however and settlement occurred in Ross, evidenced by the scatter of Norse place-names, some of which are found along the river valleys, as well as on the coast. (Crawford 1995.) (Copyright: R.M.M. Crawford)

part of Sutherland let alone the county as a whole. This paper has the very limited aim of exploring various aspects of Scandinavian place-names in south-east Sutherland, an area comprising the Parish of Dornoch and the eastern half of the Parish of Creich (Fig. 19). A major difficulty for any study of Sutherland place-names is the lack of surviving early forms; many settlement names do not appear in the documentary record until the seventeenth or even eighteenth centuries. It is also important to bear in mind the linguistic background and the history of settlement in the post-Norse era.

LINGUISTIC BACKGROUND

Crawford sets Sutherland within the linguistic region of Scandinavian Scotland containing place-names of mixed Gaelic and

Plate 10   This brooch and piece of a steatite bowl were found near the house of Ospisdale, south-east Sutherland, and are the remains of one of a small number of pagan graves which have been found in the area. These are the most southerly examples of pagan burials in north-east Scotland, and bear witness to the importance of the Kyle of Sutherland (Dornoch Firth) as the southern frontier of Norse-dominated territory in the pagan period. The woman's bronze 'tortoise' brooch is of a very widespread type, but the steatite bowl is unusual in Viking graves in Scotland (although common in Norway). Both objects are evidence of the standard nature of Norse culture within the Norse settlements around the Scottish coasts: the steatite bowl is probably from Shetland. A woman's grave is an indication of the settled nature of Norse control in south-east Sutherland. (*VA*, vol. ii, 17–18.) (Copyright: Trustees of the National Museums of Scotland)

Norse character, a legacy of the fact that the Gaelic language supplanted the Norse after the decline of Norse political power in the late twelfth and early thirteenth centuries (Crawford 1987, 93). It is likely that the feudal settlement of Sutherland by the de Moravias encouraged an influx of Gaelic speakers (Crawford 1985). However, the linguistic background is more complicated than might be supposed. South-east Sutherland was well within the Pictish heartland, as the presence of *pit-* names suggests. Furthermore, linguistic evidence indicates that it is very likely that Gaelic speakers had reached Sutherland by *c.* 800, and Gaelic was

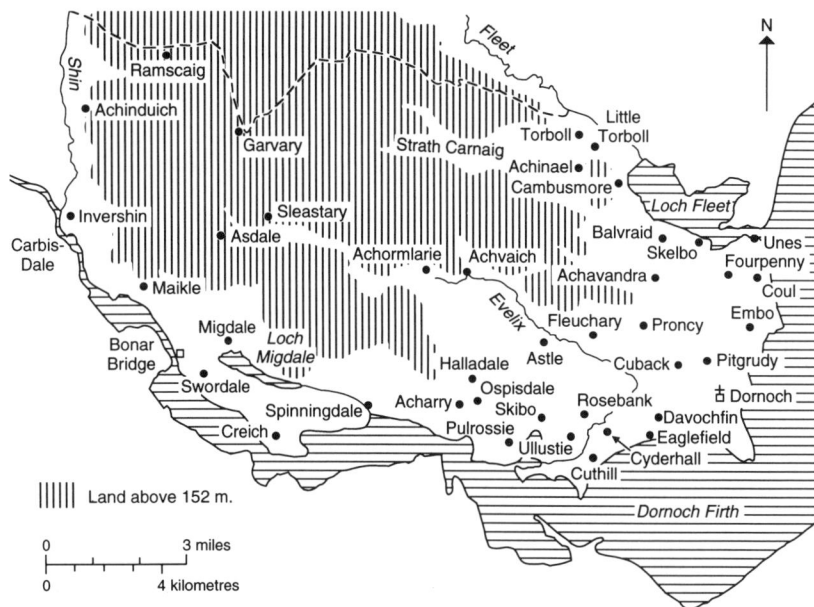

Figure 19 South-east Sutherland showing places mentioned in the text.

presumably the dominant language in Sutherland for a while. Watson claimed that 'it is highly probable that there was a good deal of bi-lingualism' during the Norse period and indeed the Norse language did have an appreciable influence on Sutherland Gaelic (Watson 1906; Dorian 1981; Fraser 1986). In this context, attention should be drawn to Cox's study of place-names in the west of Lewis which found 'substantial evidence for a continuous Gaelic speaking presence through the Norse settlement period' (Cox 1991, 483). Finally, one cannot discount the influence of Scots from about the sixteenth century.

SETTLEMENT HISTORY

Sandwiched between the Dornoch Firth and Loch Fleet (the latter a more obvious barrier before the construction of The Mound in the early nineteenth century), south-east Sutherland represents a continuation of the eastern coastal plain of Scotland. The area consists of a favoured coastal fringe surrounding undulating peat-covered hills. In the pre-Improvement period, the agriculture was both arable and stock-farming: the coastal farms placed greater emphasis on the produce of their arable lands and their rents were paid in grain, while farms at a slightly higher altitude or on poorer soil were more orientated to stock and the rents were paid partly or wholly in money. Most of the interior was common grazing and the greater part of the hill pasture to the north of Bonar Bridge lay within a commonty which may have originated during the thirteenth-century disputes between the Bishops of Caithness and Earls of Sutherland (*Bishopric*). By the mid-eighteenth century many of the peat diggings around the main settlements had been worked out, while settlement colonization was leading to a much more intensive use of the hill grazings. During the first half of the nineteenth century the settlement pattern was profoundly altered by the clearance of many townships to create large arable and sheep farms, the creation of crofts (the Dornoch Muirs formed one of the major resettlement areas during the Sutherland clearances) and the establishment of extensive plantations. The settlement history helps us to understand the environmental and historical context for settlements in the Viking period in a way in which the present settlement pattern clearly does not.

THE PLACE-NAME EVIDENCE

The number of settlements on the modern OS 1:10,000 maps with Norse names is small; most settlement names are Gaelic and a few are Pictish, Scots or English. Moreover, there do not appear to be any place-names of the types which Cox has found for the west of the Island of Lewis which might indicate the existence of extinct Norse settlement names (Cox 1989). Assessing the number of Norse names in percentage terms is a dangerous pursuit given the immense changes in the settlement pattern. Of much greater significance is the fact that several of the more important settlements, coincident with the names appearing in medieval- to sixteenth-century charters, are Norse. The main exceptions to this appear to be Proncy (1275 Promsy, 1360 Proncey), for which no satisfactory derivation has yet been suggested, Pulrossie (1464 Pulrossy: *Munro Writs*, 21), Criech, Invershin and Achinduich. It is noticeable that the Gaelic names predominate in the western or more inland parts.

Of the various Scandinavian names generally taken to mean a farm there do not appear to be any *setr*-names in south-east Sutherland. There is only one possible *staðir*-name, Ullestie, a settlement on the lands of Skibo, which Mackenzie suggests may have originally been *Ullastaðir* or 'Ulli's steading' (Mackenzie 1985). The name appears in records as: Ullest 1557 (*OPS*), Ullestie 1581 (*RMS*) and 1733 Alusty (SRO, CS) but has not been in use since at least *c*. 1800. There is some confusion over the relationship of this name to Cuthill – a charter of 1581 refers to the lands of Cuthill or Cuthill-daill or Dall-ullustie (*RMS*). It appears, however, that Ullustie was a separate settlement, possibly to the north of the River Evelix (Bentinck 1926, map facing 448).

There are four settlement names which contain the habitative element *bólstaðr* (in its contracted forms *boll, bo*):

EMBO: Ethenboll *c.* 1230 (*Bishopric*); Indboll 1606 (*OPS*); Eyndboll 1610 (*OPS*); Endbow 1623 (Dep. 175); Embow 1624 (Dep. 175). Watson's suggestion of 'Eyvind's stead' has met with general acceptance (Watson 1906, 361).

SKELBO: Scelebol 1212 × 1214 (*RRS*); Scelleboll *c.* 1230 (*Bishopric*); Skelbo 1515 (*OPS*). Fraser follows Watson in putting forward 'shell-stead', while Mackenzie favours the more plausible 'shell-sand farm' (Watson 1906, 362; Fraser 1978b, 19; Mackenzie 1985).

SKIBO: Scitheboll *c.* 1230 (*Bishopric*); Scythebolle 1275 (*Bishopric*); Skiboll 1708 (SRO, TE). Watson suggests either 'Skithi's stead' or, from ON *skið*, 'firewood-stead'; Mackenzie and Macaulay find for the former while Fraser accepts the latter (Watson 1906, 362; Fraser 1978b, 19; Macaulay 1982, 282; Mackenzie 1985).

TORBOLL: Thoreboll *c.* 1230 (*Bishopric*); Thorboll 1363 (*RRS* David II 338). Fraser and Macaulay follow Watson's suggestion of 'Thori's stead' but Mackenzie favours *torf-bol*, 'big farm made of turf blocks' (Watson 1906, 361; Fraser 1978b, 18; Macaulay 1982, 282; Mackenzie 1985).

The *bólstaðr* settlement names in this area all occupy favoured locations, in the lowland coastal fringe. Not surprisingly in view of their relatively high assessments and rental values, these settlements were to become large, well-established arable farms producing grain surpluses. Such areas had almost certainly been previously cultivated and must be regarded as the primary settlements of the Vikings. These observations, which could also be made of the two *bólstaðr* settlements in Easter Ross, Cadboll and Arboll, confirm Fellows-Jensen's characterization of places with *bólstaðr*-names (Fellows-Jensen 1984, 160). It should not be assumed, however, that the names which have survived were the original Viking names for these settlements. As has been suggested, *bólstaðr* names may have been formed as settlement expanded and large farms were split up into more manageable units, and the original names lost (Macgregor 1986, 99; Crawford 1987, 111). On the other hand, the considerable doubts which have been cast on Nicolaisen's sequence of habitative place-name elements mean that one cannot, for instance, argue that the prevalence of *bólstaðr* names means that the Vikings settled later in east Sutherland than elsewhere. Waugh's observation that in Caithness *bólstaðr* names appear to parallel Gaelic *achadh* names is only true in part for this area (Waugh 1987, 67). The *achadh* names are either small, late-established settlements in marginal areas, or the detached and smaller parts of larger units in the way that Achavandra was a part of the Skelbo estate, or Achinael part of Torboll.

Lastly, it is possible to document the process of contraction whereby endings in *-boll* gave way to endings in *-bo*. As Watson noted, the Gaelic versions of these names preserve the *-boll* form. In Gaelic Skibo is *Sgiobul* while Embo is *Eiribol* (Watson 1906, 361–2). On the other hand, in the seventeenth and eighteenth centuries Torboll was often written as Torbo (Arboll in Easter Ross is also found in this form). These examples suggest that the *-bo* forms may owe their existence to the spread of the Scots language in eastern Sutherland during the sixteenth and seventeenth centuries.

Of the various topographical place-names, those formed by the element ON *dalr*, dale, are the most common:

ASTLE: Askesdale *c.* 1230 (*Bishopric*); Haskesdale 1275 (*Bishopric*); Assastel 1360 (*RRS VI* no. 307); Aisdill 1655 (*OPS*). It is generally agreed that this is 'ash-dale'.

OSPISDALE: Hospisdaill 1628 (*Munro Writs*). Watson's suggestion of 'Ospak's dale', has met with general acceptance (Watson 1906, 362).

SPINNINGDALE: Spanegydill 1464 (*Munro Writs*); Spanegidill 1464 (*RMS*); Spayngdale (*RMS*). Watson suggests that the second syllable is ON *vik*, a bay, and that the first may be ON *spann*, a pail or measure (Watson 1906, 363). Macaulay, on the other hand, proposes ON *spong-engi-dalr*, 'round-shaped pasture dale' (Macaulay 1982, 283). Finally, Mackenzie suggests that the name may derive from ON *spang*, a single plank bridge (Mackenzie 1985).

MIGDALE: Miggeweth 1275 (*Bishopric*); Migdale 1581 (*RMS*). Macaulay suggests ON *mugga-dalr*, 'wet-ground dale', while Mackenzie puts forward ON *mjuk dal*, 'glen of soft fertile soil' (Macaulay 1982, 283; Mackenzie 1985).

SWORDALE: Swerdisdale/Swerdel 1275 (*Bishopric*); Mekill Sordell 1581 (*RMS*); Swardell 1583 (*RMS*). Watson suggests 'sward-dale' or 'grassy-dale' (Watson 1906, 362).

AUSDALE or ASDALE in district of Ardens: Mackenzie suggests ON *Olafsdal*, 'Olaf's glen' (Mackenzie 1985). However, Allt Asdale may preserve the original form, in which case this may be similar to Astle above.

HALLADALE: a cottage above Overskibo. This is probably a modern introduction.

CUTHILDALE: Cuthill or Cuthill-daill or Dall-ullustie 1581 (*RMS*); 'Cuthill and Cuthildale' 1733 (SRO, CS). There is also a reference to 'the landis now callit Cuthill' 1565 (*RMS*). This may be derived from Cutheldawach (see below).

Other Norse names include:

UNES: Owenes 1275 (*Bishopric*). Ferry Unes was the old name for the Little Ferry across the Fleet. The name contains the element *nes*, a point or headland.

CUBACK: Mackenzie suggests that this derives from ON *bakki*, a ridge (Mackenzie 1985).

CYDERHALL: Syvardhoch 1222–45 (*Bishopric*). As is well known, this is 'Sigurd's howe', the probable burial place of Earl Sigurd 'the Mighty' (Mackenzie 1985; Crawford 1986).

Mackenzie has identified a number of other Scandinavian names, some of which have been disguised as English names, including, for example, Eaglefield, thought to derive from ON *Helgavöll*, 'Helgi's field'. This is unlikely as the farm appears to have been established on a former commonty. Equally, Rosebank, which Mackenzie suggests is ON *hrossa-bakki*, 'horse's bank', is known to have formerly been Ryre and the name Rosebank appears to date from the early nineteenth century (SRO, SC).

RAMSCAIG of Achinduich may well contain ON *skiki*, a strip or small field which is Gaelicized as -*scaig* (Fraser 1978b, 21). Ramscaig, a small appendage of Achinduich occupied by one household, is first mentioned in 1739 (SRO, SC). It is also worth drawing attention to Arscaig on the west shore of Loch Shin in the Parish of Lairg which was also a small settlement. It was part of the 9-pennylands of 'Clinol'; together, the pendicles of Sallachie and Arscaig were assessed at 3 pennylands (Dep. 175; Dep. 313). This evidence would appear to support the suggestion that we are dealing with a small cultivated patch which did not comprise a separate holding.

There are several settlement names which incorporate the element *erg* which is borrowed from the Old Gaelic *airge*, now found as *airigh* (a shieling): Garvary, Sleastary, Achormlarie, Fleuchary and (?) Acharry. In contrast to some other *erg* names in Sutherland, none of the above – with the possible exception of Sleastary – have Norse initial elements. It might be argued that we should only include those examples which have been compounded with a Scandinavian specific as being of Scandinavian date (cf. Andersen 1991). On the other hand, the *erg* names from south-east Sutherland display all the characteristics which have been noted by Fellows-Jensen: they are 'generally lower, less remote and more fertile' (Fellows-Jensen 1980, 71–2; 1984) and nearly all were transformed into permanent settlements. During the eighteenth century these were places occupied by herdsmen on a permanent basis who looked after large herds of cattle. The herdsmen either occupied the land rendering herding services to the landlord's cattle or they paid rent and earned money herding cattle of the tenants. The cattle were often 'yeld' (non-milking) stock. Elsewhere in Sutherland during the seventeenth and early eighteenth centuries some of the upland grazings were occupied as 'bow-rooms': herds of cattle, or 'bows', were entrusted to herdsmen for the payment of butter and cheese (thus clearly including milking cows) – products for the laird's household or for sale. The scale of the operation sets these grazings aside from the normal shielings. It is not surprising that the more favourable sites were the first to be colonized. The evidence for 'bow-rooms' clearly parallels Higham's observation on -*erg* names in Northern England and their coincidence with vaccaries (Higham 1977).

Information on pre-Clearance field names (strictly speaking unenclosed areas of rigs) is difficult to come by. However, such lists as there are indicate that by the eighteenth century all field names in this area were Gaelic. (See for instance the 1735 list of the fields of Skibo: SRO, CS, and the 1765 list of the fields of Ospisdale: SRO, GD 153.) There are two possible reasons for this. Either there were no Norse field names, perhaps implying that the land was not worked by Norse speakers, or there were Norse field-names but they have all been replaced by Gaelic ones. Field-names are likely to have been less permanent than settlement names and indeed Gaelic users of the arable would in due course of time probably give meaningful names to the patches of arable. However, the documentary sources and the lack of earlier lists of field names do not allow us to test this.

ESTATE CENTRES

There is a remarkable coincidence within this area of Sutherland between the estate centres of the sixteenth to eighteenth centuries – Torboll, Skelbo, Embo and Skibo – and the *bólstaðr* settlements. Earlier sources suggest that these estates date back at least to the take-over of Sutherland by the de Moravia family. The estate of Skelbo (excepting outlying lands such as Invershin which were included within the barony of Skelbo) extended from Cambusmore to Coul and had been granted by Hugh de Moravia to his relative, Gilbert, later bishop of Caithness (*RRS II*, no. 520). At its centre was the castle of Skelbo, occupying a very strong position over-looking the natural harbour of Loch Fleet (the Vikings may have occupied it as a small fortified or castle site). Several settlement names within the estate refer to divisions or parts of a larger unit: Coul was formerly known as Davachdow, effectively the black davoch of Skelbo; the now long-lost settlement of Pitmain, means the 'mid-share'; and Fourpenny derives from the Norse pennyland assessment – it means a piece of land (Skelbo) assessed at 4 pennylands.

The lands of Torboll formed the centre of the barony of Torboll, an extensive possession which included lands elsewhere in Sutherland, granted by Earl William to his brother Nicholas in 1360 (*RRS VI* no. 307). The whole barony was assessed at 16 davochs, while Torboll itself, which stretched from the River Fleet up Strath Carnaig and comprised Meikle and Little Torboll, was assessed at 3 davochs. Embo was a smaller estate, assessed at 2 davochs, although there is the possibility that lands were lost to the town of Dornoch at an early period.

The lands of Skibo formed a large estate which was acquired by the bishops of Caithness possibly at the time of their move from Caithness to Dornoch (Crawford 1985). Bishop Gilbert's (1222 × 1245) constitution of Dornoch cathedral refers to the 12 davochs of Skelbo split into the 6 davochs of Skibo and the 6 davochs of Cyderhall (*CSR*, no. 9). The farm or settlement of Cyderhall itself was assessed at 12 pennylands or 2 davochs. The estate extended from the boundary between the parishes of Dornoch and Creich at the west to Davochfin, the white davoch (of Cyderhall), at the east and included Achormlarie and Achvaich to the north. It also included Cuthel, named in 1275 as Cutheldawach – a davoch of Cyderhall, which Barrow identifies as an early administrative centre, the name derived from Gaelic *comhdhail* meaning an assembly or meeting place where courts met (Barrow 1981).

The settlements to the west of Skibo were apparently contained within the lands of 'Ferincoskry' which Watson translates as 'Coscrach's land' (Watson 1926, 118). There are several Norse settlement names to the west of Skibo but the Gaelic territorial name of Ferincoskry may indicate that Norse-owned estates were confined to the eastern fringes of south-east Sutherland. This is not the same as Norse overlordship, which presumably extended over the whole of Sutherland, or Norse settlement which reached far into the interior.

The coincidence between *bólstaðr*-names and large estates should not be taken too far. While we should be looking for names signifying large land units or estates as opposed to names denoting the settlement sites within such units, it should not be assumed that all the *bólstaðr* names signify an estate. A look at other *bólstaðr* names within Sutherland such as Unapool in Assynt and Collaboll, a minor settlement contained within the lands of Lairg, warns us that we appear to be dealing with a local phenomenon. Thomson has suggested that *boer*-names in Orkney record the existence of Pictish estates which were taken over and renamed by the Norse (Thomson 1987).

Each of these estates, and those of Cadboll and Arboll in Easter Ross, formed a relatively compact block of land which contained a number of settlements with linked arable and grazings and generally including special resources of meadow-ground, woodland and fishings. Thomson, in his study of Tuquoy on the Island of Westray described an estate belonging to one of the leading members of Orkney's warrior sub-aristocracy. Indeed he argued that such multiple estates formed the basic unit of settlement rather than the family farm (Thomson 1990). The strong continuity which these estates suggest between the pre-Norse and Norse periods is mirrored by the fiscal evidence whereby the Norse pennyland assessment appears to have been based on the pre-Norse davoch (Bangor-Jones 1987).

CONCLUSION

Summaries of the Norse place-name evidence for south-east Sutherland have differed in emphasis as to the nature of the Norse settlement. Watson pointed out that the Norse element is much stronger in north Sutherland (Strathnaver) than in Sutherland proper (the earldom lands) and stated that the place-names showed 'that the Norsemen held the whole of Sutherland as its overlords but did not occupy it to the extent of displacing the native population or their language' (Watson 1906, 360). In a study of Norse settlement in the neighbouring area of Easter Ross, Small claimed that the extant distribution of Norse place-names was but a 'tiny fragment of a much larger original pattern' (Small 1986, 206). Mackenzie, on the other hand, argued that the existing Norse place-name evidence for south-east Sutherland was sufficient to indicate a thorough takeover which achieved some permanence (Mackenzie 1985).

In assessing the nature and extent of Norse settlement in south-east Sutherland, it is no longer possible to argue, as Fraser did, that topographical names are 'much less reliable pointers to actual settlement by Norse speakers' than habitative names (Fraser 1979, 20; cf. Small 1982). However, even after taking account of all place-name categories, the number and range of Norse settlement names is relatively small. It might be assumed that the marginal location of some settlements with Norse place-names indicates that the Norse settlement was more extensive than is sometimes realized. But, until a systematic study of the place-name evidence is carried out, some doubt must surround the status of settlementnames incorporating elements such as -*skiki* and -*erg* which may have continued in use well after the Norse period.

Most recent place-name studies have been based on the assumption that the re-emergence of Gaelic as the dominant language led to the disappearance of many Norse place-names: as Mackenzie put it, 'Gaelic was overlaid directly on top of Norse' (Mackenzie 1985). As has already been seen, the linguistic background was more complex than this and if the Norse period in south-east Sutherland was characterized by bilingualism, then it is possible that an unknown number of Gaelic place-names survived from the pre-Norse era. Cox's suggestion of Norse and Gaelic communities coexisting relatively isolated from each other is a real possibility (Cox 1988). It should also be noted that Norse names for major settlements are more likely to have been transmitted because it was the names of such estates, rather than minor dependent settlements, which were mentioned in charters.

There are, thus, particular difficulties in using the place-name evidence as a basis for studying Norse settlement in this area. With other areas of Norse settlement which later became dominated by the Gaelic language in mind, it may be tentatively concluded that south-east Sutherland was an area which undoubtedly experienced a Norse presence but where control/ownership may have been achieved by relatively small numbers. It is suggested that the Norse may have been restricted to the major farms and limited peasant consolidation took place. Bearing in mind the sites occupied by pre-Norse settlement names, it is probable that while individual settlements may have expanded during the Norse period, there were few new settlements created by Norse speakers. There may of course have been colonization by non-Norse speakers, perhaps because of population displacement.

It is scarcely surprising that the major Norse settlements and Norse-held estates were concentrated on the rich arable lands of the coastal fringe. Lack of documentary evidence makes it impossible to say whether these estates existed before the arrival of the Vikings (although archaeological evidence for Pictish settlement suggests that a well-organized Celtic society was in possession of the best land). It is indeed likely that, as in other areas, the Vikings utilized pre-existing economic and social structures. It would surely have been far easier to adopt the existing administrative system both for the exaction of rents and services and imposition of overlordship.

6 Norse settlement on the north-west seaboard

IAN FRASER

The coastlands of North-West Sutherland and Wester Ross contain some of the most isolated and inhospitable parts of Scotland. Their position, on the extreme Atlantic edge of the British mainland, together with their mountainous character, have resulted in low population densities, few important centres of population, and generally difficult landward communications. Yet this north-western tip of Scotland lies in a key position in terms of the historical development of Norse power in the Viking period and beside a major sea-route.

This study will examine two distinct areas of Norse settlement in this locality. The first lies between the Kyle of Tongue on the north coast of Sutherland and Loch Laxford on the west coast (see Fig. 20); the second includes the stretch of indented coastline between Loch Broom and Loch Carron in Wester Ross (see Fig 21). Both of these areas, which are characterized by mainly (but not exclusively) coastal settlement, contain significant numbers of Norse place-names.

In recent years, most onomastic attention has been paid to habitative names, i.e. names which contain a generic indicative of human habitation, such as ON *bol*, 'farm', 'dwelling', etc. Studies such as those of Nicolaisen have rightly seen the value of such generics as prime indicators of Norse settlement (Nicolaisen 1976). In one of the areas which this chapter examines, however, such generics amount to only a handful, and in the other, more southerly, they are almost completely absent. This lack of habitative names forced some commentators to suggest that these coastlands, while not prime Norse settlement zones, may well have been subjected to seasonal or temporary settlement, in order to exploit the resources which these coastlands had to offer (Nicolaisen 1976; Fraser 1978). However, Crawford makes the valid point that farms with topographical names are now recognized as being early and relatively important, at least in the Icelandic context, 'where some of the largest and oldest farms had names ending in *-dalr, -nes, -fell* and -*eyri*, as well as simplex topographical names like Foss, Holm and Tongue' (Crawford 1987, 111). So it is important that such place-names should be studied in association with, and not excluded from, habitative generics like -*bol*, -*bólstaðr* and -*setr*.

How do these areas look when such names are taken into consideration, from the point of view of the place-name scholar? Could it be that the names of topographic features, and non-habitative names, suggest other conclusions? This study hopes to draw some conclusions from the onomastic evidence for the nature of Viking settlement.

NORTH-WEST COAST (Fig. 20)[1]

It is here that an analysis of the site is all-important, together with the position of the place in a wider geographical context. When we view the fjord-like inlets of north Sutherland where many of these names are concentrated, we can appreciate the significance of Norse settlement here, forming as it does a zone of transition between the agricultural areas of Caithness to the east and the Western Isles to the west. The geographical key to settlement patterns in the area must surely lie in the presence of *Am Parbh*, from ON *hvarf*, 'turning point', the desolate and steep-cliffed promontory which we now call Cape Wrath (Taylor 1973). This must have proved a considerable hindrance to Norse navigators, especially in westerlies, necessitating careful choice of sailing weather, even in high summer.

The presence of a series of safe anchorages in such sea-lochs as the Kyle of Durness, Loch Eriboll and the Kyle of Tongue together with the associated settlements, must have been a key factor in the overall picture of Norse activity. It is therefore not surprising that the small number of habitative names that do occur in this zone are located in the most productive and strategic locations along this section of the coast.

If we examine each of these inlets, we can observe a grouping of Norse names which, taken together, suggest a consolidation of coastal settlements, with what seem to be landward communities that act as a 'hinterland', albeit in a very limited manner.

The Kyle of Durness is untypical of the others, in that it is shallow, affording only limited access to the interior for large vessels and displaying few of the characteristics of the fjord-like inlets so common in the north-west. Most of the Norse names here are to be found on the eastern shore, and the coastal portion between Faraid Head and the mouth of Loch Eriboll. Faraid Head is itself an imposing promontory, with cliffs over 300 ft high

---

1. For a recent discussion of Norse pagan graves recorded from this locality see Batey, 1994, 155–8 (ed.)

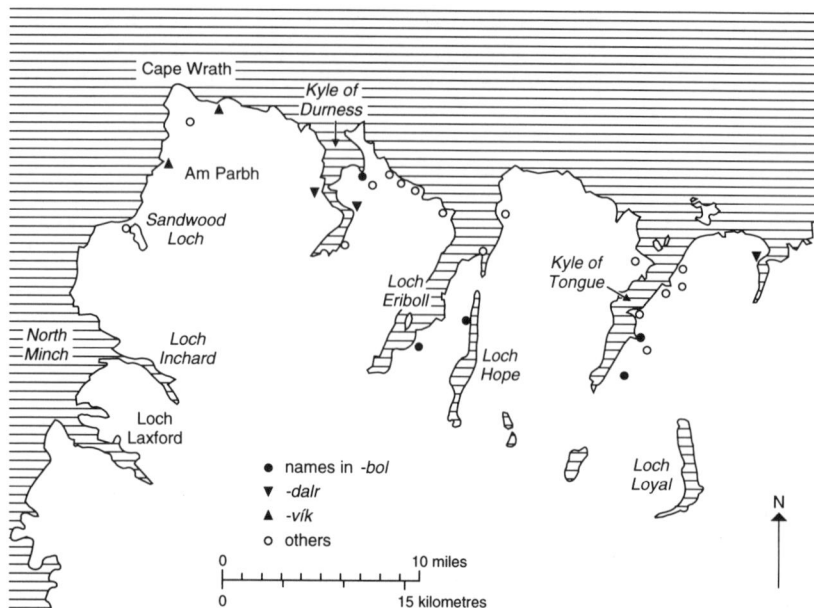

Figure 20   Scandinavian place-names in Durness and north-west mainland of Scotland.

protecting the sandy Balnakeil Bay, at the southern apex of which lies the Kirkton of Balnakeil (see Plate 11). This may well have been the site of an early *Croispol*, 'cross-stead', now commemorated only in the name of the loch which drains into the bay beside the churchyard (OS grid no. NC 391687). The village of Durness (NC 402676) is a largely modern creation, although the parish name is on record as 'Dyrnes' as early as 1230. The Norse habit of naming peninsulas in *-nes* frequently survived the transition to Gaelic, not only in Mull, Skye and the Western Isles, but in this area also.

To the east, on a series of minor inlets, lie Sangomore (NC 409674) perhaps ON *sandr-gjá*, 'sandy-cleft' with G. *mor* ending; Smoo (NC 416670) from ON *smúga* 'rift' 'cleft', still noted for a spectacular cave; Sangobeg (NC 427662) and Rispond (NC 452654) which may contain ON *hrís*, 'brushwood'. None of these contain Norse habitative generics, but they nevertheless occupy secondary sites that were obviously within reach of the central settlement at Croispol, and probably in its sphere of influence.

To the south of the present village lies Keoldale (NC 383662), found as Kauldale 1559 and Kealdil 1654. This is suggested by MacBain as ON *kaldr dalr*, 'cold valley', but W.J. Watson in his introduction to MacBain's volume considered that untenable (MacBain 1922, 17, x.). Although there is no obvious *dalr* here, the site looks southwards to the head of the Kyle, and towards

Plate 11 View across Balnakeil Bay, with the ruins of Durness old parish church centre left. The dramatic scenery of the north-west mainland of Scotland is very reminiscent of parts of Norway's west coast. It was a strategically significant piece of coast for Viking ships which had to round the headland of Cape Wrath en route from Orkney to the Hebrides. The apparent absence of pagan graves in this area has recently been rectified by the discovery of an equipped Norse boy's grave found in the dunes on the opposite side of Balnakeil Bay from the Church. (Batey, 1994, 157–8.) (Copyright. National Monuments Record of Scotland)

Sarsgrum (NC 379643), an unidentified Norse name a mile to the south. On the west side of the Kyle is Daill (NC 359682), named after the river which enters the loch near its mouth. The coastline between here and the point of Cape Wrath contains several Norse names, including Kearvaig, (NC 292728) a small *vík* with an obscure first element, at the mouth of a substantial stream; and a number of coastal names containing elements such as Gaelic *geodha* (from ON *gjá*, 'cleft') in Geodha Dubh (black cleft), Geodha Sligeach (shelly cleft) and Geodha na Seamraig (shamrock cleft). There is also Cleit Dhubh, 'black rock', from ON *klettr* 'offshore rock'. This entire coastline as far as its nomenclature is concerned is similar to Lewis in many respects, since the severe nature of the cliffs, reefs and inshore seas require a high density of names in very much the same manner as, for example, Ness or Point (Fraser 1974, 11–21).

Loch Eriboll is very different in character compared with the Kyle of Tongue. A narrow coastal strip on the western shore discouraged much settlement, and it is only on the east that a succession of small bays and headlands allows more arable farming. Eriboll (NC

432564) itself is a substantial farm and the presence of an important broch at Kempie (NC 446579, derivation unknown) is evidence of pre-Norse settlement. Another broch is marked on the OS map at NC 460605 a couple of miles north near Loch Cragaidh. Across the ridge, on Loch Hope-side lies Arnaboll, (NC 468579) (mis-placed on the Blaeu map of 1654 as actually lying on Loch Eriboll). This has a substantial number of sixteenth-century forms – Ardeboll, Arnboll, Ardnaboll and Arnobill, and appears in the Roy Military Survey of 1750–55 as 'Ardiboll'. The derivation is generally accepted as 'Arni's stead'.

The River Hope, running into Loch Eriboll is clearly from ON *hóp* 'bay', 'inlet', but whether the feature responsible for this is the small river estuary at NC 478620, or the northern end of Loch Hope itself is impossible to say. At the eastern entrance to Loch Eriboll lies Freisgill, explained as 'noisy ravine' (MacBain 1922, 16). Thus, the majority of major settlement names on the eastern shore are of Norse origin.

The third and final inlet to be surveyed in this study is the Kyle of Tongue, separated from Loch Eriboll by a wide expanse of relatively flat, peaty moorland known as A'Mhoine, 'the peat-moor'. This Kyle is similar in character to the Kyle of Durness, largely tidal with fine sand and gravel banks. The prime site is Tongue (from ON *tunga*, 'tongue of land'), probably an early Norse settlement site near the present Tongue Lodge (NC 590585). The generic *tunga* appears frequently in Iceland, sometimes in precisely this simplex form. South of this tongue of land there was a 'church-stead', Kirkiboll (NC 591565), and Ribigill (NC 583338) recorded as Regeboll in 1530 (MacBain 1922, 16), and therefore a good candidate for a habitative name in *-bol*. Two places containing ON *bakki*, 'bank', Coldbackie (NC 613600), 'cold-bank', and Hysbackie (NC 596557) perhaps 'high bank', Skullomie (NC 617613), possibly *skolli-hamar*, 'fox-slope' and Blandy (NC 620600), derivation unknown, provide further evidence for the extent of Norse settlement. On the western side, Melness (NC 585620) is the promontory lying between Achininver and the Kyle, now occupied by over a dozen small crofting townships, mostly with Gaelic names, and largely settled since 1700.

Minor coastal names in *geodha, stac* and *cleit* are common along the coastline to the west. The off-shore island, Eilean nan Ron (NC 640655) which was inhabited within living memory, lacks much in the way of Norse minor names since it was largely a product of nineteenth-century settlement. The present writer conducted a survey of this island in 1976–77, (Fraser 1978a, 83–90) and found only the usual *sgeir* 'rock', *geodha*, 'cleft', *'mol'* 'shingle or pebble beach' and the neighbouring islet called *Meall Thuilm* (on the OS map as Meall Halm, NC 629662), deriving from ON *holmr*, 'islet'. It is true to say, however, that the frequency of such terms along this coastline is reminiscent of the coasts of Skye or Lewis rather than that of mainland Wester Ross, and the impression one gets is of a landscape which retained Norse names for many of the more prominent and economically significant topographic features.

WESTER ROSS (Fig. 21)

The section of coastline between Loch Broom and Loch Carron is highly indented, with a number of sea-lochs formed by the last glaciation. These coastlands provide a variety of scenery, ranging from the typically fjord situations with U-shaped profiles, like Loch Broom, to the more open inlet conditions at Loch Ewe and Gairloch. The interior of Lewisian Gneiss and Torridonian Sandstone, however, provides a dramatic backdrop to the coast, with Ben More Coigach, An Teallach, Slioch and the Torridon hills being the principal summits. Another feature of the landscape is Loch Maree, some 21km long, occupying a major fault-line lying north-west/ south-east, and draining into Loch Ewe by the River Ewe.

There can be no doubt that this area attracted Norse settlement, since there are substantial numbers of topographic names which are clearly of Norse origin, but habitative names are confined to the single example of Ullapool (NH 125940). This occurs on Pont (1654) as Ullabill ('Ulli's farm'), on an excellent and highly-strategic site at the mouth of Loch Broom, well sheltered from prevailing winds, and with potentially good arable land close by. It is surprising, perhaps, that no other Norse names in *-bol* have survived in this part of Wester Ross, as there are many potentially fertile spots along the coast which could have supported permanent 'steads' of the kind found in north Sutherland – indeed, many of these locations are in much more favourable conditions as regards soil and other natural resources. But even as far as Gaelic habitative names are concerned, this whole zone is virtually devoid of them. Names in *baile* 'farmstead' are rare, and only one example of *cill* 'church' exists. Most settlement names, if not of Norse origin, are products of post-medieval, Gaelic settlement, using topographic terms as standard components, although *achadh* 'field' and *bad* 'place, clump of trees' are both common, and achieve the status of habitative names which they might not have attained in areas where *baile* and *cill* were common.

The number of Norse names indicative of pasturage and husbandry is low in the area. Langwell in Strath Kanaird (NC 174028) is one of the few in this northern section to contain ON *völlr* 'field'. Loch Kanaird itself (NH 110990) is suggested by Watson to be *kann-fjörðr*, 'Can-firth'; derived from the name of the broch, now ruinous, near the entrance to the loch on its western side, called Dun Canna. Its *can*-like shape struck the Norsemen, as did the *can*-like peak of the chief hill in Raasay, also called in Gaelic Dun Canna, in English Dun Can according to Watson (1904, 256). Calascaig, at the foot of Loch Achall (about NH 155954) must be from ON *skiki* 'strip'; Watson suggests 'Kali's strip'.

Figure 21 Scandinavian place-names in Wester Ross.

As we move west to Little Loch Broom (in Gaelic *an Loch Beag*, and marked on Blaeu as 'Loch Carlin', a name now lost) we encounter Scoraig, (NH 005965) suggested as ON *sgor-vík* (Watson 1904, 249), on a south-facing site, near the mouth of the loch. It is an excellent situation, on a well-drained slope with a good aspect, again commanding a loch entrance, and able to support a substantial agricultural population in a good sea-fishing zone. On the east shore of Loch Gruinard (*grunna-fjörðr* 'shallow-firth') lies Mungasdale, (NG 969931), on a pleasant, well-favoured site at the head of a small inlet known as Miotag possibly a -*vík*-name, with an obscure first element.

On the west shore of Loch Gruinard is Sand, (NG 918915) in Gaelic *Sannda*, from ON *sand-á*, 'sandy river', and Udrigle (NG 895936), Gaelic *Udrigil*, ON *ytri-gil*, 'outer ravine', a fertile area with a fine outlook over the loch.

Loch Ewe, noted for the shelter and depth of its anchorage, was one of the assembly points for Atlantic and Arctic convoys in World War II, and still acts as a bunkering station for NATO ships. Isle Ewe, still supporting a substantial arable and grazing farm, is a major feature of the loch. A number of Norse topographic names occur round its shores, including Ormiscaig (NG 858905), 'Orm's strip'; Turnaig (NG 875836), occurring as Towrnek, 1548, which although in an ideal situation for a *vík* is not necessarily such (Watson 1904, 235). On the western shore, Boor (NG 844813) is from ON *bur-á*, 'bower stream' (cf. Bower in Caithness), Inverasdale (NG 822865) contains *aspi-dalr* 'aspen-dale', with early forms 1566 Inveraspidill, 1569 Inverassedall, 1638 Inveraspedell, and 1654 (Blaeu) Inner-absdill. (Local Gaelic is *Inbhir-asdal*). Naust (NG 827834) is of doubtful origin. A reference in 1638 gives 'The Nastis', which is of little help. Watson (1904, 230) speculates on but dismisses ON *naust*, 'boat-place', as being untenable, so lacking a suitable derivation we must discard it as a genuine Norse candidate. *Smiuthaig*, a sandy bay at NG 815885 which appears on the map as Gaineamh Smo is probably ON *smúga-vík*, 'cave bay'.

A few miles to the west, the rocky coastline between the mouth of Loch Ewe and Rubha Reidh is uninhabited today, but the settlement of Camustrolvaig, now long deserted, at NG 762916, contains *trolla-vík* 'troll-bay' (Fraser 1994, 73). It overlooks Camas Mor, a steep inlet in a very exposed situation. Reasons for its being abandoned include stories of hauntings, spectres and ghostly lights, but the sheer inaccessibility and remoteness of the place must surely have been a major factor. As we round Rubha Reidh going southwards, we encounter a long, fairly even stretch of coast, with a severe western exposure. Here, settlement is limited to the small valleys which run off the peat-covered Torridonian sandstone, and which provide a very modest amount of potential arable land. The first of these is Melvaig (NG 741865), found as Malefage, 1566, and regarded by Watson (Watson 1904, 227) as *melar-vík* 'bent-grass bay'. This is not much of a *vík*, with a difficult and exposed port for boats, but it does provide relatively level space for agriculture, which must have been its main attraction. Further south is North Erradale (NG 735810), again with a rather difficult port on a wide, boulder-covered beach, but offering access to a sheltered valley with good arable and grazing. This is suggested as having the derivation *eyrar-dalr* 'gravel beach dale' which would fit the situation well (Watson 1904, 221).

At the entrance to Loch Gairloch and lying opposite the island of Longa (*lung-øy*, 'ship-isle') (NG 730775), is the township of Big Sand (NG 755788), together with the farm of Little Sand (NG 760784). In between these (which are referred to in a document of 1638 as 'the two Sandis) lies the Sand River, with a similar derivation and Gaelic pronunciation to the example noted on Loch Gruinard.

Gairloch itself is a fine, broad sea-loch, with the Gaelic derivation *gearr-loch*, 'short loch'. A number of settlements round its shores, however, have names of Norse origin. On the north side is Mial, from *mjó-völlr* 'narrow field', possibly relating to a small strip of arable land above the present township of Strath. Watson (1904, 226) records the 1566 form 'Meall', and 1638 'Meoll'. It is certainly not the Gaelic *meall* 'hill', as it is di-syllabic in pronunciation. Near the present site of Gairloch Hotel is Achadh Deuthasdal, NG 805762; this is another possible *dalr*-name, although there is very little in the way of a valley here, and it must remain a doubtful example.

The River Kerry runs into Loch Gairloch beside an important farm, Kerrysdale (NG 822734). The *dalr* formation here may be late, as the Gaelic version *A' Chathair Bheag* 'the little fairy knoll' is always used by local Gaelic speakers, but the river name itself, *Abhainn Chearraigh* is from ON *kjarr-á*, 'copse river'.

The inlet of Shieldaig (NG 806724) is the next Norse name, from *sild-vík*, 'herring-bay'. This is a sheltered inlet with deep water, still used by fishermen and yachtsmen as the safest anchorage on the entire coast of Wester Ross. Such anchorages would have been equally valuable in the Norse period, both as permanent sites for boats as well as larger ships, and as places of refuge in bad weather. The southern shore is particularly well-suited to a population which depends on the sea for its livelihood, since the inlet to the west, Badachro (NG 782736) continues in use as a centre for commercial lobster fishing and recreational sailing. The bay is guarded by the island of Isle Horrisdale (NG 785745). This is probably 'Thorir's dale', representing a now-lost name which may well have applied to the glen which runs due south from the harbour, drained by the Badachro River. Loch Braigh Horrisdale (NG 800705) further up the valley, supports this theory, as *braigh* is 'upper part', and the entire means 'the upper part of Thorir's dale.'

Two further townships to the west are Port Henderson (NG 757738), in Gaelic *Portigil*, suggesting a generic *gil* 'ravine', and South Erradale (NG 745715), which has a similar derivation to North Erradale mentioned earlier.

It is worth mentioning two Norse names on the west side of Loch

Maree containing *dalr* – Slattadale (NG 889720) and Talladale (NG 916703). Watson gives ON *slettr-dalr*, 'level dale' for the first, and quotes early forms Alydyll 1494, Allawdill 1566; and Telbadell 1638 for the second, suggesting *hjalli-dalr*, 'shelf-dale' as the derivation (Watson 1904, 231).

Near the south-east end of Loch Maree, is Gleann Bianasdail, (NG 030675), which must also be a *dalr*-name, although the specific is obscure. It is 'Pinesdale' on the Blaeu map. A short distance to the west lies the deserted Smiorasair (NH 003670). Surprisingly it appears on the Blaeu map as 'Smirsary', and Watson compares it with Smearisary in Moidart (1904, 233), giving ON *smjør* 'butter', *ás*, 'ridge' and *erg* 'sheiling' as the derivation. This is an extremely isolated place, and access must have been by boat, but it serves to illustrate the range of Norse activity in this part of Wester Ross. If this was originally a summer grazing, one can only conclude that the Norse settlement in the area must have been a good deal more comprehensive than has been suggested in the past. Three other names in ON *erg* (= 'shieling') serve to support this, although none are so remote as Smiorasair. One is Kernsary (NG 893793), now a shooting-lodge on a small loch of the same name roughly a mile east of the northern end of Loch Maree. It occurs as Carnesarie in 1548 (*RMS*, iv, nos, 204, 2273). The other two are minor names – An Aundrary (NG 844722) near the head of the River Kerry, a possible shieling site, and Loch Coire na h-Airigh (NG 804784) which in local Gaelic was *Loch Chorcasairigh*. This last seems also a good candidate for ON *erg*, as no Gaelic derivation fits. The entire area of hill-land between Gairloch and Loch Maree, in fact, contains many topographic names with *airigh*, 'shieling', which suggest intensive seasonal grazing in this area from at least the medieval period.

Returning to the desolate and rocky stretch of coastline south of the mouth of Loch Gairloch, the first Norse place-name is Diabaig (NG 798603), a sheltered, deep-water inlet, from ON *djúp-vík*, 'deep bay'. Watson (1904, 212) quotes the saying *'S'fhada bho'n lagh Diabaig, 's fhaide na sin sios Mealabhaig'*, literally translated as 'Far from the law is Diabaig, yet further is Melvaig.' Such remoteness, however, did not prevent this from being a long-established settlement, with an active fishing community which flourished because of the availability of good arable land and a secure harbour that gave shelter in most weather conditions. It was said that Diabaig fishermen, long known for their skill and resource, could operate when other ports were closed in times of bad weather.

To the south, on an arm of Loch Torridon, is Shieldaig (NG 815540), another 'herring bay' with a similar tradition. This is usually referred to as 'Sildeag na Comraich', the Shieldaig of Applecross, to distinguish it from 'Sildeag Ghearrloch', the Shieldaig of Gairloch, referred to earlier. Directly opposite this, on the Applecross side, lies Ardheslaig (NG 783560), a Gaelic-Norse hybrid with *aird* 'promontory' as the prefix to ON *hesla-vík*, 'hazel bay'. The Applecross Peninsula, as it is now called, is one of the most remote areas in the county of Ross. Although this is regarded as a Pictish name, Gaelic speakers refer to it as 'a Chomraich', 'the sanctuary', and invariably use the expression 'air a' Chomraich', 'on the sanctuary' instead of the usual *anns*, 'in', a reference to its status as an early monastic site (Watson 1904, 204 and Fraser 1984, 221.) Another *vík* name, on the west of the peninsula is Cuaig (NG 705575), 'cow-vik', occupying another sheltered inlet, while another Sand (at NG 682487) a few miles south, probably again derives from *sand-á* 'sandy river'.

At the head of Applecross Bay, the present site of Applecross Mains was of old called *Borrodale* (Watson 1904, 204), presumably *borgr-dalr*, with reference to some Celtic fort or 'broch'. A grant of 1569 by James VI to 'Sir William Stewart, chaplain of Apilcroce' lists 'Bonnadell and Longoll' (*OPS*, II, 405). The upper part of Strath Maol Chaluim, which is occupied by the Applecross River is Coire Attadale (NG 765480), *at-dalr* 'fight-dale', a name which may well have been applied to the whole strath. Yet another *dalr*-name occurs in the south-east of the peninsula, in Coire Sgamadail (NG 780390). Two further important Norse names are Toscaig (NG 712378), *hauga-skiki*, 'mound-strip', on a sheltered south-facing inlet. This was the landing-place for Applecross, with regular boat services to Kyle of Lochalsh, until the Bealach na Ba road was improved sufficiently to make regular mail services economic. On Loch Kishorn lies the farm of Russel, (NG 820404), *hróss-völlr* 'horse-field', on an excellent site, with a commanding view over the loch.

At the southerly end of this survey is Loch Carron which, with adjacent Loch Kishorn, makes up a substantial sea-loch. The major Norse names are: Slumbay (NG 895395), part of the present village of Lochcarron, which is found as Slomba 1495 and Slumba 1633, perhaps from *slaemr-vagr* 'slim bay'; Strome (NG 864357), from *straumr* 'tide-race'; Reraig (NG 838364) *reyrr-vík* 'reed bay'; Attadale (NG 925391) 'fight-dale', perhaps alluding to the presence of horse-fights, a favourite Viking sport, in this fine, level strath; and Strath Ascaig (NG 865330), from *á-skiki* 'river-strip'.

The coastline west of Strome Ferry is highly indented, with a scattering of off-shore islets, reefs and skerries. This entire western extremity of Lochalsh Parish, however, lies in one of the most strategic locations, commanding both the sea-route of Kyle Akin, and also the entrances to Loch Carron and Loch Duich. At the height of Norse power in Scotland, it is difficult to envisage this area being under any but Norse control.

We can identify a number of Norse topographic names but, again, habitative examples are absent. The bay of Erbusaig (NG 761296), 'Erp's vik', occurs as Arbesak 1554 and Erbissok 1633; Reraig (NG 810271), 'reed-vik' is on record as Rowrag 1548, Rerek 1554 and Rerag 1607; Scalpaidh (NG 777274) *skálp-á*, 'ship-river'; Avernish (NG 845265), given as Arenis 1495 and Awnarnys 1527, *afar-nes* 'bulky promontory'; and Duirinish (NG 787313) 'deer-promontory', are typical of the names in the peninsula. Further possible Norse names include Pladaig (NG 758276); Palascaig (NG 788291); and Ullava (NG 826338), a rocky islet off Duncraig.

Although most of this list applies to coastal names, several, like the names in *-skiki* and *-dalr* refer to features which suggest pastoral activities, such as stock-rearing. One can certainly imagine grain and hay crops being grown in such potentially fertile spots as Strath Ascaig, as well as in the sheltered land in Duirinish and Erbusaig.

CONCLUSIONS

Lying as they do on the direct sailing-route between the Northern Isles and the Western Isles, these northern and western coastlands must have been of prime importance to the Norse in their expansion phase of the ninth century. It is unlikely that powerful Norse fleets which operated around the Scottish coasts would have ignored a potentially profitable coastline such as this, forming as it does an important section of the Norse maritime routeway.

The relative lack of habitative names in the north-west is not, therefore, indicative of lack of permanent settlement. The clusters of names in the north coast inlets exhibit all the marks of Norse activity, which points to a range of settled farmsteads. These are mostly located in prime sites, taking advantage of all the natural features in the landscape which offer the basic resources of shelter for shipping, reasonably good arable land, timber, fish and game. The immediate hinterland of both areas provides excellent deer-hunting, a sport enthusiastically pursued by the Norse earls as mentioned in *Orkneyinga Saga*. The presence of such names as Rossal and Attadale suggests that horse-rearing was an important activity also.

Since much of the pastoral economy was geared to the use of summer shielings, it is perhaps surprising that no names in *-sætr* 'shieling' are present, at least in the coastal areas. But the *-erg* – names in the Gairloch–Loch Maree area clearly point to an extensive system of shieling sites, and if *Smiorasair* is genuine (and there is no reason to doubt that it is) then the Norse pastoral economy was a good deal more widespread than simply a few shiels near coastal settlements which were temporary at best.

The attraction of settlement on these short western sea-lochs was obviously due in some measure to the presence of good fishing grounds. Salmon, herring and white fish were all plentiful in the past. Fishermen along the west coast were often heard to say that in the 1880s, 'one could almost walk dry-shod across the sea-lochs on the herring-smacks, so close-packed were they'. Such wealth of fish is now gone, but it was clearly one of the most important natural resources of this coastline. Laxford and the two Shieldaigs are evidence of the Norse interest in fishing resources.

The presence of clusters of topographic names which date from the Norse period correlates to a large extent with the pattern of settlement which exists today. The relatively high densities of Norse names which we find on Loch Ewe, Loch Gairloch and the Kyle of Lochalsh peninsula are significant in this respect. The names in *vík* are almost all relatively isolated from other Norse names, with one or two significant exceptions. Such names as Kearvaig, Diabaig and Cuaig must have been chosen for settlement because of their value as sheltered sites on otherwise hazardous coastlines. Their use for settlement was part of a long chain of coastal locations, which were supplemented by exploitation of the resources of the interior. Sites like Ullapool have obvious strategic qualities – commanding the access to a major sea-loch, and acting as a base for shipping along an entire coastline. Links with the Western Isles may have been important in very much the same manner as its function as a ferry terminal today.

In the last century, the 'packet' link between Lewis and the mainland was between Stornoway and Poolewe, on Loch Ewe. The mail runner's route lay along the north bank of Loch Maree to Achnasheen and thence to the east coast. The presence of so many Norse names on Loch Ewe suggests an emphasis on settlement close to such routeways, most, but not all, on coastal locations.

It can be argued, then, that Norse place-names in important sites along this coastline can be regarded in the same light as habitative names in areas of Norse settlement where *-bólstaðr*, *-sætr*, and *-staðir* abound. This is not necessarily to upgrade sites like Diabaig and Shieldaig to the status of, say, such Lewis examples as Tolsta, Shawbost and Bayble, or Skye names such as Monkstadt, Carbost and Colbost. But in an area where settlement of any kind is limited by topographical considerations, such as is very evident here in the north-west, the status of a settlement is largely measured by the resources which it has to offer.

Overall, the number of Norse generics is small. *Dalr, vík, nes, fjörðr, skiki, völlr, erg* and *á* together make up 90 per cent of the total. These generics are all distinct and recognizable, were easily assimilated by Gaelic speakers, and must retain in pronunciation many features of the original Norse. The three instances of *Sand-á* 'sand river', for example, continue to be pronounced [saʌ'ndʌ], while non-Gaels use the normal Englished form Sand. This is testimony to the enduring nature of these names, simply because of the concise and toponymically graphic nature of their structure. It could be argued that any habitative names coined in the area might not have survived in some cases, and were replaced by Gaelic names in *achadh-* and *bad-* purely because they were lexically opaque, and, in a declining Norse linguistic milieu, were therefore less likely to have been perpetuated. The *vík-* and *-dalr* names on the other hand, had the advantage of being in striking locations, forming part of a continuing tradition of settlement, so that they did survive, despite the fact that Norse speech had long ceased to be used and Norse associations were long forgotten.

The lack of information on Norse taxation for Wester Ross is also a puzzling phenomenon, although it operated in the form of ouncelands and pennylands in the Sutherland area (Crawford 1987, 86–7). It may well have been that the settlement pattern of Wester Ross presented problems to the Norse, so as to make a structured system of taxation and levying uneconomic to control (Crawford 1987, 91). The lack of habitative names in the area may therefore reflect the fiscal policy, rather than any lack of overall political dominance.

In conclusion, a contrast between the two areas of Norse settlement appears to emerge from the place-name evidence. While the vocabulary of place-name material is much the same in both, the toponymic evidence from the Wester Ross firthlands suggests that Norse control was sporadic, and not so fully dependent on the trade-routes as was the Durness-Tongue area. In the overall strategy of Norse maritime activity, the north coast fjords were far more important, and their permanent settlements formed links in the chain of Norse presence from the Northern to the Western Isles.

Moving to the Hebrides we enter a very different cultural sphere: the existing Gaelic society certainly survived Viking raids on the west coast of Scotland, and Gaelic culture spread quickly back into the Inner Hebrides, although more slowly to the Outer Hebrides, to judge by the surviving pattern of Norse place-names. Archaeological evidence[1] in the form of pagan graves gives dramatic proof of the intensity of Viking settlement in some of the islands, which, along with the deeply-indented coastline of the Scottish mainland, provided the Norwegian Vikings with a world so similar to the one they had left behind. This fact may account for the evidence of early Viking domination. Some support for this is provided by the most famous of the Icelandic sagas in which the conqueror of the Hebrides, Ketil Flat-nose (flat-nefr), is remembered as having been the progenitor of some of the most important early settlers of Iceland. Although his appearance in the west is linked by the sagas with Harald Fine-hair (King of Norway c. 870–940) this would seem to be a later rationalization of his conquest, and other evidence suggests that Ketil's floruit was nearer the middle of the ninth century, not the end of it:

> After having landed in the west, Ketil fought a number of battles, and won them all. He conquered and took charge of the Hebrides, making peace and alliances with all the leading men there in the west.
>
> (Eyrbyggja Saga, Chap. 1)

---

1. See distribution map of Norse graves in Crawford 1987, Fig. 31.

Contemporary Irish annals record the activities on both sides of the Irish Sea of a Viking-led force of Gall-Gaedhil (='Foreign Gael') from the mid-ninth century, initially under a certain Ketil Find (='the White'):

> A victory was gained by Ivar and Olaf over Ketil the White with the Gall-Gaedhil, in the lands of Munster.
>
> (Annals of Ulster, s.a. 857)

We can assume that Ketil the White and Ketil Flat-nose are probably one and the same[2] and the Gall-Gaedhil (the 'Foreign Gael') may be regarded as the inhabitants of the Hebrides (or Innse Gall ='islands of the Foreigners' as the Irish called them) and who were of mixed Norse and Gaelic stock.

The mingling which is evident from the terminology of the Irish Annals is also evident in the place-names of the Hebrides. The blending of the two languages resulted in a very confused nomenclature, although the percentage of Norse and Gaelic names varies from north to south and from the Outer Hebrides to the Inner. It also varies according to the quality of the land, so that the more fertile islands like Coll and Tiree appear much more heavily Norse-influenced than the more mountainous like Mull, although this appearance may be deceptive. Coll and Tiree had a value apart from the quality of the land for, lying as they do out in the main sailing lane, they served as very important staging posts on the route through the islands and would have provided strategic control points for whichever Gall-Gaedhil chieftain exercised authority as rí Innse Gall (='king of the Islands of the Foreigners'). Gilli of Coll was one such who seems however (according to saga tradition) to have been subject to the earls of Orkney, in the period of Orkney control in the Hebrides in the late tenth century; and he was given the designation of 'jarl' (=earl) in the sagas. He was tied by marriage to the Orkney earl Sigurd 'the Stout' and was active in the events leading up to the battle of Clontarf in 1014, according to Njal's Saga.

The Orkney earls' control in the Hebrides did not last for very long, and throughout the Norse period these islands were never brought under any one overlord permanently. They were the domain of Viking warlords 'par excellence' who provided their naval skills and galleys for whoever was willing to pay the best money. Earl Sigurd could call on the men of the islands to follow him to Clontarf because they saw this as an opportunity for gain. A later account of those who are said to have accompanied him to Ireland lists them according to their island or coastal stronghold; from Man and from Skye, from Lewis and from Kintyre and Argyll; as well as from the 'Land of snow' (? Iceland) (ES, i, 537). Their promised

---

2. See my summary of the evidence (1987, 47) and Smyth's arguments (1977, 115, 124; 1984, 156–7).

Plate 12 A few representative coins and silver ingot from a Viking hoard found on Tiree in the late eighteenth century. The coins (numbering several hundred originally and later dispersed) are Anglo-Saxon and date the deposition of the hoard to c. AD 970. Hoards such as this have been found in many parts of Scotland and are evidence of the wealth of the Norse communities who used the coins as bullion in their trading exchanges. They also no doubt melted many down to form silver ingots like the one in the photo. Such silver hoards probably indicate disturbed conditions and were hidden for safe-keeping. (Graham-Campbell, 1975–6, 128; Blackburn and Pagan, 1987, no. 171.) (Copyright: British Museum)

reward would have been in silver, although Earl Sigurd's death at Clontarf probably meant there was little positive benefit from the expedition. Earl Gilli is said to have given 'a load of silver' to one of his followers after news of the disastrous defeat was received (Njal's Saga, Chap. 157).

It was loads of silver such as this which oiled the oars of the Viking sailing ships. Some might be buried in the ground for safe keeping and never recovered; the distribution of such Viking silver hoards encompasses all the areas of Norse influence in the British Isles. Many have been found in the Hebrides, such as that from Tiree dating from the late tenth century (see Plate 12) not so far in time from the battle of Clontarf which involved so many of the 'wild foreigners' from the Hebrides (see recent discussion of the Tiree hoard by Graham-Campbell 1995, 97–9).

7 Norse settlement patterns in Coll and Tiree*

ANNE JOHNSTON

The Inner Hebridean islands of Coll and Tiree lie some 50km west of the Argyll mainland. Their location at the western extremity of the chain of islands on the sea route running south from Orkney and Shetland to Ireland ensured that they were settled quickly and densely by the Norse colonists. This examination of Norse settlement on Coll and Tiree traces the evolution of colonial settlement within each island concentrating on the onomastic framework and linking this to the stages of settlement growth. The methodology employed is both interdisciplinary and retrospective, allowing successive layers of occupation to be 'peeled back' in order to expose the pattern of settlement as it may have existed in the Norse period.

The constraints of the physical environment exert the greatest influence on settlement. Geographically and geologically the islands are very different in character. Tiree is flat and low-lying with only the hills of Beinn Hough, Ben Hynish and Beinn Ceann a' Mhara rising above 140m. These form a sharp contrast to the gently undulating expanses of machair found around the coastline and in a large plain, the Reef, which cuts across the island from north to south effectively dividing it into two parts. The accompanying widespread occurrence of calcareous soils has resulted in areas of great fertility in all parts of the island although the low-lying nature of the land and frequent high winds mean that large areas are adversely affected by sandblow. The neighbouring island of Coll is characterized by broad belts of machair and extensive dune formations on the west coast, both of which have encroached inland during historic times. The land bordering the east coast forms a stark contrast; here the underlying rock formation gives rise to an

---

* The following unpublished records have been used in the preparation of this chapter:

SRO, GD RHP 8826/1–2   J. Turnbull, 'A general description of the islands of Tirij in Argyllshire', 1768–9.

SRO, GD RHP 3368   Langland, 'Plan of the island of Coll', 1794.

Plate 13 View of the flat and fertile landscape near Hough, Tiree, with Beinn Hough in the distance. The stone circle, just visible in the centre foreground bears witness to the prehistoric settlement which preceded the intensive Norse settlement on the island. (RCAHMS, Argyll, 3, no. 107.) (Crown Copyright: Royal Commission on the Ancient and Historical Monuments of Scotland)

indented coastline with acidic parent soils resulting in large tracts of moorland.

Three layers of pre-Norse settlement are discernible. There are the brochs, forts and duns of the Iron Age, a few traces in the documentary records of the administrative organization of the Dalriadic kingdom, and the recorded monastic complexes of Celtic religious communities. Evidence for Iron Age structures on Tiree is abundant with five forts, fourteen duns and two brochs ringing an island measuring no more than 15km from north-east to south-west and 9km at its widest extent. On Coll the Iron Age monuments show a marked concentration in the central, most fertile, portion of the island. The first written source to attest to settlement in this area comes from the *Senchus Fer nAlban* a twelfth-century copy of an eighth-century document – part survey, part census – which describes the organization of the Irish Dalriadic settlement in Scotland, an area roughly corresponding to that of modern Argyll (Bannerman 1974). It gives no concrete indication as to the exact location of settlement within Coll and Tiree but indicates that the organizational system of Dalriada was based upon groupings of 20-house units, which may have originated in an existing local land assessment. The Irish Annals, Saints' Lives and Monastic Chronicles are more informative as to the site and situation of eighth-century monastic foundations on the island. Adomnan's Life of Columba mentions two communities on Tiree (Anderson 1961, 483, 525) although physical remains have only been identified at St Patrick's Temple, situated on poor land at Ceann a'Mhara (RCAHMS 1980, 28).

The impact of the first Norse raids into these already populated and, presumably, prospering islands is first glimpsed through the monastic records which chronicle, in 798, that 'the Hebrides and Ireland were plundered by the heathen' (*Annals of Ulster s.a.* 253). The inevitable bias of the evidence towards the monastic houses means that little else is known of the initial incursions of the Norse into Celtic territory and we are left with a picture of the Norse, drawn by their victims, as marauding barbarians intent upon pillage and destruction. There is no contemporary literature from the Western Isles in the Norse period to counteract this view. *Orkneyinga Saga*, which is most pertinent to Norse settlement in the Scottish Islands, is primarily concerned with the establishment and subsequent history of the Orkney Earldom and, like the Icelandic Sagas with their subtle blend of fact and fiction, recounts the traditional stories of repeated raiding excursions to the west. It is possible that the place-name Annat (G *anndoit*) as in the field-name Annat (Caolas) Tiree indicates a monastic site abandoned in the ninth century, perhaps due to the Viking threat.[1] Further indication as to the date and character of the initial phase of raiding prior to permanent settlement must be based upon archaeological approximation and the tenuous evidence of folk tradition. On Tiree the Gaelic ballad called the 'battle of the sheaves' (*Blàr nan Sguab*)[2] purports to recall a mighty confrontation between Norse and native centred upon the township of Cornaig where, in the nineteenth century, swords, shields, helmets and a spear were found, possibly of Viking date (Anderson 1872–4, 555). It is important to distinguish between the various phases of Norse activity in the islands; sporadic raiding parties led to a period of semi-permanent habitation as the Norse 'during the winter stayed in the islands beyond the sea' (*Heimskringla* 1964, 77).

Archaeological interest in the Norse period in the Inner Hebrides

---

1. In the Outer Hebrides and the Northern Isles there is evidence to suggest that the Norse recognized Celtic Christian sites. In these areas place-names incorporating the ON noun *papa* 'priest' are found. It has been suggested that the Norse applied the term *papa* to any church site temporarily abandoned (MacDonald 1977, 30). *Papa* names are entirely absent from the Inner Hebrides but it is possible that G *annaid* was a comparative and complementary term fulfilling much the same function in designating an early abandoned church site.
2. Sound archive of the School of Scottish Studies, University of Edinburgh, SA 1968/247/B: the variant versions of this Ballad are discussed by MacDonald (1984, 272).

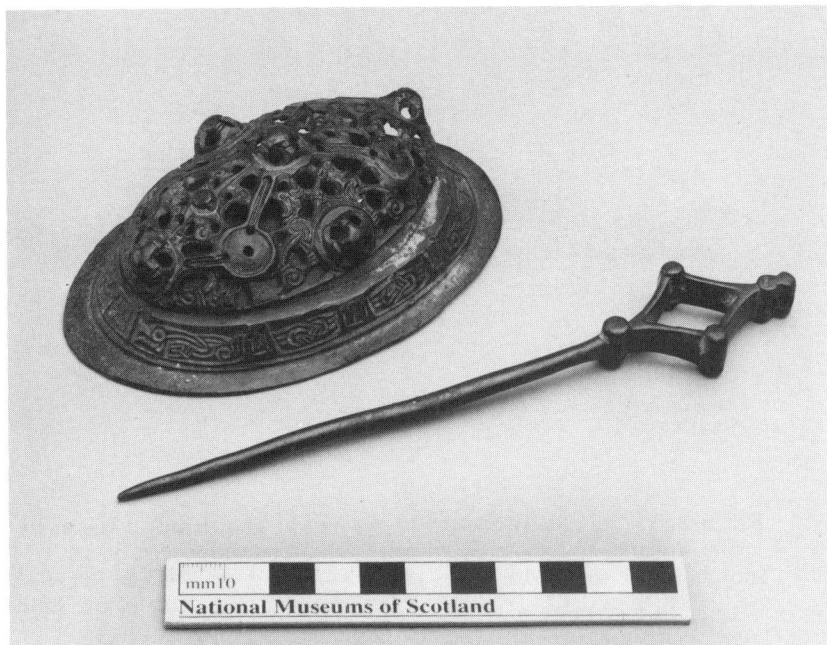

Plate 14a One oval (tortoise) brooch and a bronze pin from a Viking woman's burial on Tiree. The pin is a very fine and unusual specimen of the third brooch pin often found in Viking women's graves (the second tortoise brooch is missing). It may have been made from a piece of Celtic metalwork. (*VA*, vol. ii, 62–3; RCAHMS, Argyll, 3, no. 236.) (Copyright: Trustees of the National Museums of Scotland)

has lagged behind that of the Northern Isles. No settlement sites have been excavated and archaeological assessment relies on an analysis of loose finds, such as the discovery of pennanular brooches at Cliad, Coll, and artefacts suggestive of a male burial at Grishipoll (see Plate 14b) on the same island (Beveridge 1903, 1–3, 38). Detailed fieldwork is called for, particularly in those areas of Coll and Tiree where sandblow frequently changes the face of the landscape.

Place-names arguably provide the richest source for a study of Norse settlement in this area. Both Coll and Tiree show a particularly high ratio of Norse to Gaelic settlement names where Norse names account for 50 per cent of the total compared to figures of 30 per cent for Islay, 15 per cent for Mull and Lismore, 12 per cent for Arran and less than 10 per cent for Rhum, Eigg and Canna. The range and type of these names give an indication of the relative chronology of the various phases of settlement and the character of the Norse community over several centuries. The high proportion of Norse names may also suggest that at some period the islands' inhabitants were entirely Norse speaking. This in turn

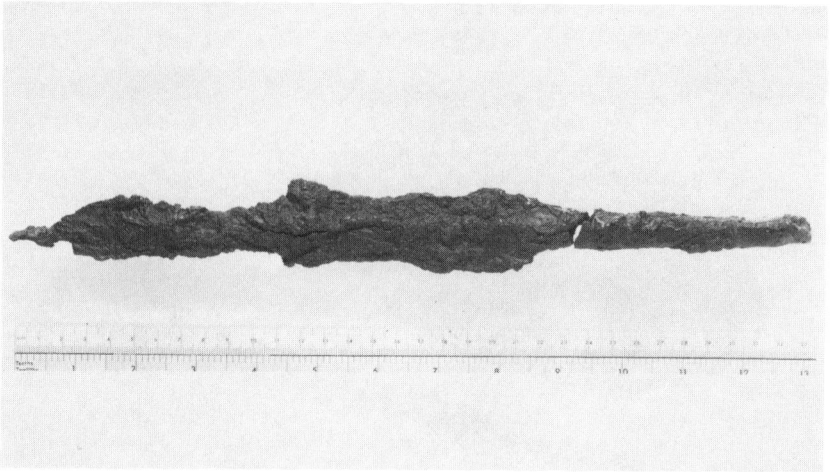

Plate 14b This badly-preserved spearhead was found in the early 1950s in sand-hills near Grishipoll, Coll, apparently part of an inhumation burial, which was probably Viking. (RCAHMS, Argyll, 3, no. 235.) (Copyright: Trustees of the National Museums of Scotland)

would indicate that the landscape must have been described purely in Norse terms. Yet, before and after the Norse period in the Inner Hebrides, Gaelic was spoken in the islands. None of the Gaelic names can be said with any certainty to date from the pre-Norse period and it may be assumed that the majority of Gaelic settlement names discernible today stem from the post-Norse era. Many such Gaelic names, however, mask the presence of earlier Norse names either by the addition of Gaelic elements to existing Norse names, as in the case of Ballyhough on Coll where Gaelic *baile* 'township' forms an addition to the Norse noun *haugr* 'mound' or by the Gaelic renaming of settlements originally known by a Norse name, as may have happened in Tiree where the Gaelic name Caolas (G *caolas*) 'strait' masks the earlier Norse name Skipnes (ON *skip nes*) 'ship headland'. Additionally, a Norse name may have become so gaelicized that it is difficult to ascertain in which language it originated. For this and other reasons it is important to trace settlement names in the documentary record to their earliest written form.

Analysis of the onomastic material has to be considered in conjunction with fiscal sources, an evaluation of land quality and the geographical situation of a settlement. Cartographic material has proved a valuable source, particularly eighteenth-century estate maps made prior to the agricultural improvements which so changed land-use in the islands. Tiree was surveyed in 1768–9 by James Turnbull (Turnbull 1768–9) who produced an extensive written description recording the quality and quantity of land throughout the islands, the extent of sandblow, nature of harbours/

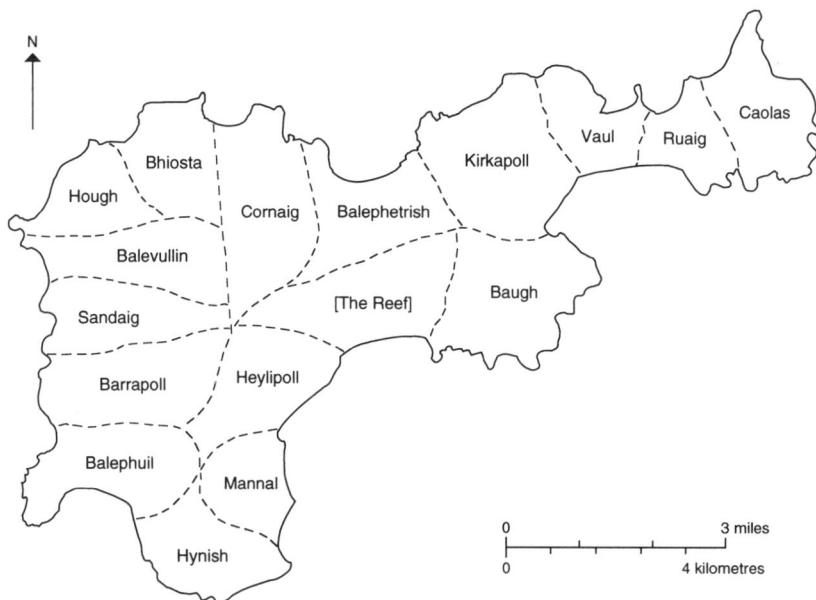

Figure 22 Primary settlement units and ounceland divisions, Tiree.

beaching points, settlement boundaries and areas of infield, outfield and rough grazing pertaining to each settlement with the valuation afforded it. His accompanying map provides a clear and detailed representation of the information contained in his written account (see Fig. 23). Turnbull's survey is unparalleled and the cartographic material for Coll, surveyed by Langland in 1794 (Langland 1794), seems poor by comparison (see Fig. 25). Cartographic material of this type also helps pinpoint settlements no longer in existence as in the case of Mibost, Coll, lying in an area now devastated by sandblow, or Bhassapoll, Tiree where a Norse settlement name (ON *vatns bólstaðr*) 'fresh water farm' is now retained only as a landscape name.

PRIMARY SETTLEMENTS AND THE OUNCELAND UNIT

When considering likely locations for initial permanent occupation in the islands all settlements mentioned in the sources have to be considered – whether they are physically discernible or not. Several qualitative and quantitative favourability factors can then be evaluated (soil quality and extent of arable land, distance from the sea, nature of harbour facilities, presence or absence of ecclesiastical monuments), allowing classification of settlements into three categories: primary, secondary and peripheral. Primary settlements

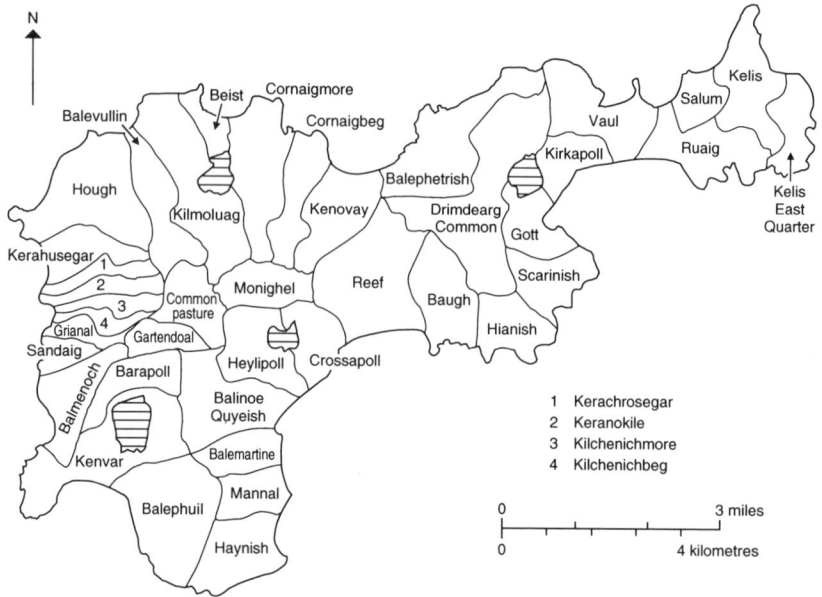

Figure 23   Tiree: settlement units as shown on Turnbull's map of 1768–9.

represent the earliest settlement in a given area (see Figs. 22 and 24 for Tiree and Coll) while secondary and peripheral ranking settlements point to expansion resulting in the division of original units. One of the clearest indications of the former status of a settlement is seen through its fiscal evaluation. In the charters, retours, sasines and particularly the rentals of the Scottish period, it is not the annual payment of rent or dues which is important but the fixed valuation of the settlement. This is variously expressed in terms of ouncelands, pennylands, merklands, maillands (Tiree only) or monetary denominations. All these evaluations, which were originally measures of land quality rather than of size or extent forming a basis for both taxation and rent, remain remarkably consistent. On the analogy that a high valuation is indicative of high quality land and that high quality land often attracted early settlement, it follows that a settlement with a high valuation is likely to predate a settlement, in the nearby vicinity, with a lower valuation.[3] According to such criteria ten settlements on Coll may

---

3. The value of fiscal analysis in settlement studies was established in Norway where it has been used to date settlement name generics chronologically (Sandnes, 1973, 12–28). The basic principle involved is that the higher the average (median) annual payment of rent or tax for a given generic group of names in relation to other generic groups, the older the former was in relation to the latter. An adaptation of this form of fiscal analysis can also be used to give a relative 'date' for individual groups of settlements.

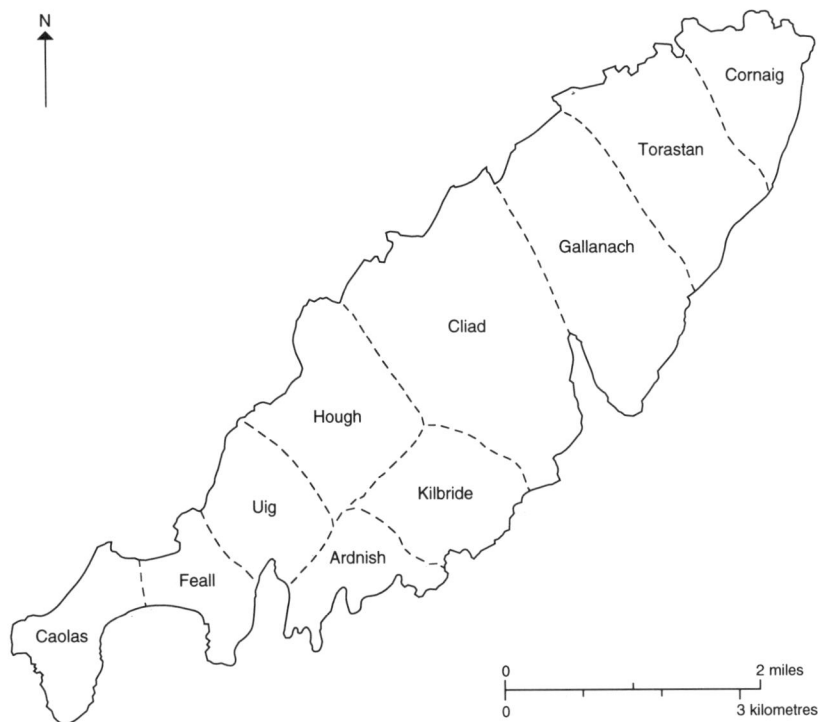

Figure 24 Primary settlement units and ounceland divisions, Coll.

be classified as primary (see Fig. 24). Seven of these primary settlement names are Norse and over half are in the form of simplex topographical names describing prominent coastal features or landmarks easily recognizable from the sea: Uig (ON *vík*) 'bay', Hough (ON *haugr*) 'mound', Feall (ON *fiall*) 'hill', [Ard]nish (ON *nes*) 'headland' and Cliad (ON *klettr*) 'rocks'. Of the remainder of the Norse primary names, Cornaig (ON *kornvík,*) 'cornbay' describes the settlement in terms of the quality of the land while Torastan (ON *Thorstaðir*) 'Thor's farm' preserves the personal name of a Norseman who may have been among the first settlers on the island. Three primary settlement names are Gaelic of which Caolas (G *caolas*) 'strait' shows a similar preoccupation with a distinctive seascape feature.

The use of such topographical names as settlement names may indicate the naming of both topographical features and settlement at one and the same time. Alternatively it may indicate the transference of a topographical name from a physical landmark to a habitation site. In the early Viking period of Norse exploration, which preceded permanent settlement, raiders spent the summer months in the islands returning to Norway for the winter. Prominent landscape and seascape features would be named and

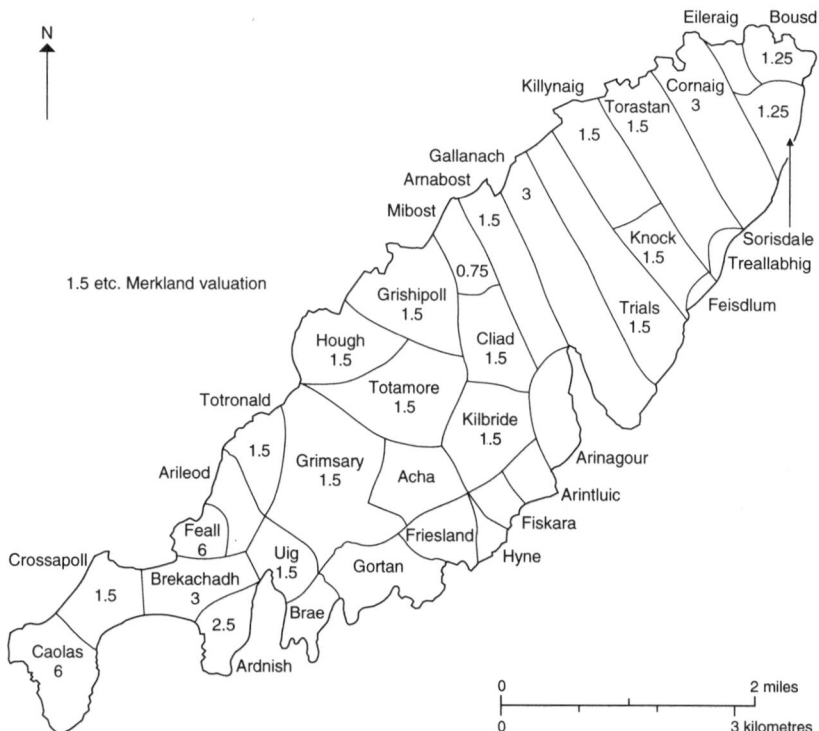

Figure 25   Coll: settlement units based on Langland's survey of 1794.

used as navigational markers on these sea voyages long before such sites were settled. Additionally, it would be the easily-defended sites, isolated headlands and deep sheltered bays which were the first semi-permanent bases for the Norsemen when they started to overwinter in the islands. The existence of headland dykes in some Orkney islands suggests that a process of ness-taking (ON *nes nám*) occurred, the object of which was to provide bases for raids (Crawford 1987, 47). There are no known remains of such enclosures in Coll and Tiree, although the large number of settlement names compounded with ON *nes* in Tiree may point to the early colonization of headland sites.

The isolation of such primary settlement sites gives an indication as to the location of the primary settlement *units*, i.e. the total area pertaining to the primary settlement in terms of infield, outfield, rough grazing, shoreland and harbours. On Coll the physical discrepancy between the fertile areas on the west coast and the more inhospitable terrain on the east coast has resulted in a distinctive demarcation of primary settlement units with narrow and elongated divisions stretching from coast to coast, giving each settlement access to the machair on the west coast and the outfield and rough grazing to the east. On both Coll and Tiree this primary unit corresponded to the Norse administrative division called the ounceland, known in later written sources by the Gaelic term *tirunga* (lit. 'land ounce') and the latin noun *unciata*.[4] This is the unit which seems to have had significance in the administrative, fiscal, religious and socio-economic organization of the Norse communities not only in the Western Isles but throughout all areas of Norse settlement in Scotland (Macgregor and Crawford 1987).

A Tiree rental of 1622 states that 'a tirung [ounceland] is a 6 merkland, and is divided into 20 pennylands' (Campbell 1911–12, 344).[5] There are several discernible 6 merkland/1 ounceland units on Tiree. These centre on the townships of Caolas, Kirkapoll, Heylipoll, Mannal, Hynish, Balephuil, Barrapoll, Ruaig, Hough, Balevullin, Bhiosta and Vaul (see Fig. 22). All rank as primary settlements. Regrouping of other settlements reveals an additional four 1-ounceland units: Baugh and Scarinish, Balephetrish and Earnal, Balemeanach, Sandaig and Grianal and Cornaig (more and beg).[6] There are thus sixteen settlements which merit classification as primary and over half of these have Norse names. As on Coll several of these primary settlements are known by simplex topographical names: Hough (ON *haugr*) 'mound', Vaul (ON *fjäll*) 'hills', and Baugh (ON *vágr*) 'bay' while others are compounded with the ON generic *nes*. Both Coll and Tiree have single examples of the habitative generic *staðir* associated with a primary settlement. On Tiree the name Bhiosta (the prefix is obscure) is retained only as a landscape name while the settlement of Torastan (? Thor's *staðir*) on Coll occupies a prime site on the island. In Shetland *staðir* compounds are believed to denote 'high status sites which were probably colonised after the most favourable coastal sites had already been settled' (Macgregor 1987, 465). On Tiree this would certainly hold true for Bhiosta. The only other primary ounceland

---

4. The name suggests that the ounceland was an area of land originally rendering one ounce of silver in tax.

5. The ounceland provided the basis for all subsequent re-evaluations of land. With the Treaty of Perth in 1266 and the cession of the Hebrides by the Norwegians to the Scottish Crown it was necessary for the latter to know exactly how much revenue would be forthcoming from the newly acquired estates. This resulted in the imposition of a new unit of land assessment, the merkland. In Tiree and Coll the ounceland was re-evaluated at 6 merks to the ounce, giving a valuation of 6 merklands for each ounceland.

6. Documentary and cartographic material from the Scottish period gives a picture of settlement in the islands several centuries removed from the Norse era and after extensive settlement expansion had occurred. In Norwegian settlement studies geometrical analysis has been employed with some success. The shape of holdings is studied and fitted together in an effort to retrace the original boundaries of settlement units (Farbregd 1984, 33–50). The regrouping of component parts of original settlement units in the Hebrides can sometimes be achieved through tracing settlement boundaries in conjunction with the fiscal evaluation of the settlements in question.

unit found in an 'inland' location is at Barrapoll where the generic is clearly derived from ON *bólstaðr*.[7] The ounceland settlements of Kirkapoll (ON *kirkju bólstaðr* 'church farm' and Heylipoll (ON *helgi bólstaðr*) 'holy farm' may, however, also conform to this pattern of prime sites established shortly after the initial wave of settlement. The small size of Coll accounts for the absence of this form of early settlement expansion on that island.

To what extent did the Norse settlers actively avoid or choose to settle those areas which were utilized by former inhabitants? The distribution of forts and duns on the islands, concentrated on areas of agricultural favourability, may be taken as giving as near a representation as possible of settlement focii in the eras preceding the Norse incursions. On Islay the distribution of Iron Age defended settlements and Norse habitative toponyms have been found to have little correlation leading to the conclusion that Norse settlement on that island was essentially an infilling around areas already settled by earlier groups (Nieke 1983, 313). On Skye likewise little similarity was found between the distribution of Iron Age forts and duns and Norse habitative toponyms, resulting in the hypothesis that Norse and native occupied distinct and separate areas of the island and that a relatively peaceful coexistence occurred (Small 1976, 36; see Crawford 1987, 110 for a critique of this study). Nor does the distribution of Norse habitative generics relate well to that of the Iron Age fortifications on Coll and Tiree – the reason being that it is the topographical rather than the habitative names which should be used as the most reliable indicators of Norse primary settlement units. On both islands these topographical names correlate well with the primary ounceland divisions. This suggests that the Norse may have reutilized pre-existing units and the corresponding boundaries, which conformed to the natural divisions inherent in the landscape, and named them after the most outstanding physical feature when establishing primary settlements during the 'landnam' period.

The neatness and permanence of the ounceland demarcations on Coll and Tiree suggest that the imposition of the ounceland system may have been contemporaneous with, or followed swiftly upon, the establishment of the primary units. It is possible that the ounceland divisions came about as the result of a conscious decision to demarcate the island into several interlocking units for administrative purposes. This in turn suggests the presence of a strong central authority having control over one or both of the islands. Alternatively the ounceland system may have been imposed at a later date on existing settlement units which had developed as a

---

7. In the Outer Hebrides *bólstaðr* contracts to *-bost* and in the Inner Hebrides most frequently to *-poll* or *-boll*, with the exception of Islay where the modern form of the suffix is *-bus*. Tiree is unusual among the Inner Hebridean Islands, for the names Murtost and Bist show the contraction of *bólstaðr* to *-bist* and *-bost* as well as *-poll* and *-boll*.

result of organic growth. In either case, the binding together of the component parts of the original primary unit by an obligation to pay a common tax or other dues ensured a cohesiveness such that the ounceland unit formed the basis for all subsequent evaluation. The tight network of interlocking ouncelands and their correlation with natural boundaries ensured that the basic settlement demarcations on Coll and Tiree were still geographically discernible at the time the islands were mapped in the eighteenth century.

SETTLEMENT EXPANSION AND DIVISION WITHIN THE OUNCELAND UNIT

Secondary and peripheral expansion from the primary settlement on Coll and Tiree can be seen to have taken place within the ounceland unit. The division of the primary unit to incorporate secondary expansion occurs in two ways. First, by the division of the primary settlement into two or more equal parts, equal in land quality but not necessarily in size, with each division having a portion of infield, outfield and rough grazing. In this case all the resulting units may be regarded as secondary, even if the original core is recognizable. The name of the primary settlement is often apparent. A second form of secondary expansion sees the separation of a land parcel from a primary settlement. The parcel retains a substantial portion of agricultural potential. The adjacent 'mother' settlement may still be regarded as a primary unit if it retains superior favourability factors.

Expansion from the primary unit shows a clear-cut and distinctive form on Coll, suggesting that it developed according to a set pattern rather than as a result of haphazard growth. Several of the primary units show a division into two or more secondary units, where all the secondary divisions are of equal status and the name of the primary unit is retained by one of the new divisions. This is particularly clear in the case of Cliad (see Fig. 26). Here a primary settlement known by a simplex topographical name was subsequently divided into four secondary settlements. Cliad retained the most favourable portion of the land, and also the name of the primary unit, while the remaining secondary divisions came to be known by habitative names incorporating the generic *bólstaðr*. Other ounceland units also conform to this form of development where, like Cliad, the name of the primary farm remains as the name of one of the subdivisions:

Hough	Ballyhough	1.5 merklands[8]
(1 ounceland)	Totronald	1.5 merklands
	Grimsary	1.5 merklands
	Totamore	1.5 merklands

---

8. The merkland valuations are those recorded in the sixteenth century.

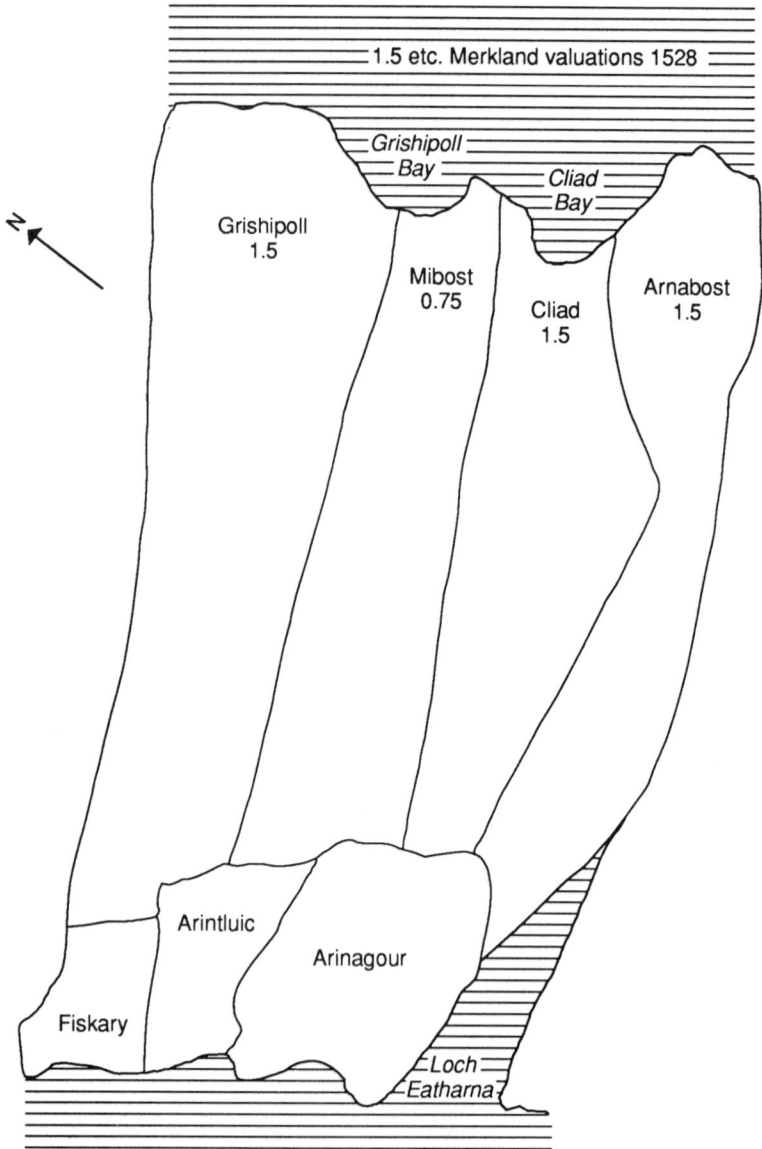

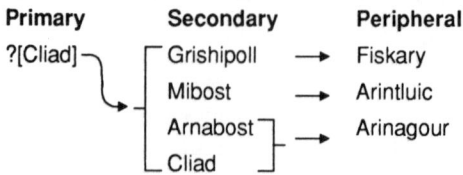

Figure 26 Coll: settlement unit of Cliad.

Torastan	Torastan	1.5 merklands
(1 ounceland)	Knock	1.5 merklands
	Killynaig	1.5 merklands
	Gar	1.5 merklands

The majority of Norse secondary settlement names on Coll are compounded with the habitative generic *bólstaðr* (in its contracted forms *bol* and *bost*): they are Crossapoll, Grishipoll, Arnabost, Mibost and ?Bousd. Again the specifics describe some distinguishing feature of the farm: ownership at Arnbost (ON *Arnabólstaðr*) 'Arni's farm'; shape of the settlement at Mibost (ON *mjórbólstaðr*) 'middle farm'; a distinctive landmark at Crossapoll (ON *krossbólstaðr*) 'cross farm'; and the type of activity carried on there at Grishipoll (ON *gríssbólstaðr*) 'pig farm'.[9] Only at Bousd is a descriptive specific lacking suggesting that the name was self-explanatory to the namers in that it conveyed a particular type of farm. Its derivation may therefore stem from ON *bústaðir* and not *bólstaðr*. Grishipoll, Mibost and Arnabost are situated in close proximity to one another, therefore necessitating the addition of a discriminatory specific to qualify the generic. Of the secondary settlements bearing Gaelic names, two show how the secondary unit originated: Goirtean (G *goirtean*) 'clearing' testifies to the clearance and enclosing of land while Acha (G *achadh*) 'field' was initially applied to a cultivated field and then to a farm established in a cultivated area. Both would point to settlement expansion after the close of the Norse era.

On Tiree secondary expansion from a primary settlement is likewise seen to have taken place within the framework of the ounceland. A pattern which mirrors that described above for Cliad is also found on Tiree with the division of a primary unit into several component parts. The primary *staðir* farm, Bhiosta, shows a division into the four *bólstaðr* settlements of Bhirceapoll, Bhassapoll, Murtost and Bist. An additional form of secondary expansion occurs on Tiree with the separation of a parcel of land from the primary farm which itself remains intact, as is seen at Kirkapoll and Gott and Heylipoll and Crossapoll (see Fig. 27). In the east of the island at Ruaig, Caolas and Vaul, where the land is among the poorest on the island, the original primary unit continued as a single independent unit until modern peripheral settlement occurred.

Peripheral settlement expansion on Coll has primarily taken the form of the development of seasonal shielings into permanent habitation. The shielings are found almost exclusively along the east coast as at Fiskary, Arintluic and Arinagour. Grimsary is a notable exception being situated on the west coast where its good

---

9. The specific *gríss* may, alternatively, derive from the male personal name *Griss* 'boar/pig'.

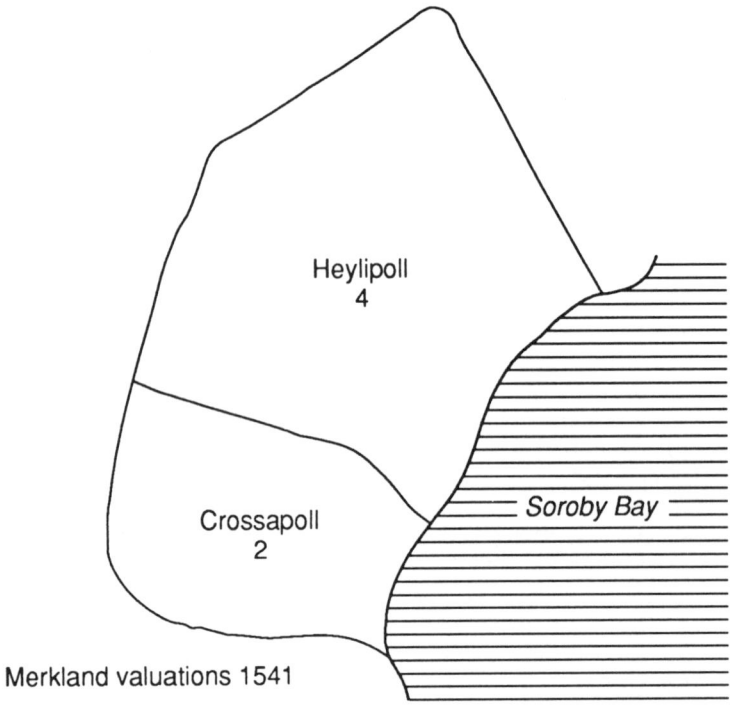

SUGGESTED EXPANSION OF SETTLEMENT

Primary		Secondary
Heylipoll	→	Crossapoll

Figure 27   Tiree: settlement unit of Heylipoll.

harbour, large areal extent and high valuation merit its classification as a secondary settlement. Both the names Fiskary and Grimsary are compounded with the Norse generic *ærgi* while the remaining shielings on the island are known by the Gaelic form *airidh*. The near total absence of the Norse noun for a shieling in the Inner Hebrides suggests that shieling drift, as it was known in Norway, and which involved a considerable amount of time spent away from the home farm, was not practised in the island. The Gaelic shieling name Airigh-aon-Oidche 'one night shieling' suggests that time spent away from the main farm was the exception rather than the rule. Shieling names on Coll in many cases describe the type of activity connected with them, as at Fiskary 'fish shieling' and Arinagour 'goat shieling'. Others refer to ownership as in the name Arileod 'Ljótr's shieling'. Additional peripheral settlement expansion has taken the form of the development of small units at the head of east coast bays, as at Treallabhig and Fislan. The name Treallabhig (ON *Þrall vík*) 'bay of the thralls' suggests the existence of unfree members of society and, if so, it might indicate the presence of a subjected native population. Peripheral settlement also came about through the elevation of pendicles of land to settlement units in their own right in the post-Norse period, as happened at Usairt and Feranagoinen. Several Gaelic names, for example, Clachard, Feadan and Ballard, refer to nineteenth-century settlements which essentially represent a late infilling of the settlement pattern.

Neither the Norse nor Gaelic toponyms associated with peripheral settlement growth on Tiree allude to any density of shielings on the island. Two Gaelic shieling names are found: An Aridhean and Airidh aon Oidche. One possible instance of ON *sætr* is apparent, preserved in the name Dun Hiader. Clearly the flat and fertile land precluded any necessity for seasonal transhumance. Much of the modern, tertiary development of settlement has been an infilling of the essentially Norse pattern by low ranking settlements having Gaelic names, many of which incorporate the habitative generics *baile* and *cill*. Missing entirely is the Gaelic generic *achadh* which occurs throughout the southern Hebrides.

DATING AND THE CHARACTER OF NORSE SETTLEMENT ON THE ISLANDS

So far, discussion of the chronological development of settlement in Coll and Tiree has used the terms primary, secondary and tertiary to differentiate between the various phases of settlement expansion, both within the framework of individual settlement units and within each island as a whole. Such categorizations are of limited value when comparing Norse settlement in Coll and Tiree with other areas of the Western and Northern Isles. The use of a purely relative chronology *is* useful in some instances; for example, the tertiary settlement phase on Coll characterized by the habitation of Norse shielings on a permanent basis cannot be equated with the tertiary settlement phase in some areas of Tiree where the site, situation and Gaelic names of the peripheral ranking settlements suggest that they developed in the post-Norse era. Clearly the introduction of absolute dates into such a vague chronology would be helpful. Nicolaisen's general survey of the distribution of Scandinavian settlement in Scotland mapped the incidence of the three habitative generics *staðr*, *bólstaðr* and *setr* and concluded that 'the names in *staðir* provide a picture of what Norse settlement was like before and up to the middle of the ninth century whereas *setr* names speak of colonisation and expansion well into the second half of the century. The map of *bólstaðr* supplies an overall vision of Scandinavian settlement in the north and west as its most extensive' (Nicolaisen 1976, 96). On Coll and Tiree the lack of a large enough sample of these three habitative generics most commonly associated with Norse settlement makes it inadvisable to attempt the formulation of such a chronology firmly anchored to define historical periods. The date given in the Irish Annals for the first raids on monastic houses may indicate a Norse sea-faring presence in the area in the last decades of the eighth century and sporadic raids may have led to overwintering in easily defended locations. The first phase of semi-permanent settlement characterized by the coining of simplex topographical names, may, tentatively, be dated to the last decades of the eighth century and the beginning of the ninth century. The suggestion of hypothetical dates for the development of secondary and tertiary settlement units in the islands would be of little value and these phases of settlement are best viewed relatively.

The range and type of generics found on Coll and Tiree, both habitative and topographical, are not so diverse as those found elsewhere in the Scottish islands. A comparison with the Northern Isles, particularly Orkney, shows that names describing many different habitation types are missing. Only single examples of *staðir, setr/sætr, hus, garðr, býr/bú* and *bustaðir* exist, there are no examples of the generics *skali* or *kví* and none of such fixed compounds as *huseby*. The lack of such names in the Inner Hebrides possibly reflects a society where wide differentiation in the status of settlement sites did not exist. Differentiation between different types of settlement (or a lack of differing types of settlement?) was, for some reason, not so necessary in the Inner Hebrides where the use of a single habitative generic, *bólstaðr*, seems to have sufficed to denote a 'farm'. The range of specifics coupled with the *bólstaðr* names in the Inner Hebrides also varies from those of the Outer Hebrides and the Northern Isles where personal names and directional specifics are most common. Two fixed *bólstaðr* compounds are found in Coll and Tiree, *kirkjubólstaðr* 'church farm' and *krossbólstaðr* 'cross farm' and it is likely that these had some significance in relation to the developing ecclesiastical network of the island.

Another indication as to the character of the Norse community on Tiree comes from the lost place name Bee, recorded in 1541 (*ER*, xvii, 648) and evaluated at 3 merklands. The settlement of Bee is no longer extant, nor is there any real indication as to where it may have been situated, unless the name may be equated with the suffix of the name Rossbhu, Kennoway. The simplex name Bea is also found in Orkney where it is believed to derive from ON *bú*. Several of the Orkney *bú* names are associated with the residences of Earls or local rulers. Although the valuation afforded Bee, Tiree, is low and there is little to suggest that it was once a high ranking settlement there is a (remote) possibility that the name may be a relic of the place of residence of local rulers on the island, such as Holdbodi, described as 'a great chieftain' in *Orkneyinga Saga*, who lived on Tiree in the early twelfth century (*OS*, trans. Taylor 1938, 244, 264, 374). Equally elusive is the residence on Coll of Earl Gilli, a man of substantial means allied by marriage to Earl Sigurd of Orkney in the early eleventh century (*Njal's Saga*, 182).

Such evidence from the documentary record points to control by strong Norse rulers in these two islands which, coupled with the imposition of the ounceland system following upon the establishment of primary settlements, suggests that the islands had close contact with the Orkney Earldom over several centuries. The similarity in the settlement names of Coll and Tiree and those of the Northern Isles would indicate that these Inner Hebridean Islands were not peripheral outposts but formed an integral part of the Norse world.

Ireland was a Mecca for Viking raiders and traders. Although it lies outside the scope of this volume, the history of Ireland's influence on the course of events relating to the Scandinavians of northern Britain has always to be borne in mind.[1] From the first raids in the late eighth century to the battle of Clontarf in 1014 – and later – the religious centres of Ireland and the commercial possibilities loomed large in the Viking 'quest for moveable wealth' (Crawford 1987, 45). The establishment of urban trading centres around the coasts of Ireland and particularly at Dublin[2] had an exceedingly important effect all round the Irish sea zone, as the chapters on south-west Scotland and north-west England show (below Chaps 8 and 12).

Tenth-century silver hoards (already referred to above p. 107) provide one archaeological trail for the commercial activity of Scandinavian traders and entrepreneurs around the British Isles. Further archaeological evidence for this tenth-century trading activity has recently been brought to light (Hill 1991) by excavations at Whithorn in Galloway, showing that a proto-urban industrial and trading base was developing at the ancient ecclesiastical and episcopal centre of Galloway. In its later tenth-century and eleventh-century phase, this community had Scandinavian links and was clearly part of the Irish Sea trading nexus. The term 'Hiberno-Norse' is used for this phase of the Scandinavian impact on the British Isles and the Hiberno-element revolved around the fortunes of the trading city of Dublin and the kings who ruled it, sometimes conjointly with the city of York.

The name Galloway itself probably derives from the term Gall-Gaedhil ('Foreign Gael') (although see Brooke 1991) and, if it does, is surely evidence for a settlement of Hebrideans of mixed race who moved into the south-west peninsula of Scotland in the tenth

---

1. See Edwards (1990 Chap. 8) for an overall assessment of the Vikings in Ireland.
2. See Wallace and O'Floinn (1988) and Bradley (1988).

century. The place-names of Scandinavian character clustered around Whithorn may relate to that population element, or may have closer links with the Danish settlers who established themselves at the head of the Solway Firth. It is surely not coincidental that these incomers around Whithorn settled in the locality of an ancient ecclesiastical centre. Whether they were invited in or whether they moved in uninvited, the existence of such centres had clear attractions for these entrepreneurs (Higham 1993, 197). Their presence, added to the mixture of cultures reflected in the place-names of Galloway, makes this one of the most complex areas of north Britain for linguists and historians to attempt to elucidate.

We are even beginning to perceive some Hiberno-Norse influence in eastern Scotland, as Simon Taylor reveals in Chap. 9, which may be further evidence for the Norse use of the waterways and firths of south Scotland to an extent at which we can only guess (Crawford 1994, 169).

8 Scandinavian settlement in south-west Scotland with a special study of Bysbie

RICHARD D. ORAM

Placed at the pivotal point between the Norse-dominated Hebrides and their southern colonies in Man and at Dublin, the south-western corner of Scotland is poised to control the sea-lanes which linked these two major areas of Scandinavian settlement. This strategic position and its proximity to several centres of Norse power in the Irish Sea zone has meant that the region has been long regarded as a probable area of Scandinavian colonization. Indeed, it was seen by some as one of the principal centres of Viking activity in mainland Scotland south of Caithness and Sutherland, and the home of the hybrid Norse-Gaelic people known to the Irish chroniclers as the *Gall-Gaedhil* (Foreign- or Stranger-Gaels). It was from the latter, moreover, that the name of the region was supposedly derived: Galloway – the Land of the Gall-Gaedhil (Smyth 1984, 157; cf. Brooke 1991).

Historians accepted these reasons almost without question and developed the view that Galloway *must* have been an important centre of Norse power simply because it was unthinkable that any right-minded Viking could ignore such strategic shores. Chronicles and sagas were plundered ruthlessly for any material that would strengthen this argument, mythology and folk-lore intertwined, and an elaborate 'history' of Scandinavian Galloway was evolved. Eventually, the region came to be seen as a Norse jarldom and as part of the *riki* of Thorfinn the Mighty, which the Orkney earl had built up in the first half of the eleventh century (Huyshe 1914, 105). The twelfth- and thirteenth-century lords of Galloway were claimed to be of Norse descent, and their subjects represented as a people in whom Scandinavian ancestry was strong.

In the last ten years this traditional interpretation has come under closer scrutiny and a major revision of our beliefs is under way. A combination of detailed archaeological research – e.g. at Whithorn – and a more critical examination of all types of historical and place-name evidence has led to a reassessment of the role of the Scandinavians in the development of Galloway. One historian, indeed, has gone so far as to question whether, in fact, they were ever significant players in the settlement pattern and population structure of the Scottish south-west (Cowan 1991). Such revisionism, however, goes too far. While the historical documentary evidence cannot be used to show that the Norse and Danes had any impact on the region other than as passing raiders, both archaeology and place-names indicate that they cannot simply be dismissed as irrelevant and that they were here in sufficient numbers certainly to influence the place-name map and possibly the local political structures as well.

Place-names are at present – despite the remarkable archaeological discoveries at Whithorn – the principal source of evidence for the spread of Scandinavian colonists throughout Galloway. The names themselves are scattered the length of the coastline, from the Rhinns in the west to the estuary of the Nith in the east, but with two major clusters in the Machars peninsula and in the district around Kirkcudbright (see Fig. 28). Very few names other than purely topographical ones are found in the interior of the region, and this coastal distribution points very much towards a secondary sea-borne colonization from the earlier Norse settlements in Man and the Hebrides. Some of the archaeological remains uncovered at Whithorn further demonstrate this Norse aspect and point to contacts with the Norse west (Hill 1988, 19). At the eastern end of the Solway, however, the place-names may represent part of the north-westward push of Danish colonists from York who, it has been suggested, crossed the Pennines into the plain around Carlisle and spread from there into Dumfriesshire (Fellows-Jensen 1991). Two separate colonizing movements thus seem to be present: one moving north-westwards by land from northern England, the other east and south by sea from Ireland, Man and the Hebrides.

Both types of Scandinavian place-name forms can be recognized in Galloway: the purely topographical and the habitative. The former are applied mainly to coastal navigational features, e.g. ON *nes* (coastal promontory), as in Almorness, Borness, Eggerness, Satterness; ON *holmr* (a low-lying island) Estholm (Hestan Island), and ON *bryggia* (landing-place) as in Lybrack (*Lybrig* in the Exchequer Rolls for 1456), which suggests name-forming by a seafaring people familiar with the main features of the Solway coastline. Away from the sea there are fewer certain names, but elements such as ON *garðr* (field or enclosure), as in Fairgirth, or ON *vað* (ford), as in Anwoth, indicate that some colonizers penetrated to the interior. Another possible element is ON *eik* (oak), which may be represented in Rerrick and Southwick where, despite the modern forms of the names, the generic does not seem to be ON *vík* (Fellows-Jensen 1991, 81). There are other ON elements such as *bekkr* (stream), *þveit* (paddock/clearing), *gil* (ravine), *fjall* (hill) and *dalr* (valley), but these are more common in Dumfriesshire than in

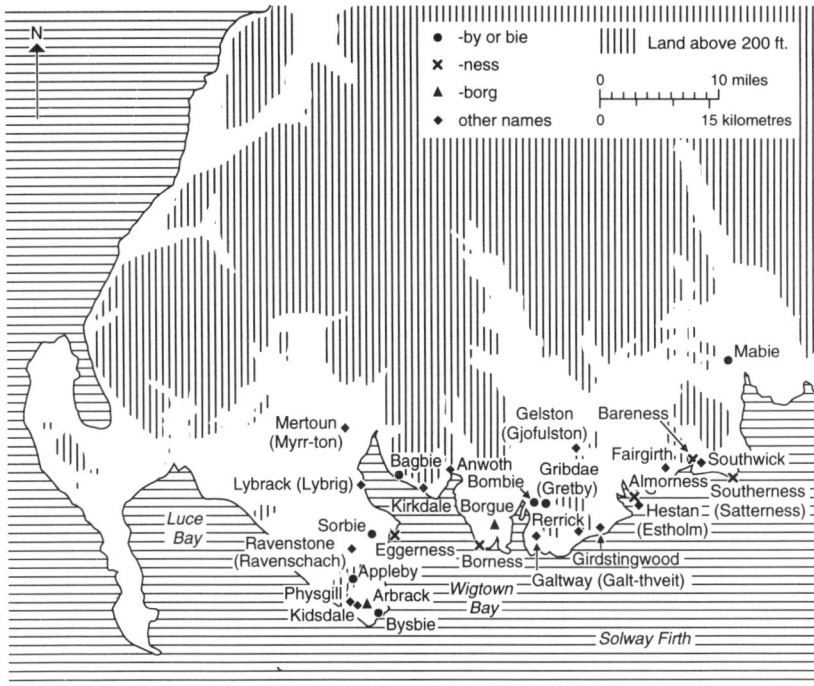

Figure 28 Scandinavian place-names in Galloway.

Galloway, which suggests that they may have been largely the product of the Danish landborne colonists from northern England. It should also be noted that all four forms passed quickly into the northern English dialect as loan-words and as a result of this they are of little use in attempts at the creation of a chronology for Scandinavian settlement in this region. Many names may have been coined in the twelfth century when Galloway experienced a substantial Anglo-Norman colonization from northern England.

In contrast to topographical names, those containing habitative elements are rather scarce. Evidence for intensive settlement and the evolution of a place-name hierarchy, as represented by the *staðir, sætr* or *bolstaðr* farms of the Scandinavian north and west of Scotland, is wholly absent in Galloway, and there is a markedly thinner distribution of habitative name forms than occurs in the Danish-settled areas of Dumfriesshire. Other than two *borg* names (stronghold) as in the simplex form Borgue near Kirkcudbright and the farm of Arbrack (recorded as *Arborg* in the Exchequer Rolls in 1456) the only positively-identified form contains *býr* or *boer* (farm), which is mapped by the suffix *-by* or *-bie*, e.g. Bagbie, Bysbie or Sorbie. The distribution of this element is restricted to the estuaries of the Cree and the Fleet, with most occurring in the Machars. Only seven definite names of this form are recorded in Galloway, which further undermines the old arguments for a Scandinavian conquest and subsequent colonization of the region. The thin and geographically-restricted distribution points rather towards a limited number of colonists and the infilling of gaps in what is otherwise a place-name map dominated by Brythonic, Gaelic and Anglian name-forms.

Other factors, however, have probably contributed to this picture of a thin and scattered settlement and have led to an understatement of the scale of the colonization venture. The place-name map in Galloway was still highly fluid until the sixteenth century, with many names recorded in the twelfth and thirteenth centuries disappearing in the course of the fourteenth century to be replaced in the fifteenth century by a wholly new name. For example, the Brythonic parish and settlement of *Trevercarcou* in the Glenkens district of northern Kirkcudbrightshire, disappeared as a result of the social dislocation caused by the devastation of the region by the army of Robert I in the early years of the fourteenth century. When the settlement reappears in the early fifteenth century, it had been recolonized from outwith Galloway and renamed in Gaelic *Balmaclellan* (Brooke 1984, 41–3). This is an extreme example, but illustrates how it is possible for names of ancient usage to disappear almost without trace. Such may have been the fate of some Scandinavian names where later, non-Scandinavian owners changed the settlement name to one in their own tongue. The dramatic Gaelicization of Galloway, which occurred in the eleventh and twelfth centuries, may have seen the replacement of some Norse names by Gaelic ones. A second and vitally important factor is the possibility that some estates were taken over in their entirety by Norse settlers and their existing, non-Norse name preserved by the new owners. There are some indications that this may have occurred in eastern Galloway and Dumfriesshire (Fellows-Jensen 1991, 86), and at Glasserton in the Machars an Anglian estate may have been partitioned by an important Norse settler to form holdings for his dependents (see below pp. 138–39). It is highly probable, therefore, that the scattering of *-bie* and *-by* names which has survived represents only a portion of an originally more extensive settlement.

Within the *-bie* and *-by* suffixed names there is a probable geographical – and originally linguistic – divide. Those in the east of Galloway, such as Mabie on the western side of the Nith estuary, derive probably from the old Danish *-by* rather than Old East Norse *-býr*, as they appear to constitute the western limit of the Danish colonizing movement from the Vale of York. The examples around Kirkcudbright, e.g. Gribdae ('Gretby' in 1356) and Bombie, and Wigtown Bay (e.g. Bagbie) and particularly those in the southern parts of the Machars peninsula (e.g. Appleby, Bysbie and Sorbie) argue in favour of an introduction of the generic by Norse-speaking – or Norse-influenced – colonists who arrived by sea. The noun itself, in both forms, can be used to describe almost any type of settlement from single farmsteads to important towns, but the examples in Galloway refer solely nowadays to small farming communities.

The origin of these *-by* and *-býr* settlements in Galloway is still subject to debate. Unlike the examples known from Cumbria and Dumfriesshire, the specific element used in name-forming in *-by* in Galloway was never a personal name. It has been argued that personal-name prefixes are indicators of grants of land to, or seizures of property by, specific individuals and occurred where larger estates were being broken up (Fellows-Jensen 1991, 85–6). Appellatival specifics, that is where the qualifying element is not a personal name, are seen as indicative of the complete takeover of the pre-Scandinavian unit itself. In Galloway only appellatival specifics are recorded, which implies that the settlers were moving into an already defined settlement pattern and taking over complete units within it, although there is some evidence in the southern Machars for the break-up of a pre-Norse estate to form smaller units (see below pp. 138–39). The scarcity of personal-name forms associated with any of the various generics indicates that the immigration was not sufficiently intensive for these initial settlements to be speedily broken down into smaller farms. Indeed, it could be argued that the scale of the settlement was so clearly limited that it is possible that the Norse were being invited into the region rather than arriving as unwelcome colonists. In the Machars peninsula, and in particular around Whithorn, the manner in which the Scandinavian settlement sites are slotted in between estates possessed by the monastery and form an arc around the northern and western boundaries of the outlying ecclesiastical manors appears to support such an hypothesis (see Fig. 29).

An additional (but not strictly habitative) element which has been used in the past in studies of the place-names of Galloway to argue for more significant Scandinavian colonization is the noun *kirkja* (church), especially in its inversion compound form. This occurs when the Scandinavian generic *kirkja* is paired with a non-Scandinavian – usually Gaelic in this area – specific in non-Scandinavian word order, i.e. *Kirk-X* as opposed to *X-Kirk*. The 'kirk-compound' place-names of southern Scotland have long been a source of debate, and fresh argument has been kindled in recent years which has brought into doubt once more the direct Scandinavian role in the name-forming process and called into question the chronology for the name type which had been proposed by earlier scholars. John MacQueen, for example, favoured a tenth-century context for these names and sought to link them to the supposed Gall-Gaedhil settlement of Galloway (MacQueen 1973). Nicolaisen himself raised the possibility of a derivation of some of these forms from Anglian examples and avoids reference to Gall-Gaedhil, but preferred an origin where Scandinavian and Gaelic peoples rubbed shoulders (Nicolaisen 1976, 108–111). Most recently, however, Daphne Brooke has highlighted the great

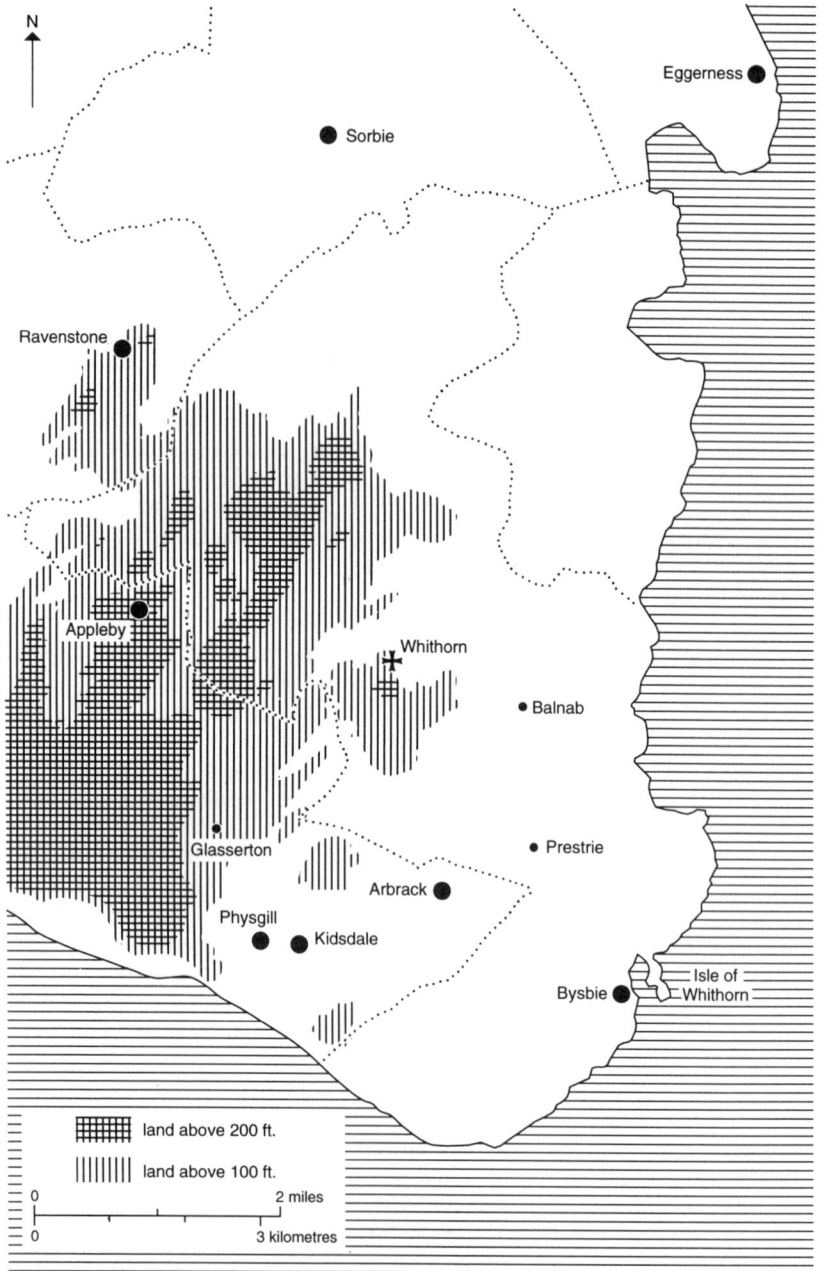

Figure 29 Southern part of the Machars, Galloway, showing place-names discussed in the text.

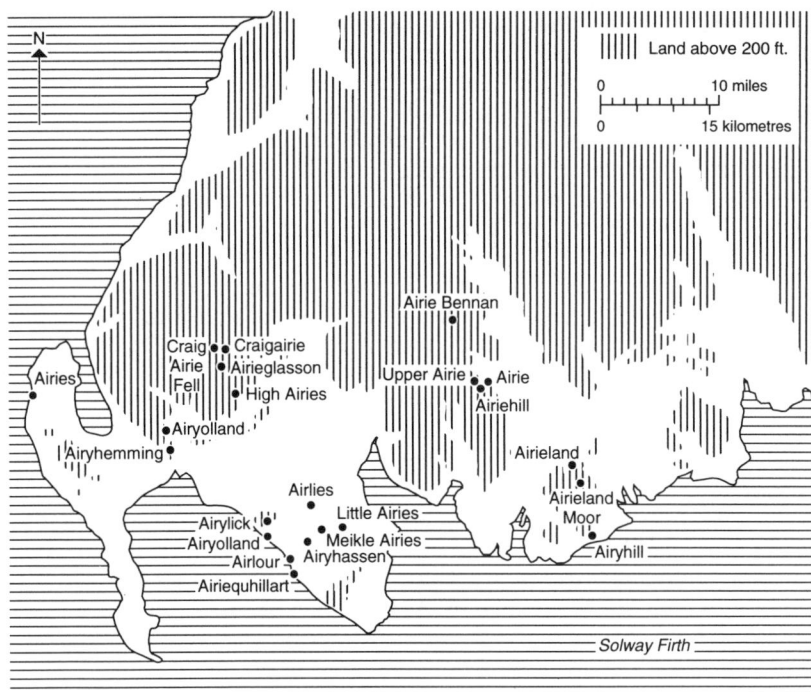

Figure 30 *Airigh* names in Galloway.

fluidity of place-name forms in Galloway throughout the Middle Ages and, focusing in particular on the *kirk-* and *kil-* elements in parish names, has argued a strong case for a late date for the formation of the kirk-compounds (Brooke 1983).

While place-names of purely Scandinavian derivation are comparatively rare in Galloway, one element of Gaelic origin, long recognized as commonplace in regions of Norse or mixed Norse-Gaelic settlement, occurs with great frequency. This is the generic *airigh* (a shieling), which represents the adoption of a native Hebridean/Manx Gaelic term by the incoming settlers (Fig. 30). It has a widespread distribution throughout Galloway, Man and Cumbria, where the common link would appear to be some degree of Norse settlement from primary colonies in the Hebrides. In Cumbria it is clearly an import, but in Galloway and Man there were pre-existing Gaelic-speaking populations who may have used the word in the pre-Norse period. The origins and development of the shieling system have been studied in depth in various regions, but particularly in Man and Cumbria. Eleanor Megaw demonstrated the Gaelic origins of the Manx *eary*, and proposed a pre-Norse origin for the majority of those which developed into permanent settlements (Megaw 1978). The absence of *-sætr* names (the Norse equivalent term) indicates that the newcomers found a fully-developed summer-grazing system and adopted the existing Gaelic terminology. Both *sætr* and *airigh* occur in Cumbria, which may indicate that the latter had not entirely replaced its counterpart in the vocabulary of Norse colonists arriving there from the older colonies in the Isles. The absence of *sætr* from Galloway parallels the Manx situation and is probably indicative of a pre-Norse origin for the pattern of shielings which developed there.

Megaw's research in Man produced two distinct strands of evidence. First, where modern *eary* names in what is now enclosed agricultural land indicated the former existence of a seasonally-occupied shieling. Second, un-named and abandoned sites. The former were found to lie mainly at or around the 600 ft contour at the limit of cultivation. Most were recorded in some of the oldest Manx manorial records, which revealed a past existence as upland holdings commonly linked to a lowland farm. Individual possession, moreover, was implied by the fact that many of the surviving *eary* names had personal names as specifics. Many developed into fully-fledged farms themselves, and continue to function as such today. Much less could be said for the abandoned, un-named sites. These survive today as little more than the conspicuous grassy shieling mounds which speckle areas of open moorland. Most lie well beyond the limits of modern agriculture, normally between the 900 and 1000ft contours, and none developed into a permanent farm site.

Manx estate documents show that the named *earys* on the island developed throughout the Middle Ages, with many becoming permanent habitation sites by *c.* 1500. Some are known to have been valuable pieces of property in their own right, quite distinct from the parent farm which they served. Some, indeed, which were valued as a *treen* or *ounceland*, also possessed a chapel, and seem to have been among the earliest to develop as permanent settlement sites. It has been implied that where such transformations occurred the *eary* was probably of pre-Norse origin. The development, however, was probably triggered by the arrival of the Norse, which led to an infilling of the settlement pattern as pressure grew on the available resources of land, with a move to occupation on a permanent basis of previously seasonal settlements. Since the bulk of such sites lie near to the primary farming zone, at low altitudes, Megaw compared them with the later Norwegian and Scottish 'home-shieling', which was used in spring and autumn when poor weather rendered the summer upland shielings unusable. The un-named upland shielings, therefore, may be the original summer sites, occupied for only a few months annually, and fading into oblivion as the system of transhumance pastoralism which gave rise to them passed out of use.

In Galloway the medieval estate records are markedly inferior to the Manx examples. Indeed, documentation concerned with the *airie* or *airy*, as the Galwegian sites are known, is non-existent before the sixteenth century. Most of the named *airigh* sites in Galloway are now long-established farms, but in some cases the term is applied to tracts of land rather than settlements, as in the district called The Airies on the western side of the Rhinns peninsula. The physical distribution of the Galwegian form is closely similar to its Manx counterpart, with none lying above the 750ft contour and most lying at the limits of the arable, on good pastureland. The majority lie in western Galloway and like the *-by* names occur in their greatest density in the Machars, where the arable is interspersed with tracts of higher, rockier grazing. In eastern Galloway *airigh* names are restricted to those former parishes with a high proportion of mixed farming, and lie mainly in the Parishes of Kelton and Rerrick, in close proximity to the cluster of Scandinavian place-names around the Dee estuary.

It needs to be said that the linguistic structure of the Galloway *airigh* names is almost exclusively Gaelic, in that the specific follows the name-forming generic, or occurs in its simplex form. This, together with the absence of *sætr* names, argues for a pre-Norse, Gaelic ancestry, yet their greatest concentration lies in the region of heaviest Norse settlement. This parallels the Manx situation, with the incoming Norse providing the catalyst for the transformation from seasonal to permanent habitation sites. Their concentration in the regions where *-by* names are most common would indicate a speedy taking-up of the best available land, with settlement of the former seasonal sites representing a secondary expansion from the original farms.

BYSBIE AND ITS CULTURAL SETTING

The implication of the above is that in Galloway most of the Scandinavian settlement that took place was of generally late date and was a secondary expansion from areas of primary colonization. The colonists, moreover, appear mainly to have come from earlier Norse settlements in Gaelic-speaking districts of western Scotland and to have been familiar with the types of farming and farming nomenclature common to those areas, although the affinities between material and structures from Norse Whithorn indicate that Norse colonies in Ireland, particularly at Dublin, may also have played a part, rather than those from the Danish settlements in the northern part of England. It is also clear from the number and type of the surviving settlement names that the colonizing movement was no mass influx of population with a resulting displacement of the native communities through seizure of land by the newcomers. What we see instead is the slotting-in of a few incomers into an already crowded landscape and their absorption into the settlement pattern.

What occurred was indeed absorption, not obliteration, for the newcomers made a lasting physical impact on the local nomenclature and transformed the nature of the regional economy. This can best be seen in the Machars district of south-eastern

Plate 15 An aerial view over Whithorn, looking south-east towards Bysbie and the Isle of Whithorn. The Church, with the extensive grave-yard, can be seen in the foreground, to the right of which the recent excavations have taken place. (Copyright: Peter Hill, Whithorn Trust)

Wigtownshire, that long promontory bounded on the east by the Cree estuary and Wigtown Bay and on the west by Luce Bay. At the south end of the Machars, in the area around the early Celtic and Anglian ecclesiastical centre at Whithorn, was one of the principal zones of Norse colonization in Galloway. Excavations around the site of the medieval cathedral-priory at Whithorn (see Plate 15) have produced remarkable evidence for an 'Hiberno-Norse' trading and manufacturing community which has striking parallels with the Norse settlement at Dublin, although on a much smaller scale. This community appears to have developed to serve the trading needs of the late Anglian monastic and episcopal centre on the hill at Whithorn, both utilizing the abundant local raw materials and drawing finished goods from elsewhere in the Norse-dominated west. Unlike similar emporia on the western seaboard and in Ireland, however, it flourished on an inland site, several miles away from the coast, but linked to the sheltered harbour of the Isle of Whithorn by long-established roads (Hill 1991, 39–40 and Fig. 3.11; Alcock and Alcock 1990, 130).

Whithorn was an ancient settlement long before the arrival of the Norse and had flourished in the eighth and ninth centuries when Galloway was a province of the Anglian Kingdom of Northumbria. But even before then it had been one of the principal ecclesiastical centres of the Brythonic Kingdom that had stretched along the northern shore of the Solway. This antiquity can be seen in the pattern of settlement and parish names in the area around Whithorn, where most of the old parochial centres developed out of estates that had belonged to the monastery. The link between the monastery and the lands is reinforced by the survival of sculptured crosses of the type known as the 'Whithorn School' at most of the medieval parish church sites (Craig 1991). The place-name map of parishes in the district also betrays the pre-Norse character of settlement in the Whithorn area, being dominated by Brythonic and Anglian names such as Glasserton or Cruggleton, Loncastle and Menhungion, all of which highlight the antiquity of the settlement pattern in this part of Galloway. The pattern, however, is not exclusively Brythonic and Anglian, for into it are inserted a group of Scandinavian names, but these, too, seem to be dependent upon the Whithorn community. The most significant names are the parish and settlement name Sorbie (ON *saurr-býr*='swamp or mud farm'), and the farm names Appleby (ON *apel-býr*='apple farm') and Bysbie (ON *biskup-býr*='bishop's farm'), but they are just the examples which are most recognizably Scandinavian in a group which forms a wide ring around Whithorn. Sorbie has an interest of its own in that it is a name form with an unusually wide distribution, occurring also in Scotland in Dumfriesshire, Ayrshire, Fife and Argyllshire, the Isle of Man, and – most extensively – in Yorkshire, Lancashire and Cumberland in England. The meaning of the name can be interpreted in a variety of ways, as the *saurr* may refer to nearby coastal mudflats – and these do occur to the east of Sorbie on the swampy margins of Wigtown Bay – or be taken to imply that the incoming Norse were not seizing the good land, but were seeking to make a living from marginal land reclaimed from the marshes. Icelandic examples of *saurr-býr* are associated with the cult of the fertility goddess, Freyja, so a possible interpretation is to identify them with cult centres, but the proximity of Sorbie to the major Christian centre at Whithorn renders this identification unlikely (Nicolaisen 1976, 101–102). Bysbie, however, is perhaps the most intriguing of the place-names and provides an opportunity to examine the relationship between the Norse and their ecclesiastical neighbours.

The interpretation of the name Bysbie as 'bishop's farm' is based on the form recorded in 1305 in a charter of Edward I to Dundrennan Abbey (*CDS*, 2, No. 1702). In this it appears as 'Biskeby', where the specific is interpreted as deriving from *biskup*, the Scandinavianized form of the Old English *bisceop*, a bishop. Nine years earlier in 1296, however, it was recorded as 'Buskeby' when its tenant, William de Buskeby, submitted to Edward I after the defeat of the Scots in that year (*CDS*, 2, 214). This form, which is based on a disputed interpretation of the original 'Ragman Roll' text, raises the possibility of an earlier form, *Buski-býr* (shrub-farm), as is suggested for the Ayrshire and Renfrewshire place-name Busby (Fellows-Jensen 1989, 43, 50–51). Unfortunately, due to the poor survival of medieval documentation from Galloway in general, there is no earlier form of the name preserved. The vagaries of medieval scribal recording of place-names are such as to allow no categoric rejection of one or other form, but there is strong circumstantial evidence in favour of 'bishop-farm'.

Bysbie nowadays is a single cottage, formerly a farm, and in the Middle Ages apparently a substantial piece of property held by a man deemed of sufficient social status to have his submission to the victorious English recorded in the Ragman Rolls. It lies just above the shore on the western side of the natural harbour of the Isle of Whithorn (NX 475359), looking southwards to the Isle of Man (see Fig. 29). From later Medieval sources we know that it was Church land throughout the Middle Ages, William de Buskeby of 1296 probably being a tenant of the Cistercian abbey of Dundrennan in Kirkcudbrightshire, which had certainly gained possession of the estate before 1305. It is a remote portion of the monastic estate, detached from the abbey's main centres of landed wealth in eastern Galloway, and probably represents a gift of property near to the seat of the see of Galloway at Whithorn, made to the abbey at or soon after its foundation in 1142 by one of the twelfth-century bishops of Whithorn – most probably the pro-Cistercian Bishop Christian (1154–86). The Norse name, however, suggests that it may have been Church property at a much earlier date and it is possible that it originally formed part of a multiple episcopal estate built up in the Anglian period, when the see of Whithorn was established on a firm, territorial basis. There are two other farm-names nearby which betray such an origin, the Brythonic Prestrie (*Prest-tref* = 'Priest's Farm') and the Gaelic Balnab (*Baile an Ab* = 'Abbot's Farm'). A 'bishop's farm' would complete the sequence neatly. The dating of the Norse name poses certain problems, however, as there is no recorded bishop at Whithorn between the last known of the Anglian succession, Heathored, in c. 833 and the appearance of Gilla-Aldan in c. 1128 (Watt 1991, 24). It should be stressed that it is by no means certain – although likely – that the episcopal succession failed completely in the intervening three hundred years, but it is probable that there had been no bishop at Whithorn for over a century by the time of the establishment of a Norse colonist at Bysbie in the tenth century. What is important is that, although it was probably not the bishop in person who was founding the farm or establishing a Norse-speaking colonist on his land, the land may still nonetheless have been recognized locally as forming part of the episcopal property, and the settler acknowledged the connection.

A study of the place-names around Bysbie shows that it formed part of a complex agricultural and economic pattern. There were several other properties belonging to the bishop or the monastery of Whithorn in the near vicinity, strung out along the old routes from the episcopal centre to the Isle of Whithorn and it is possible that

Bysbie originally represented a portion of the episcopal demesne at the port through which the commercial life of the monastic community and its dependent civil settlement was channelled. As such, it had probably formed a very important element of the bishop's revenues in the Anglian period, and the evidence for significant trading activity from Whithorn through the Isle to other centres in the Irish Sea basin in the tenth and early eleventh centuries suggests that it remained a strategic and economically important site. Would it be stretching the evidence too far to indulge in a piece of social reconstruction and suggest that Bysbie became the farm of the Norse tenant of Whithorn established by them to control and run the lucrative trade through the port?

Other Norse settlements were located nearby, at Arbrack on the Whithorn road, at Kidsdale and Physgill some two miles to the west, and at Appleby due west from Whithorn. Together with Bysbie, these settlements form an arc along the southern and western sides of Whithorn itself. None, however, formed major estates in their own right, but were portions of larger properties which certainly belonged to the Church in the later Middle Ages, or had passed before the middle of the twelfth century into the hands of the lords of Galloway. Although they were valuable in their own right – Kidsdale was regarded as one of the Balliol family's principal estates in Wigtownshire in the later thirteenth and fourteenth centuries – all with the exception of Bysbie (which lay in Whithorn Parish) were secondary estates carved out of the earlier Anglian manor of Glasserton, the Parish of which encompassed both Kidsdale and Physgill. Here we may have some evidence for the separation of blocks of territory from a pre-Norse unit, but the new settlements appear to have been recognized implicitly from the beginning as simply subordinate subsections of the principal centre at Glasserton. Is this evidence for the takeover of a pre-Norse manorial unit by a Scandinavian colonist and the subsequent partitioning of the estate to provide farms for his dependents? Certainly, when the local hierarchy of lordship crystallized in the mid-twelfth century, all four farms were probably tenancies of the ecclesiastical lords of Glasserton. Along with Sorbie to the north, and possibly Ravenstone ('Ravischach' in *c.* 1306 = ?*Hrafns-skogr* – Raven's Wood), these were probably the first permanent farms, located on the best available land which the incomers were able to acquire. With the exception of Sorbie, none represented the principal farm of the larger estate in which they lay, a factor which further argues against their violent seizure by an incoming tide of land-hungry Vikings, although the suggestion of the subdivision of an earlier estate at Glasserton into a number of smaller Norse-owned (and named) holdings might suggest that the relationship between the Scandinavians and the native Brythonic and Anglian-speaking population was not entirely harmonious.

Beyond these main farms, in a broad arc around the northern and western periphery of the settled land, lay the *airigh*s which formed the summer shielings (see Fig. 30). Like their Manx counterparts the Wigtownshire shielings are clustered heavily in what was formerly marginal land in areas of rocky and high ground. The centre of the Machars is hardly mountainous, but it was a region in which arable cultivation was limited to a few pockets of low-lying territory until the agricultural improvements of the eighteenth and nineteenth centuries opened up former areas of intractable bog and moorland. Nevertheless, by the middle of the fifteenth century, several of the early *airigh* sites had developed into permanent farms. Regrettably, the poverty of the documentary sources for Galloway in the early Middle Ages does not allow us to link particular *airigh*s with particular 'mother-farms', as the patterns of land-holding have fragmented and changed in this region with distressing regularity between the twelfth and eighteenth centuries. The full extent of the Bysbie land-holding, then, remains unknown to us.

The picture that is beginning to emerge of the Norse colony in the Machars is a great deal more complex than was believed in the past. It is still very easy to overstate the size of the colonizing venture – at either end of the scale – and the material from the Whithorn excavations may serve to further distort the impression gained. It is also very tempting to conjecture about the origins of the Norse colony in the area, to provide reasons for their establishment in a zone of intensive Brythonic and Anglian activity adjacent to the political and ecclesiastical centre of western Galloway, but all such hypotheses remain no more than guesswork. What we can see is the establishment of a few families around the monastery itself, craftsmen and traders attracted to the site by its economic potential, perhaps serving also as mercenaries. Beyond them, on outlying portions of the ecclesiastical estates, often on the poorer soils as in the marshes around Sorbie, a few colonists slotted into gaps in the established pattern or were installed in vacant properties to act as agents for the clergy. While they adapted in many ways to meet their new situation, they also adapted their new environment in ways that were familiar to them, bringing with them the system of summer shielings that they had encountered in Man and the Isles. Although they may not have been numerous, these Scandinavian incomers left their permanent mark on the place-name map of Galloway.

9 The Scandinavians in Fife and Kinross: the onomastic evidence*

SIMON TAYLOR

Despite all the bad press the Vikings have received, or more likely because of it, people are eager to see them associated with their area, and Fifers are no exception. Take the little village of Dunshelt, or Dunshalt, in Auchtermuchty Parish. Anyone approaching it either by road or footpath will see the name vary between these two forms from one sign to the next; and the

---

* The following symbols are used in this chapter:
† lost or obsolete name.
/ 'in the parish of', in Fife unless otherwise stated.
unrecorded hypothetical form.
Counties have been abbreviated by the three-letter system used by Nicolaisen *et al.* 1970 and by Nicolaisen 1976.
The following maps and records have been used:

Ainslie 1775	'Map of the Counties of Fife and Kinross' compiled and engraved by John Ainslie 1775
Gordon, *Fife*	Map of 'The Sheriffdom of Fife' based on James Gordon's survey of 1642, printed in *Atlas Novus* ed. W. Blaeu (1654), reproduced in *Illustrated Maps of Scotland*, ed. J. Stone (1991), Pl. 27
Pont, *East Fife*	Map of 'The East Part of Fife' from the original Pont Manuscript of the 1590s, printed in *Atlas Novus*, reproduced in *Illustrated Maps of Scotland*, ed. Stone, Pl. 29
Pont, *West Fife*	Map of 'The West Part of Fife' from the original Pont manuscript of the 1590s, printed in *Atlas Novus*, reproduced in *Illustrated Maps*, ed. Stone, Pl. 28
Retours	*Inquisitionum ad Capellam Domini Regis Retornatarum . . . abbreviatio* (Rec. Com., 3 vols., 1811–16), I Fife and Kinross
RHP	Register House Plan: various maps and plans kept at West Register House, Charlotte Square, Edinburgh
Sasines	Register of Sasines, kept at East Register House, Princes Street, Edinburgh
SGF 1828	Map of *Counties of Fife and Kinross, surveyed in the years 1826 and 1827*, ed. Sharp, Greenwood & Fowler, reprinted by Wychwood Editions, 1992

villagers are equally divided. Those who subscribe to the form 'Dunshalt' explain it as follows: when the Danes were attacking Fife long ago, the River Eden, which now flows unobtrusively by the village, was much wider, like a large estuary stretching into the heart of Fife. But at Dunshalt it became more difficult to negotiate, so that is where the Danes halted, giving rise to the name 'Danes-halt', which later became corrupted to Dunshalt.

This is a good example of what the Irish call *Dinnseanchas*, or popular etymology, and like so many stories which explain place-names, it is pure fantasy. However, Scandinavians of one kind or another *were* in Fife and Kinross, and have left real traces behind them in the names of places, even though there is no firm historical evidence for any Viking settlement.

In Fife the most unambiguous place-name element which signifies settlement by speakers of a Scandinavian language derives from the OScand *bý(r)*. In OWScand it meant 'farmstead', in OEScand it developed the meaning 'village'. There are at least six places in Fife which contain this element: Corbie, Gedbys †, Humbie, Sorbie, Weathersbie † and Weddersbie, details of which are given in App. I and on Fig. 31.

All these places are, or were, isolated farmsteads, on marginal land, and all are above 300ft or on steeply rising ground. It is therefore possible that they were cleared and settled by those who named them. None is more than four miles from the sea, although not all look out over the sea.

There is a second indicator of Scandinavian presence in Fife and Kinross. This is the Gaelic place-name element *gall*, the basic meaning of which is 'foreigner, stranger'. Its use in the Highlands through the ages is fully discussed by MacInnes 1989. In north-west Scotland *gall* was used at an early date to refer to the Norse, and *Innse Gall* was the usual Gaelic term for the Hebrides after the Norse invasions in the ninth century.

However, what foreign group was meant by the word *gall* in the Scottish Lowlands during the Gaelic-speaking period? It was not the English, who have always been referred to as *sassunach* (MacInnes 1989, 93). That this was also the case in medieval Fife is indicated by the Kirkcaldy place-name Balsusney, which probably contains this Gaelic word *sassunach*, 'English'. In the neighbouring Parish of Kinghorn there is the farm Balbarton, *Balbretan* 1372 (*RMS* i no. 415), which means 'estate of (or associated with) the Briton(s)' (Watson 1926, 208), so this people, too, was recognized and named. It is highly unlikely that it refers to the Anglo-Normans, as they came into Fife as major feudal vassals, and at a time when Gaelic was on the wane as a language in which new settlement-names were being coined. The only other important racial group to whom the word *gall* might refer are the Scandinavians, and there is no reason to think that the Lowland Gaelic-speakers differed in their use of this term from their cousins in the north and west.

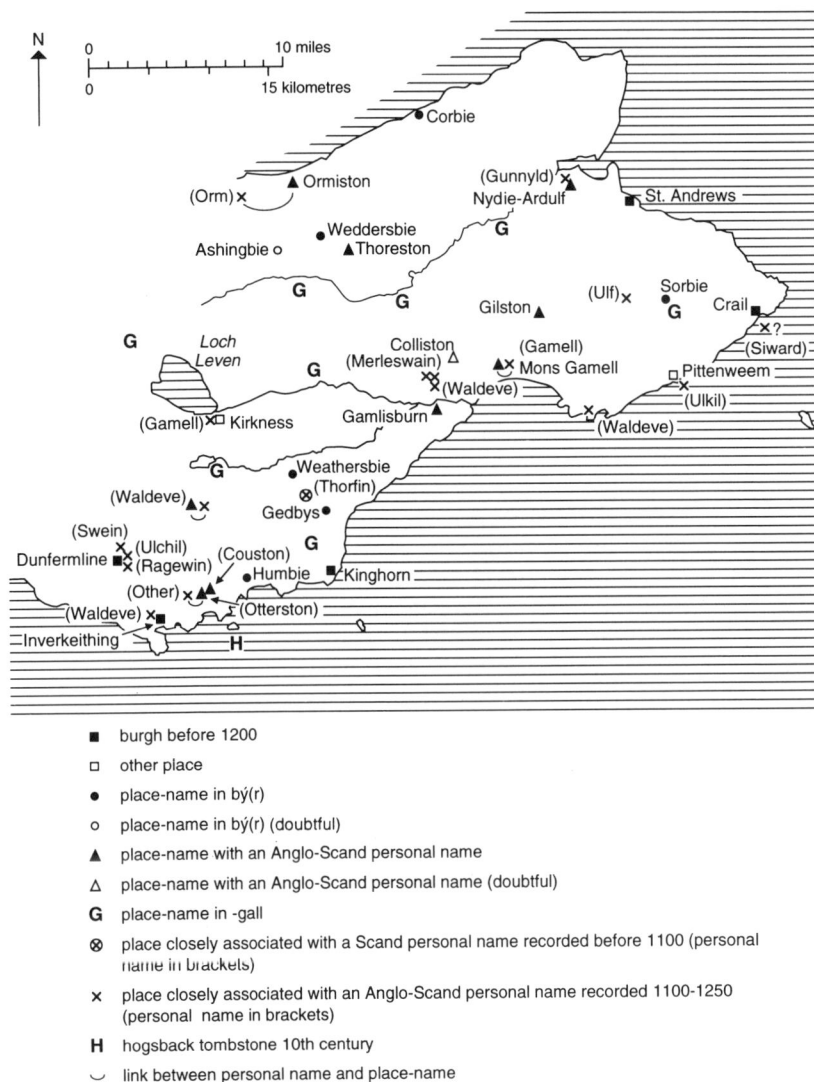

N

0   10 miles

0   15 kilometres

Corbie

(Gunnyld)   St. Andrews

(Orm) ×   ▲ Ormiston   Nydie-Ardulf

     G

• Weddersbie

Ashingbie o   ▲ Thoreston

     G   G   (Ulf) ×   Sorbie

Gilston ▲   G   Crail

G   Loch   Colliston   (Gamell)   × ?

Leven   (Merleswain) △   ▲× Mons Gamell   (Siward)

     G   ×× (Waldeve)   □ Pittenweem

(Gamell) ×□ Kirkness   Gamlisburn ▲   ×   (Ulkil)

                                (Waldeve)

   G   • Weathersbie

(Waldeve) ▲×   ⊗ (Thorfin)

         Gedbys •

(Swein)   G

Dunfermline ■× (Ulchil)

× (Ragewin)   (Couston)

            • Humbie   ▲ Kinghorn

(Other) × ▲▲

(Waldeve) ×■   (Otterston)

Inverkeithing   H

■   burgh before 1200

□   other place

•   place-name in bý(r)

o   place-name in bý(r) (doubtful)

▲   place-name with an Anglo-Scand personal name

△   place-name with an Anglo-Scand personal name (doubtful)

G   place-name in -gall

⊗   place closely associated with a Scand personal name recorded before 1100 (personal name in brackets)

×   place closely associated with an Anglo-Scand personal name recorded 1100-1250 (personal name in brackets)

H   hogsback tombstone 10th century

‿   link between personal name and place-name

Figure 31 Scandinavian place-names in Fife and Kinross and other elements discussed in the text.

There are at least six Fife and Kinross place-names which contain this specific, five of which are compounded with the Gaelic habitative *baile* 'estate, farm' to form *Ballegallin* † or *Ballingall*. For full details of these see App. II and Fig. 31. These two groups of place-name are the *only* unequivocal evidence we have for Scandinavian settlement in Fife, as the historical record, with one possible exception, is silent in this regard. However, from this fragmentary record a general picture can be reconstructed of Scandinavian activity in and around Fife throughout the whole of the so-called Viking Age, from the mid-ninth until the mid-eleventh century.

This activity began in earnest with Olaf the White's campaign against Fortriu in 866. Smyth (1984, 191–2) suggests that this and other attacks on the Picts and the Strathclyde British around this time were supported or at least connived at by the Scottish King Constantine I as part of his campaigns against these two peoples. If this was the case, then he was later to be hoist by his own petard, as he was defeated by a Danish army at Dollar (CLA) in 875; and two years later was killed in a battle against the Danes at a place called *Inverdufatha*, possibly Inverdovat/Forgan in north-east Fife (*ES* i, 353).[1]

Local tradition, first recorded by Andrew of Wyntoun, who was writing in Fife around 1400, tells of the massacre by Vikings of St Adrian and his companions on the Isle of May in the Firth of Forth, and Skene (*Chron. Picts-Scots*, 425) and would assign this event to these campaigns of the 870s.[2]

Smyth (1984, 195) followed by Crawford (1987, 51 and 1994, 109) sees this Viking activity in southern central Scotland as part of a concerted effort on the part of the Danes of York and Dublin to secure the major route linking the two centres via the Firths of Forth and Clyde. These plans collapsed in the 870s, with the death or departure of all the more experienced Danish leaders (Olaf the White, Ivar I and Halfdan), and the next recorded Viking activity near Fife is in 903, when Ivar II of Dublin plundered Dunkeld, and in the following year was killed in a battle in Strathearn (*ES* i, 399). This campaign smacks more of desperation than of careful strategy, as in 902 the Annals of Ulster record that the 'Gentiles' (i.e. the Hiberno-Scandinavians) had been expelled from Dublin. Nevertheless, this did not make their intentions any less serious, and it is quite possible that they were aiming at conquest, or at least at establishing trading bases (Crawford 1987, 59).

After 910 the claim on York of Ragnald of Dublin, another of Ivar I's descendants, again brings the Forth-Clyde route into prominence. After an initial period of hostility between Constantine II, King of Scots, and Ragnald culminating in the battle of Corbridge in 918, we see the Scottish King settle down into an alliance with Ragnald and his successors against the expanding power of Wessex until the 940s (Smyth 1984, 198 and Duncan 1975, 92).

This period came to an end when King Edmund of England took York in 944, followed shortly after by the turbulent reign in York of

---

1. According to Smyth (1984, 195) Constantine I's last battle was against the remnants of Halfdan's army which had suffered a crushing defeat by the Dubliners in Strangford Lough earlier that year.
2. But compare Barrow, 1973, 186 note 100, where he identifies Adrian with the seventh-century Pictish saint Ethernan.

the Norwegian King Erik Bloodaxe (947–8 and 952–4). During these upheavals the Scottish King Malcolm I gave every assistance to the Dublin King Olaf Cúarán in his attempt to take York. It was unsuccessful, and English control of York was finally established after Erik's death in 954.

This long period of close collaboration between the Scots and the Dublin-York Scandinavians is reflected in the names borne by one of the main branches of the Scottish royal family. King Constantine II (900–43), who dominated northern politics during most of the first half of the tenth century and whose daughter probably married Olaf Guthfrithsson of Dublin, gave his eldest son a Scandinavian name. This was Indulf, King of Scots from 954–62, probably Scandinavian Hildulf or Hildólfr. King Indulf's elder son, Culen, who reigned from 966–71, had the Scandinavian nick-name *Ring*, from OWScand *hringr*, 'ring-giver', while his second son had the thoroughly Scandinavian name Olaf (Crawford 1987, 60).

This points to close dynastic and cultural links between Scots and Scandinavians over two generations at the highest level. This may in turn have created the kind of Scandinavian-friendly environment which would explain at least some of the Scandinavian place-names in Fife.

In this context it is relevant also to mention the hogback monument. This is a house-shaped recumbent stone grave-cover usually about 4½ft long, with a marked convex roof-line which gives it its name. It was an innovation of the Hiberno-Scandinavian settlers in north Yorkshire from about the second quarter of the tenth century. They are fully discussed by Lang (1972–4, 206 ff. and 1984, 87 ff.). Early (i.e. tenth-century) examples are to be found chiefly in northern England (except in present day County Durham and Northumberland), with a scattering throughout southern Scotland, mainly close to maritime routes, with the heaviest concentration in the estuaries of the Forth and Clyde. A particularly early example, closely related to northern English types, is found on Inchcolm/Aberdour, an island off the Fife coast in the Firth of Forth. Lang (1972–4, 227) dates it to the mid-tenth century, that is to a period of Scottish-Scandinavian alliance, and of much coming and going between Dublin and York.

The distribution of hogbacks in Scotland has been linked to the importance of the estuaries of the Forth and Clyde as a trading and communication route between the Scandinavian settlements in Ireland and Yorkshire in the tenth century (see, for example, Crawford 1987, 172–4). At the very least the Inchcolm hogback points to an influential Scandinavian presence in the area in the mid-tenth century, and may be linked to the cluster of *-bý(r)* names in the adjacent part of west Fife (see Fig. 31).

All the later references to Scandinavian activity in and around Fife are of hostile incursions, and these are unlikely to have led to any permanent settlement. Sometime in the early 1030s (according to *OS*, 55), Earl Thorfinn the Mighty of Orkney marched south with a conquering army to Fife, where he spent some time fighting and razing villages to the ground.

In 1031 King Cnut of Denmark and England, and overlord of Norway, led an army into Scotland, possibly as far as the Tay, and secured a submission from King Malcolm II and 'the princes in the north from the middle of Fife', as the contemporary poem puts it (*Heimskringla, Olafs Saga Helgi*, 225).

It is possibly a conflation of these events which gave rise to the plethora of stories of battles between Danes, Norwegians and Scots in King Duncan II's reign (1034–40) recorded by historians such as Wyntoun, Fordun, Bower, and Boece, many of which allegedly took place in Fife.[3]

It was no doubt during this unsettled period in Fife that some passing Scandinavian hid his hoard of ill- or well-gotten silver at Lindores/Abdie, and for some reason failed to come back to collect it. It has been dated to around 1030 (Blackburn and Pagan, 1987, 298).

From King Macbeth's reign (1040–57) we have our first direct documentary evidence for Scandinavian presence in Fife. An unnamed son of one Thorfin had held that part of the lands of Bogie which King Macbeth gave to the Culdees of Loch Leven (*St A. Lib.* 12, 15 and 43: *Bolgin filii Thorfini* etc.). Thorfin is very much a WScand personal name, and is closely associated with the earldom of Orkney.[4] Bogie is in the Parish of Kirkcaldy, less than a mile from Gedbys † and two miles from Weathersbie †. We cannot assume that, because a son of Thorfin held part of Bogie, Thorfin himself had held land there. However, the Scandinavian connection in the heart of mid-eleventh-century Gaelic Fothrif (west Fife) cannot be ignored, and may be linked to the possible tenth-century influx of Scandinavian-speakers alluded to above. However, it may also be linked to the increased contact, not all of it hostile, between the kingdom of Scotland and the earldom of Orkney at around this time.

---

3. See for example Bellenden, *Chronicles* ii, Book 12, chapter 2, which mentions the battle at Kinghorn between the Scots (under Macbeth and Banquho) and the Danes. Incidentally, it is following the account of this battle that we find the first written reference to the Inchcolm hogback (see above p. 145), and it is noteworthy that at this time (the early sixteenth century) it was clearly identified as a Danish funerary monument.
4. This OWScand name *Þorfinnr* forms the specific element of the name Corstorphine MLO (earliest occurrence *c.* 1128), for which see Nicolaisen 1967, 228.
   We find another Thorfin in Fife about 100 years later: *c.* 1150 one Macbeth mac Torfin is one of those who perambulate the marches of land in the East Neuk of Fife (*May Recs.* no. 3). Around the same time this Macbeth also witnesses David I's second confirmation charter to Dunfermline (*Dunf. Reg.* no. 2).
   This personal name is exclusively WScand, closely associated with the Norse Earldom of Orkney, although it also occurs several times in Domesday Book, only in Yorkshire (Björkmann 1910, *s.n.*; Feilitzen 1937, 392).

Another possible link between Fife and the Scandinavian world from Macbeth's reign is the place-name Kirkness/Portmoak, now in Kinross, formerly Fife. This is by far the earliest Germanic place-name recorded in the Fife area. According to *St A. Lib*. 114, King Macbeth and Queen Gruoch gave *Kyrkenes* to the Culdees of Loch Leven. The name has a very Scandinavian ring about it, and can be paralleled by similar names from Scandinavia itself (e.g. Kirkenes in northern Norway). However, on linguistic evidence alone the name could equally well be Anglian, although I can find no equivalent place-name from the Anglian world.[5]

This same charter which records Macbeth's grant of Kirkness (*St A. Lib*. 114) also narrates how some Irishmen (*Hibernienses*) had come to Kirkness, having been given by the king a saltpan there, caused trouble and were burnt to death, thus giving rise to a local place-name recorded in Latin as *Saxum Hiberniensium*, 'Rock of the Irishmen'.[6] It is a fascinating piece of *Dinnseanchas*, which deserves to be better known. There is however a problem about its dating, as it purports to explain the name 'Rock of the Irishmen', which is one of the marches of the land of Kirkness given by Macbeth to the Culdees, but states that the Irishmen were introduced into the area by King Malcolm, son of Duncan, i.e. Malcolm III, who ruled after Macbeth.

What we seem to have is a local legend attached to a place-name, and founded on some historical incident, which the thirteenth-century scribe has tried to place in a firm historical context. He failed because he was not familiar enough with the sequence of eleventh-century Scottish kings. The original king might have been Malcolm I (943–54), son of Donald II, or Malcolm II (1005–34), son of Kenneth II, or may not have been mentioned at all. The scribe chose to associate the story with the early Scottish king who would have been most familiar to him, and he was caught out only because of the resulting anachronism.

But who were the *Hibernienses* of the story? Did they perhaps belong to that Hiberno-Scandinavian group which had played such a prominent role in Scottish politics during the tenth century? As far as the inhabitants of south-east Scotland were concerned, they would have been as much Hibernian as Scandinavian, coming as they did from Ireland. The fact that this story specifically associates these Irishmen with Kirkness, a unique Germanic, apparently Scandinavian, place-name in an otherwise totally Gaelic-speaking area, further suggests that these were no ordinary Irishmen.

---

5. The next Germanic place-name to be recorded in Fife is from about 70 years later. It is Goatmilkshire/Kinglassie (*schiram de Gatmilc, Dunf. Reg.* no. 1), one of the lands given to the church of Dunfermline by Alexander I (died 1124). This name is either Anglian or southern AS, and was presumably coined by the English Benedictine community established at Dunfermline by Queen Margaret.
6. It may be the huge, conspicuous erratic block immediately north-east of Capeldrae Farm/Ballingry.

Finally, less than two miles south of Kirkness, in the Parish of Ballingry, lies Inchgall – 'island of foreigners' – the peninsula in Loch Ore which later became the site of a castle and the administrative centre of a medieval barony (see App. II).[7]

Before drawing any conclusions from the above, some linguistic and semantic points need to be made.

First, if we posit a tenth-century date for at least some -*bý(r)* names in Fife, during a period in which Scots and Hiberno-Scandinavians were close allies, and which saw the erection of the hogback monument on Inchcolm (see above), then it would be remarkable for these names to have come down to us relatively unchanged. For if they are so early, they not only would have been coined in an almost exclusively Celtic-speaking environment, but also would have continued to exist in such linguistically hostile conditions for at least 250 years. However, they show no signs of Gaelicization such as is found in the Scandinavian names of the Western Highlands and Islands. For example, #*Saurrbý(r)*, which becomes *Sorbie* (FIF, DMF and AYR), has become Soroby in Tiree (ARG), Soroba near Oban (ARG), and in the Craignish district (ARG) a *Soropa* is recorded in 1512 (MacBain 1894, 224).[8] In fact, any changes they do manifest are ones which are totally in keeping with other -*bý(r)* names in Anglian-speaking Lothian and northern England. They could, it is true, have been 're-Germanicized' by Anglian-speakers in the late twelfth and thirteenth centuries, a process possibly aided by the fact that some of the first in Fife would have come from areas where -*bý(r)* names were thick on the ground, i.e. Yorkshire. Also many Anglian-speakers from Lothian would have been familiar with them. However, it is a point that should be borne in mind, given that any previous discussion of Scandinavian names in Fife and Angus has tacitly assumed a linguistic matrix similar to that obtaining further south. Whereas -*bý(r)* names can only have been coined by speakers of a Scandinavian language, -*gall* names, although most likely referring to Scandinavians, were coined by speakers of Gaelic.

There are several possible explanations as to how these two very distinct groups originated. One is that the -*gall* place-names were so named not while the Scandinavian settlers lived there, but after

---

7. Note also the presence of an old Irishman (*hiberniensis*) at a dispute regarding the marches of the vill of Kirkness c. 1128 (*St A. Lib*. 118). His name, Morrehat, is probably Celtic, but this does not preclude him from being of Hiberno-Scandinavian extraction, as Celtic names were common among Scandinavian settlers in Ireland.
8. Gaelic was probably still being spoken in areas of Fife and Kinross remote from the burghs in the early fourteenth century. See Barrow 1989, 79 note; and my doctoral thesis *Settlement-Names in Fife* 56–7 (Edinburgh Ph.D.). Also my article 'Babbet and Bridin Pudding' in *Nomina*.

Gaelic-speakers had taken them over, or after the descendants of the original settlers had become Gaelic-speaking. This would perhaps suggest that -*gall* names were coined in an earlier period than those which retained their Scandinavian names. Another possibility is that Ballingall, for example, could refer to a farm where one member of the household belonged to that race, but which was otherwise part of the majority linguistic community. A third possibility is that Ballingall could refer to a farm neighbouring one whose inhabitants were *Gall*.

Yet another possibility must be considered, especially in the light of the place-name Rumgally/Kemback. This name would seem to belong to the first phase of Gaelic-speaking settlement in Fife. It forms part of a chain of rath-names around the Eden valley which contains important people names, such as Ramornie/Kettle, 'rath of member(s) of clan Morgan' (Watson 1926, 239); Rathillet/Kilmany, 'rath of the people of Ulster' (*ibid.*); Rummond/St Andrews, *Rodmanand* 1144 (*St A. Lib.* 122), 'rath of (the people of) Manau', the district at the head of the Firth of Forth; and possibly Radernie/ Cameron, 'rath of ?(the people of) Eireann'. If Rumgally does indeed mean 'rath of the sons of the *Gall*', then it suggests that among the first Scottish settlers there were Gaelic-speakers who considered themselves as being descended from the *Gall*. And it is just these people who may well have given rise to those other place-names containing *gall*.[9]

It is significant that the names in *gall* have a different distribution pattern from those in *bý(r)*, with the latter being nearer the coast, while the former are predominantly inland around the Lomond Hills and along the Eden valley. This may also support the theory that the -*gall* names belong to a different period of name-formation. However, it may also have to do with the different linguistic environment of the coastal areas compared to the landward ones. Exposed as they would have been to more outside influences, it is possible that non-Celtic names had a greater chance of survival near the coast compared with more monoglott inland areas.

There are two exceptions to this inland distribution of -*gall* names: the poorly recorded Inchgall † / Kinghorn, and Ballegallin † / Carnbee. As suggested in App. II *s.n.*, Ballegallin may have been named because of its close proximity to Sorbie, a Scandinavian-speaking settlement, and then underwent part-translation into Anglian, surviving as Gaston. We know from independent evidence that the introduction of Anglian-speakers into the district around Crail was particularly thoroughgoing in the second half of the twelfth century, through the efforts of Ada de Warenne, the queen

---

9. Note Smyth 1984, 190–1, who suggests that Alpin, father of Kenneth I and Donald I, under whom we can assume at least some of the Gaelic settlement of Fife took place, had formed a dynastic alliance with the *Gall*.

mother, whose burgh Crail was.[10] Alternatively Sorbie may even have been the same place as Ballegallin, with two names – one used by the Gaelic-speaking community, the other by a minority Germanic-speaking community – with the Germanic name surviving because of the relatively early introduction of Anglian into the area.

If this tells us nothing else, it warns us of the complexities of these names, and of how tentative any conclusions drawn from such incomplete evidence must remain.

THE TWELFTH AND THIRTEENTH CENTURIES

There was another later and quite separate period of Scandinavian-related settlement in Fife. This has left behind it place-names which generally contain an Anglo-Scandinavian personal name combined with an Anglian generic, usually -*tūn*, 'estate, farm, enclosed piece of land'. These are listed in Appendix III.

It must be stressed from the outset that they in no way imply direct contact with Scandinavia, nor with any Scandinavian language. They are best seen partly in the light of movement within the kingdom of the Scots itself, particularly from Lothian, and partly in the light of movement from England, particularly northern England.

Thus the decision to exclude places which contain purely Anglo-Saxon names might seem rather arbitrary, and is dictated ultimately by lack of space. However, their inclusion would not fundamentally alter the picture obtained by focusing only on the Anglo-Scandinavian ones. Also there are far more Anglo-Scandinavian personal names than Anglo-Saxon ones, not only as eponymous specifics in place-names, but also as individuals who appear in contemporary documents, mainly as witnesses. This further underlines the relative importance of Lothian and northern England as places of origin of these twelfth-century incomers.

If we study the distribution map, we find two main clusters of such place-names, one around Kennoway, the other in west Fife around Inverkeithing. In the twelfth-century record, there is a significant presence in both these areas of land-holders with Anglo-Scandinavian names. In the second half of the twelfth century, the lord of Inverkeithing was Waldeve, probably a relative of the earls of Dunbar (Stephen 1938, 49–50). He held land on both sides of the

---

10. In the second half of the twelfth century mention is made of various Northumbrians holding land there, such as Ralph of Morpeth and Ralph of Allerwash (*St A. Lib.* 208); and the farm-name Wormistone/Crail contains the Anglian name *Winemer*, who was given the land *c.* 1180 (*RRS* ii no. 196). See also *ibid.* p. 434: 'The parishes of Kingsbarns, Crail and Carnbee seem to have been extensively settled by royal servants and minor officials in the twelfth and thirteenth centuries'. Many of these will have been Anglian-speaking.

Forth, and his father, Gospatrick, had some controlling interest in the ferries at Queensferry, which we can assume Waldeve inherited.[11] Waldeve or Waltheof is an Anglo-Scandinavian name common in Northumbria and Lothian from the early eleventh century. Björkmann (1910, *s.n.*) considers it to be an Anglianization of the common WScand name *Valþjófr*. Three places containing Anglo-Scandinavian personal names lie within a few miles of Inverkeithing. They are Otterston, Couston and Beath-Waldeve †. They were probably settled by men closely associated with Waldeve, lord of Inverkeithing, and their immediate provenance is most likely to have been Lothian.

Lothian had received an influx of Northumbrians, who were themselves heavily Scandinavianized, during the turbulent times immediately following the Norman conquest of England, especially after the collapse of the Danish-Northumbrian rebellion against William the Conqueror in 1069–70. This is epitomized in the Scoto-Northumbrian family of Gospatrick Maldredson who became Earl of Dunbar in 1072, and to whose family Waldeve of Inverkeithing was related. Moreover, David I, before becoming King of Scots in 1124, had been for the previous ten years lord of large tracts of territory south of the Forth, and inevitably men would follow him north when he succeeded his brother Alexander I on the Scottish throne. This perhaps explains the presence of one Swein as *prepositus* (reeve) of Dunfermline as early as the 1120s.[12] However, it was not all one-way traffic, and the other main Fife ferry, the Earl's Ferry from Elie to North Berwick, was enabling the opposite effect: the earls of Fife owned land around North Berwick, and even the land on which North Berwick Priory was founded in the late twelfth century was called *Gillecolmestun*, a settlement name with an Anglian generic element in predominantly Anglian-speaking Lothian, but with a thoroughly Gaelic personal name as the specific.

The other significant cluster of Anglo-Scandinavian place-names is around Kennoway. These are Colliston/Scoonie, on the boundary of Kennoway and Kettle Parishes, Gamlisburn † between Wemys and Markinch Parishes, *mons* Gamell † by Lundin, and probably Gilston, both in Largo Parish.

In the 1160s and 70s the name of the lord of Kennoway was Merleswain son of Colban, whose successors bore the name of Merleswain or Waldeve until the mid-thirteenth century (see Appendix IV *s.n.*). Merleswain, or Mærleswegen, is a rare name, apparently containing both Anglo-Saxon and Scandinavian

---

11. Waldeve, who was dead by 1199, was lord of Inverkeithing FIF and Dalmeny WLO; see *Dunf. Reg.* no. 165 and also *Inchcolm Chrs.* no. VII and notes. According to Stephen 1938, 49–50, this Waldeve was related to Earl Waldeve of Dunbar. His father was Gospatrick 'lord of the sea ferries' at Queensferry (*RRS* i no. 126).

12. *Dunf. Reg.* no. 18. See *RRS* i, 44 for a discussion of the meaning of *prepositus*.

elements.[13] It was the name of the sheriff of Lincolnshire at around the time of the Norman Conquest – an important member of the Anglo-Danish nobility who held lands from Cornwall to Yorkshire. He was among the many who took refuge in Scotland after the abortive rebellion against William the Conqueror in 1069–70. He was in good company, for among those refugees were Edgar Atheling and his sisters Christina and Margaret, the latter soon to become Queen of Scots (Freeman 1867–79, iii, 423 and iv, 169; *ES* ii 23–4; see also Duncan 1975, 122). Although we hear no more of this Merleswain, it is possible that he acquired Kennoway at this time and passed it on to his family, along with his name. However, the situation may be more complex, for the father of Merleswain lord of Kennoway had the thoroughly Scandinavian name of Kolbeinn, which was Gaelicized as Colbán (see Jackson, 1972, 75). There is good reason to think that he was Colbán earl of Buchan. Colbán himself could have been descended from an exiled Anglo-Scandinavian family, or he could have had Orkney connections (he had another son called Magnus!). But his, and therefore Merle-swain's, interests in Fife may have had more to do with the Celtic side of his family, rather than with any direct link with noble exiles from England in the 1070s (see Appendix IV under Colbán).

Whatever the immediate background of Merleswain lord of Kennoway, whether from the north or the south, he does seem to have stimulated Anglo-Scandinavian settlement in his vicinity, as Fig. 31 shows. The influx of southern settlers was further strengthened in the later twelfth century by the flourishing of the recently-founded royal burghs of Inverkeithing, Kinghorn and Crail, as well as of the ecclesiastical burgh of St Andrews, which brought in merchants from both Lothian and northern England. Ecclesiastical connections with northern England also brought in many from the same area. A good example is the household of Bishop Robert of St Andrews (1127–59), who was originally from Nostell Priory in Yorkshire, which shows many Germanic names – Anglo-Scandinavian, Anglo-Saxon – but chiefly Norman.

The single most important contributory factor in this settlement from the south was the feudalization of the Lowlands by members of the Anglo-Norman and Continental Norman aristocracy, which reached its peak during the second half of the twelfth century. They brought with them a host of retainers and household members, mostly with Norman names, some however with Anglo-Scandinavian or Anglo-Saxon ones.

---

13. Björkmann 1910, *s.n.* considers the second element to be from Scandinavian *sve(i)n(n)*, but is doubtful about the first. It is possibly an Anglo-Saxon name-element found in Marlborough, WLT and Malborough, DEV (see also Ekwall 1960, *s.n.*).

CONCLUSION

There are thus two main periods of Scandinavian influence on Fife and Kinross: one direct, the other indirect. For the early period of direct influence the complexity and paucity of evidence allow for only the most tentative of conclusions. However, it can be said that names coined by Scandinavian-speakers are more likely to have survived near the coast, whereas their inland settlements are recognizable more usually by the Gaelic element *gall*. The exception to this, Kirkness/Portmoak (KNR), may be due to the fact that the estate was given to a religious institution. This meant that the name was written down at a relatively early date, which kept it alive until the introduction of Anglian ensured its long-term survival. Some of the names in *gall*, particularly Rumgally/Kemback, may belong to the very earliest period of Scottish settlement in Fife.

The tenth century seems to be the most likely period for Scandinavian settlement in Fife, as well as in Lothian and Angus.[14] This coincides with the spread of the earliest of the hogback tombs, found in all three areas, with a particular cluster of *-bý(r)* names in the vicinity of Inchcolm, with its important early hogback. This was also when relations between the Hiberno-Scandinavians and the Scots were important for prolonged periods of time, and the land may have been given in return for some mercenary activity.[15] However, the place-names themselves reflect more peaceable activities such as sheep- (Weathersbie † and Weddersbie) and goat-rearing (Gedbys †), and dog-keeping (Humbie), while the story told in *St A. Lib.* 114, if it is indeed about the Hiberno-Scandinavians, alludes to their involvement in a salt-making industry! This story suggests also that the decision to bring them into Fife was taken at the highest level, by the king himself.

The later, twelfth-century, period of indirect Scandinavian influence is related to the influx into Lowland Scotland north of the Forth from Lothian and northern England of speakers of a northern Anglian dialect with Scandinavian features, many of whom had Scandinavian names. This was a by-product of the growing Anglo-Norman feudal influence on both the secular and religious life of Scotland. Although there was no major political or cultural upheaval dividing these two phases, both were relatively independent of each other.

Analysis of onomastic evidence in any part of Scotland is at

---

14. For *-bý(r)* names in Lothian, see Nicolaisen 1967. *-bý(r)* names north of the Tay are Ravensby near Carnoustie ANG, and *ly* Grymmysbe †, described in 1525 as being in the town of Arbroath (*Arb. Lib.* ii p. 440).

15. As suggested by Professor G.W.S. Barrow, personal correspondence; see also Fellows-Jensen 1991, 54–5, where a 'coast-watchers' theory is put forward. The problem with this is that the sea can be seen neither from Weathersbie nor Weddersbie, although they, like the *-bý(r)* names with a view of the sea, command very open outlooks.

present severely hampered by the lack of a full country-wide place-name survey. This is certain to turn up new evidence, particularly relating to the elements *bý(r)* and *gall* in eastern lowland areas, which will in turn shed new light on Fife and Kinross, and, it is hoped, give more satisfactory answers to at least some of the questions posed in this chapter.

APPENDIX I NAMES IN *-BIE* OR *-BY* FROM OSCAND *BÝ(R)*

Corbie/Balmerino lay on the estate of Birkhill on the Tay, and the name survives in nearby Corbie Den, and Corbiehill. It appears as *Corbi c.* 1231 (*Balm. Lib.* no. 1), *Corbiden* 1234 (*ibid.* no 56), *Cortiby* or *Corciby c.* 1240 (*ibid.* no. 7). Also *c.* 1212 one Odo de *Corby* witnessed a charter relating to lands in Balmerino (NLS Adv. MS 15.1.18 no. 46).[16]

It seems likely that the first element is the personal name 'Corcc', which the Hiberno-Scandinavians borrowed from Irish, where the name is well attested (Fellows-Jensen 1989–90, 74). It would then be exactly parallel with Corby CMB, which appears in the twelfth century as *Chorkeby* and *Corchebi*, and in the fourteenth as *Corcabi* (Ekwall 1960, *s.n.*; those places in Lincolnshire and Northamptonshire called Corby derive from the OScand personal name Kori, *ibid. s.n.*).[17]

Gedbys †/Kirkcaldy (OS 6" 1st edition sheet 32, NT 260922) first appears as *Gaidbie* in 1647 (*RMS* ix no. 1833); in subsequent *RMS* charters of the seventeenth century as *Gaitvie* and *Geddy*. It may contain the OScand *geit*, 'she-goat'. It lay on the north-eastern slopes of Raith Hill, on the lands of Abbotshall. Adjacent to Gedbys is The Scars, also on OS 6" 1st edition, with which Gedbys is always associated in the *RMS* charters. Both names are now obsolete.

Humbie/Aberdour is first recorded, as Humbie, in 1574 (*Inchcolm Chrs.* 219). It is one of five Humbies in southern Scotland, with East Lothian, Midlothian, West Lothian and Renfrewshire each having one. The earliest occurrence of the name is *Hundeby*, ELO *c.* 1250, and WLO *c.* 1290. It probably contains the genitive plural of OScand *hund(r)* 'dog, hound'. This is certainly the derivation favoured by Fellows-Jensen (1991, 51), where she adds that they can probably be seen as places where hunting-dogs were kept. Thus a later Scots parallel might be Dogton/Auchterderran near the medieval royal hunting forest of Cardenden. Compare also Hunmanby YOE and Hunsonby CMB, both of which contain OScand words for 'dog-keeper' (Ekwall 1960, *s.n.*).

Given the frequency with which this place-name occurs, however, it has also been suggested that we are dealing here with a

---

16. This is an original charter. A copy of its counterpart appears in *St A. Lib.* 271, where the place-name has been miscopied as *Corhri*.
17. We can reject the tentative suggestion of a hybrid (AS and OScand) derivation made by Fellows-Jensen (1989–90, 52) if only on the grounds that the name was not coined in an Anglo-Saxon-speaking environment.

Scandinavian common noun which has been borrowed into OSc, perhaps meaning 'kennels'.[18]

However, it may also contain the Norse personal name *Hundi*.[19] This is less likely, given the frequency of the place-name, and the infrequency of the personal name in independent record.

Sorbie/Crail does not occur before the OS recorded it in the mid-nineteenth century (OS 6" 1st edition). It is to be found in seven other places in Scotland, four of which are in Argyll. It contains the Scandinavian noun *saurr*, 'mud, dirt, sour ground'. For a full discussion, see Nicolaisen 1976b, 101–2, and Fellows-Jensen 1985a, 40.; see also Ballegallin †/Carnbee App. II.

Weathersbie †/Auchterderran in the hills south-east of Cardenden, between the 350ft and 400 ft contour (NT 235948), first appears as *Weathirsbie* in 1659 (*RMS* xi no. 80), and again on the magnificent plan of Raith estate of 1757 (RHP 1710), where we find *Weathersbie* and *Weathersbie Tofts*, and where the land is described as 'thin soil, carpet grass . . . sheep pasture'. It occurs also on OS 6" 1st edition, but mistakenly as *Weathers Brae*, and the small building to which this name is attached is described as 'in ruins'.

It contains the Scandinavian *veðr* 'wether, castrated ram', with the singular used to represent a plural, and, along with Weddersbie/Collessie, underlines the importance of sheep-farming among the small group of early Scandinavian colonists in Fife.

Weathersbie † lies between two Gaelic place-names which contain the word *mult*, 'wether': three miles to the south-west in Kinghorn Parish lies Balmuto, *Balmultauch*' 1319 (*RRS* v no. 144), 'wether farm' and five miles to the north-east in Markinch Parish, on the south bank of the River Leven, lies Auchmuty, *Admulty c.* 1240 'wether ford'. This indicates a high degree of integration into the local pastoral economy.[20]

---

18. I owe this suggestion to Professor G.W.S. Barrow, personal correspondence.
19. See Ekwall 1960, *s.n.* Hanby and Humby, which he derives unequivocally from this personal name; as does Nicolaisen (1967, 225–6 and 1976 [1979 impression], 113–4); see also *ibid.*, the page of additional information opposite p. 1, for the less likely suggestion that it contains OWScand *húrn* 'hump, hill'.
20. I think we can rule out the suggestion that we are dealing here with a nickname, or a form of the Scand proper name Viðarr/Withar (Feilitzen 1937, 406), because of its dual occurrence within Fife. This is far more easily explained by supposing the singular appellative meaning 'wether' used in a collective sense (Fellows-Jensen 1989–90, 51).

Weddersbie/Collessie appears to be linguistically and semantically identical with the previous name, where it is discussed in full. Its early forms are *Wedderisbe alias vocat. Wester Cullessy* 1509 (*RMS* ii no. 3363) and *Wedderisbye* 1515 (*Fife Ct. Bk.* 1).[21]

---

21. Note also Ashmabee/Ashingbie †, part of the lands of Leckiebank/ Auchtermuchty, which occurs in the Sasines 1781–1820 in ten independent entries, five of which are spelt *Ashmabee*, and five *Ashingbie*. Although in its form Ashingbie it bears a resemblance to such Scandinavian or Anglo-Scandinavian names as #Asheby †LNC and CHE (Fellows-Jensen 1985a, 26), which contain the Scandinavian or Anglo-Saxon word for 'ash-tree', the peculiar variations in its spelling prevent any serious attempt at an etymology. I have found no trace of it before this date, and it is now obsolete.

APPENDIX II NAMES CONTAINING THE GAELIC *GALL*

Ballegallin †/? Carnbee first appears in *c.* 1150, when David I gives
to the Isle of May Priory half of *Ballegallin*, along with common
pasture in the shires of Kelly and Crail (*May Recs.* no. 3). It lay in
the shire of Kelly, which is now roughly the Parish of Carnbee,
apparently near its march with Crail. We know that it lay in
Kellyshire, rather than Crail, not only because Malmure the thane
of Kelly is one of those who perambulate the marches for the king,
but, more importantly, because Ballegallin's teinds were payable to
the abbot of Dunfermline (*St A. Lib.* 392–3), whose monastery
owned the church of Kelly (*RRS* i no. 157).

In Crail parish, very near its march with Carnbee (previously
Kellyshire), is a place called Gaston. This first appears in 1278 as
Galliston (Balm. Lib. nos 42 and 43), when one William de *Galliston*
resigns the neighbouring estate of Drumrack to Sir John de Hay.
Could this name contain the Gaelic element *gall*, and could it be a
part-Anglianization of the Gaelic *Balegallin*, which disappears from
the record by the thirteenth century? In this context it may be
significant that only half a mile north-west of Gaston is Sorbie.[22]

Ballingall/Kettle. On OS 1" 1st edition only Wester Ballingall is
marked, which on modern maps appears as Balmalcolm Farm;
Gordon *Fife* has *Balnage*. It appears as *Balnegal* 1294 (Stevenson
Documents, 416) as one of the lands of the earl of Fife. It next
appears as *Bangall* 1457 (*RMS* ii no. 608), then as *Ballingale* 1487
(*RMS* ii no. 1683).

Ballingall/Leslie first appears as *Ballingall* 1504 (*RMS* ii no. 2788),
as land belonging to the earl of Rothes; then as *Bongall* 1512 (*ibid,*
no. 3511). The family Ballingall of that ilk first appear in 1478
(SRO Calendar of Charters no. 475), and seem to be connected with
this Ballingall rather than the one in Kettle, although it is not
totally clear.

The Ballingall Burn/Strathmiglo and Falkland runs between the
village of Strathmiglo and the Lomonds, joining the Falkland Burn
to flow into the Eden near Dunshelt. On the 1826/1827 Counties
Map (SGF/1828) a small steading named Ballingall is marked on
the banks of this burn on the lands of Woodmill/Falkland. It does
not appear on any subsequent map. By 1909 the field where
Ballingall lay is called Boerland (Falkland Estate Cropping Book
penes Falkland Palace). Two fields on Wester Cash farm which

---

22. However, Gall(e) appears as a surname in Fife as early as *c.* 1290 in the vicinity
    of Cameron/Markinch (Fraser, *Wemyss* ii, no. 2).

march with the Ballingall Burn are called East and Mid Baiglie (*ibid.*), which is probably a corruption of Ballingall.[23]

Ballingall/Orwell KNR, *Estirbalnegalle* 1372 (*RMS* i no. 413); *Balnagal* 1404 (*Pitfirrane Writs* no. 11); *Bennagall* 1619 (*Retours* I Kinross no. 5).

Inchgall/Ballingry, *Inchegalle* 1393 (*Pitfirrane Writs* no. 8), is the name of the island or peninsula in Loch Ore where the medieval castle of Lochore stands (now in ruins). The castle itself is thought to date from the twelfth century (Pride 1990, 72), and was known as Inchgall. A charter of Governor Albany was issued *apud Inchegall* in 1407 (*RMS* i no. 901).

Inchgall †/Kinghorn formed part of the sunny half of North Pitteadie, a farm two miles north-west of the burgh of Kinghorn. This is how it is described in 1819 in the Sasines, where it appears both as *Inchgall* and, erroneously, as *MacGall* (Sasines no. 12399). It appears also on Ainslie 1775 as *Inchgaw*.

Rumgally/Kemback, *Ratmagallyn* early thirteenth century (*St A. Lib.* 310), *Radmagalli c.* 1240 (Barrow, 1974, 31); ? 'rath of the sons of the *gall*'. The early loss of final *n* makes this more likely than 'sons of Gal(l)an', a proper name which occurs in Adamnan, as well as once in the royal genealogy of the MacErcs in *Senchus Fer n-Alban* (*ES* i, cli). See also above.

---

23. These names are no longer in use. In the Sasines 1781–1820 there is a place called *Mingal(l)* mentioned in eight separate entries, the first one being in 1788, no. 1856. Now obsolete, Mingal(l) formed part of the lands of Peathill, which lay two kilometres due east of the lost Ballingall farmstead, in the flat, marshy land around Lathrisk. It might just represent #*mòine nan gall*, 'peatmoss of the foreigners'. Unfortunately I have been unable to trace any earlier forms of this name.

APPENDIX III PLACE-NAMES CONTAINING ANGLO-SCANDINAVIAN PERSONAL NAMES CHIEFLY WITH AN ANGLIAN GENERIC

Beath-Waldeve †/Beath: 'terram de *Beeth* quam Waldeuus tenuit' *c*. 1200 (*RRS* ii no. 396 = *Dunf. Reg.* no. 66); *Beeth Waldef* 1278 (*Dunf. Reg.* nos. 86 and 87). Waldeve held this land before *c*. 1200, when Sayer de Quincy gave it to Dunfermline Abbey (*Dunf. Reg.* nos 66 & 154). This same Waldeve also held Strachan KCD (*St A. Lib.* 276–7). He witnesses a charter of Dunfermline in the 1230s (*ibid.* no. 202). His heirs finally renounce all rights to the land in Beath in 1278 (*ibid.* no. 86). The site of Beath-Waldeve is now lost, but we know it was not part of Wester Beath (*RRS* ii p. 385; and *Dunf. Reg.* no. 207).

At around the same time another part of Beath was also held by a man of non-native stock, one William (the) Fleming. However, whereas Waldeve appears to have been a free tenant, William (the) Fleming was in some way thralled to Dunfermline Abbey (*Dunf. Reg.* no. 326). The part he held became known as Beath-Fleming † (*Dunf. Reg.* nos 177 and 178). For a discussion of these manorial names see, e.g. Barrow 1980, 42 note 43. Beath is unique in Fife for its proliferation of proprietorial names in various forms up until the early modern period. It seems to have been following a trend set already in the twelfth century.

? Colliston/Scoonie: ? *Collystona* 1359 (*ER* i p. 560: this may refer to Couston/Aberdour), *Coliston* 1478 (SRO Calendar of Charters no. 475), *Collistoun* 1517 (*Fife. Ct. Bk.* 398). This may contain Kol(r), the same personal name as in Couston/Aberdour, see next name. However, the retention of the medial unstressed syllable suggests rather the Gaelic personal name Colin, found in Colliston/Orwell KNR (*Collinstoun* 1553 *RMS* iv no. 794). Colin(us) appears several times in Atholl and southern Perthshire in the early thirteenth century, e.g. *Dunf. Reg.* no. 332 and *St A. Lib.* 246, 349, 363 and 364.

Couston/Aberdour: *Colestun* 1189 × 99 (*Spalding Miscellany* V p. 243) *Coleistoun* 1240 (*Inchcolm Chrs.* no. XIX), *Coustoñ* 1457 (*Dunf. Reg.* no. 452) and Colstouñ 1466 (*ibid.* no. 458). This contains the Anglo-Scandinavian personal name Kol(r), which most likely comes from the OScand Ko(l)l(r), see Feilitzen 1937, 307. It appears (as Col) only once in Domesday Book, in Lincolnshire. However, there is evidence that it was also an Anglo-Saxon name, see Ekwall 1960, *s.n.* Colesborne GLO.

Couston is adjacent to another place-name in *-tūn* containing an Anglo-Scandinavian personal name *viz* Otterston/Dalgety.

Gamell #Law †/Largo: *mon[s] Gamell* early thirteenth century (*RMS* iii no. 2132). This was apparently situated somewhere on the west side of Lundin. Note that a man called Gamell witnesses a charter of Walter son of Philip de Lundin regarding land in Lundin/ Largo *c.* 1170 (*St A. Lib.* 264; see also *RRS* ii no. 167).

There are at least four other men called Gamel(l) in Fife from around the same period. In Domesday Book this name is significantly more common in Yorkshire than anywhere else in England (Feilitzen 1937, 257). It appears twice in Lothian place-names (Nicolaisen 1967, 229).

Gamlisburn †/Wemyss or Markinch: *Gamlisburn c.* 1290 (Fraser *Wemyss* ii no. 2), a burn which forms a march of the lands of Over Cameron/Markinch. For the personal name Gamel(l), see Gamell #Law † above.

Gilston/Largo: *Gylstoun* 1538 (*RMS* iii no. 1859), *Gelstoun* 1540 (*ibid.* no. 2147), Gilstoun *c.* 1550 (*N.B. Chrs.* p. xxiii). Because of the lack of early forms, it is impossible to say which personal name is involved here. It may however be the OWScand Gilli, found in Gilston MLO (Nicolaisen 1967, 229).

Nydie-Ardulf †/St Andrews: Nydie Mains was called *Nidin Ardulf c.* 1220 in a lost terrier of St Andrews Priory lands (BM, MS Harl. 4628, fo. 242v.). The other Nydies mentioned along with it are *Nidin Rusticorum* and *Nidin Ecclesie* (the *Bonde Nidin* and *Kirke Nidin* of *St A. Lib.* 316).

The name is probably Anglo-Saxon Eardwulf, with Scandinavian influence (see Björkmann 1910, 6). In Domesday Book Ardulf occurs only in Yorkshire (Feilitzen 1937, 243).

Ormiston/Abdie: *Ormestoun* 1564 (*Lind. Cart.* no. ccci). This is derived from either a) the local surname Orme recorded in the early sixteenth century (*ibid.* 297–8), one of whose members was Henry Orme abbot of Lindores 1502–23+ (*ibid.* 310–12). The surname itself may well signal descent from Orm son of Hugh son of Gillemichael earl of Fife, lay abbot of Abernethy in the later twelfth century (*RRS* ii no. 152); or b) Orm son of Hugh himself.

In Domesday Book this name occurs almost exclusively in Yorkshire (Feilitzen 1937, 337). It occurs in five different place-names in Lothian and the Borders (Nicolaisen 1967, 231).

Otterston/Dalgety: 'terram de *Kincarneder* quam Other tenuit' *c.* 1199 (*Inchcolm Chrs.* no. VII); 'terram . . . que dicitur le *Corsakir* in terra de *Oterston* sita' 1349 (*ibid.* no. XXXIV), *Oterstoñ* 1395 (*St A. Lib.* 5).

The personal name Other comes from the OScand Óttarr/Ottar (Björkmann 1910, 104). In Domesday Book it occurs almost exclusively in Devon, the exceptions being one occurrence in Yorkshire and one in Shropshire (Feilitzen 1937, 342).

Thoreston †/Collessie Parish: 'in campo de Thoreston' 1248 (*Lind. Cart.* no. cxxxvii). This is the only occurrence I have found of this place-name. It lay either within or adjacent to the vill of Kinloch, near a ford over the Collessie Burn; *campus* means 'field' or 'piece of enclosed ground', and may in this case translate Scots *tūn*.

The only Thor on record from north Fife is one Thore father of Gamel, the latter of whom witnesses three charters of Earl Duncan II of Fife 1154 × 72 (*St A. Lib.* 242–4).

APPENDIX IV SOME PERSONAL NAMES CONNECTED WITH FIFE SHOWING ANGLO-SCANDINAVIAN INFLUENCE BEFORE 1250

Colbán early twelfth century, father of Merleswain I, lord of Kennoway *q.v.*, is probably Colbán earl of Buchan, who witnesses both the charters of Merleswain I son of Colbán concerning Kennoway, the Earl's only extant non-royal charters. One of his sons is called Magnus (Jackson 1972, 75). Also the earls and countesses of Buchan continue to be closely linked to the family of Merleswain and their interests in Fife well into the thirteenth century (see, e.g. *St A. Lib.* 252, 253–4; also *Inchcolm Chrs.* nos xxv and xxvii). This link between Fife and Buchan may go back to the marriage of Ete daughter of Gillemichael to Gartnait mormaer of Buchan, since Ete's father may have been Gillemichael earl of Fife, who died *c.* 1136 (Duncan 1975, 165 n. 56).[24] The daughter of this marriage, Eve, married Colbán, who thus became mormaer or earl of Buchan (Jackson 1972, 34, 35 and 76). Kennoway may have formed part of Ete's 'tocher' (= dowry).

This leaves open the question of Colbán's provenance, whether from Fife, Buchan or from a Scandinavian-speaking region such as the Orkneys. It is discussed by Young (1993, 179–80), who comes down in favour of Fife. At the same time, however, he admits that the Fife connection may have been established earlier, at the time of Gartnait's marriage to Ete. If this connection was indeed established then, there is no particular reason to assume that Colbán came from Fife. Colbán's family, and the Fife connections with the earldom of Buchan, are fully discussed by Young (*ibid.*, 179–81 and 194).

Merleswain I son of Colbán, second half of the twelfth century, lord of Kennoway, witnesses royal charters of Malcolm IV and William I. Mereuin son of Colbain, who witnesses David I's second confirmation charter to Dunfermline Abbey *c.* 1150 (*Dunf. Reg.* no. 2), is almost certainly an error for Merleswain, due not to scribal error but to confusion with the similar Anglo-Saxon name Merewin, which we know was being used in east Fife *c.* 1200 (*St A. Lib.* 383). He grants some lands in Kennoway, along with the church, to St Andrews Priory *St A. Lib.* 258–9 (before 1178); in this charter it implies that a now lost place called *Pethchaschen* had been given to Kennoway church by an earlier Merleswain; however, in the next charter *ibid.* 259–60, which appears to have been issued at the same time, it is clearly stated that it was Merleswain son of Colbán

---

24. Relevant to this early link between Fife and Buchan is Maeldomnig son of Macbeth, *judex* of Fife and Fothrif, who witnesses a charter of Gartnait and Ete to the abbey of Deer in Buchan in 1131 or 32 (Jackson 1972, no. 3 and pp. 62–3; see also Barrow 1966, 23 under 'Meldoinneth').

who had been the donor of this land. He is granted Ardross/Elie by King William *c.* 1172 (*RRS* ii, no. 137).

His father Colbán may well have been earl of Buchan (see above *s.n.* Colbán). His son is also called Merleswain (II) (see *St A. Lib.* 259–60). Waldeve son of Merleswain, who witnesses various Fife charters between *c.* 1199 and 1220 (e.g. *St A. Lib.* 272, 318–9 and 381), is the son either of Merleswain I or Merleswain II. The name itself is discussed above pp. 151–2.

Merleswain III son of Waldeve son of Merleswain, is compelled by William Cumin Earl of Buchan *c.* 1212–31 to stand warranty (*warantizare*) to the canons of St Andrews for the land of Kilmux in Kennowayshire (*St A. Lib.* 252, also 254). This was part of the lands given to St Andrews Priory by his forebear Merleswain I son of Colbán. For further discussion of this, see *Inchcolm Chrs.* p. 127. In 1239 he is involved in a dispute with the bishop of Dunkeld concerning the patronage of the church of Fithkil (= Leslie FIF) (*ibid.* no. XVIII). He is dead by *c.* 1263, when he is styled Merleswain of Ardross/Elie (*ibid.* no. 139). From this same charter we know he had a daughter, Scolastica.

He was also styled Lord of Innergelly/Kilrenny, as in 1281 Bishop William of St Andrews gives a charter to Margaret of Ardross, daughter of Merleswain the late lord of Innergelly (*Dryb. Lib.*, no. 20). He is the last member of this family to bear the name Merleswain.

Ragewin is one of the three men given to the church of Dunfermline by David I 1124 × *c.* 33 (the other two being Gillepatric and Ulchil, a Scandinavian name), *Dunf. Reg.* no. 19. This name is not recorded elsewhere. It would appear to be a mixture of the Scandinavian *Rage-* and the Anglo-Saxon *-wine.*

APPENDIX V RED HERRINGS

Bonnington etc., a common place-name, is frequently quoted as probably or possibly containing the Scandinavian personal name *Bóndi*, (e.g. Nicolaisen 1967, 226–7 and 1976, 114–5; and Crawford 1987, 100). Fellows-Jensen (1989–90, 50), however, more convincingly derives the majority of these names from the Anglian, later Old Scots, common noun *bond(e)*, ultimately a borrowing from the Scandinavian *bóndi*. This was the husbandman of later Scottish charters, whose characteristic holding was as much as 26 acres of arable (see Barrow 1981, 8–9), and whom Sanderson (1982, 41) calls the backbone of rural tenantry in the later Middle Ages.

In Fife, where the personal name is never recorded, it occurs as a place-name specific six times combined with *tūn*: Bonytoun †/Abdie, Bonnyton/Carnock and Largo, Bonnyton † (of Garvock)/Dunfermline, Bonnytown/St Andrews and Bonnington/Saline.

It occurs also in the following places:
The 'Bondhalf † of Auchtermuchty' (1517 *RMS* iii no. 168, and frequently thereafter) is no doubt connected with the modern street name 'Bondgate', east of the burn.
'Bonfield', between Strathkinness and Nydie/St Andrews, appears as *Bonde Nidin* and *Nidin rusticorum c.* 1220 (for the references see Nydie-Ardulf App. III *s.n.*).
'Bonnygate', one of the main streets in Cupar, leads from 'Bondfield', to the west of the town, which latter is probably *Bondland* 1294 (Stevenson, *Documents*, 415). The form with 'field' first appears as *Bonefeld* in 1452 (*RMS* ii no. 580).
'Newtoun-Bondis' † is an alternative name for Wester Kincaple/St Andrews recorded in 1551 (*RMS* vi no. 17).

Carnbee is the name of a small village, as well as a large inland parish in the East Neuk of Fife. The parish was originally called Kellie, which was also the name of the local shire. This name is still preserved in Kellie Castle, Kellie Law, and the farms of Easter and Wester Kellie. The parish changed its name sometime in the late thirteenth century, and this change probably came about because the church itself was sited at the place called Carnbee, although the whole area continued to be known as Kellie(shire).

Even putting aside the Celtic first element, the modern pronunciation of Carnbee, with both syllables bearing equal stress, suggests that we are not dealing with a Germanic name. Its earliest occurrence is in *St A. Lib.* 277, when one sir Richard de *Karnebehyn* witnesses an early thirteenth-century charter.

Other early forms of the name are *Garnebrin* and *Karneby* 1274–5 (*Bagimond's Roll*, 37 and 62); *Carnebeyn* 1278 (*Balm. Lib.* no. 42); and *Karnebe c.* 1351 (S.R.O. Calendar of Charters vol. i no. 119A).

After this date the name appears consistently as *Carnbe*, or more often *Carnbee* (e.g. in 1443, *RMS* ii no. 373, or in 1528 and 1535 *ibid.* iii nos 706 and 1450 respectively), the double '*e*' possibly representing the secondary stress.

The first element of the name is obviously Gaelic *càrn* 'cairn, heap of stones, etc.'. I do not know what the second element means. The final *-yn/in* of the early forms is probably not an organic part of the name, but rather some kind of locative inflexion. Unlike organic *n* it never survives in modern forms.[25] Bagimond's earlier form *Garnebrin* appears to contain the *p*-Celtic *pren* 'tree', but Bagimond is not the most reliable of sources, and as the second *r* occurs only here, we must regard this as a rogue form.

Crombie/Torryburn is listed in the OS map of *Britain before the Norman Conquest*, 1973, as a name in *-bý(r)*. However, as Fellows-Jensen (1991–92, 41) correctly points out, it is a Gaelic place-name derived from *crom*, 'bent, crooked'. Throughout the medieval period it is #Abercrombie, first appearing as *Abercrumbin* 1157 × 60 (*Dunf. Reg.* no. 144 = *RRS* i no. 157, where it is mistakenly identified with Abercrombie, St Monance Parish, which shares the same etymology). For the *-in* ending of the early forms, see Carnbee above, and fn. 25. The earliest occurrence of the name without *aber* is 1525 *Laing Chrs.* no. 350.

Drumnagoil/Beath, the name of a ridge in Blairadam Forest; Liddall, 1896, *s.n.* derives it from Gaelic *druim a' ghoill* 'ridge of the foreigner' (*goill* being the gen. sing. of *gall*). I have found no record of the name earlier than the nineteenth century, but it would seem rather to derive from *druim na goile* 'ridge of the swirling stream' (*goil-e* f. 'boiling, swirling of a stream'), with reference to the Drumnagoil Burn which runs along its south side.

Forganby appears on the OS 1" 1st edition for the parish name Forgan. It is a completely unhistorical form, and I can find no trace of it either earlier or later, not even in the OS Name Books.

Forgan is in fact a Celtic place-name, first recorded in the early thirteenth century as *Forgrund* (*St A. Lib.*, 260). There is no reason to doubt Watson's etymology of the place as 'on' or 'above a bog' (Watson 1926, 380), although the *Foregrundscihire* he mentions *ibid.* is in fact Longforgan PER, on the opposite side of the Tay estuary.

---

25. This *-in* ending is frequent in twelfth- and thirteenth-century forms, e.g. *Abercrombin* for Abercrombie, *Uctermukethin* for Auchtermuchty, *Kilglassin* for Kinglassie, *Kircaledin* for Kirkcaldy, *Nidin* for Nydie, *Petconmarchin* for Pitconmark, *Rathelpin* for Rathelpie, *Sconin* for Scoonie and presumably *Ballegallin* for #Balgall or #Balgally. It is best explained as a kind of locative case, which perhaps shows either the dative or the genitive ending of OIr *n*-stem nouns: the dative after such propositions as OIr *in(d)* 'in', the genitive with a word such as 'land of' understood. MacDonald (1941, 5) calls the twelfth-century form *Cragin* for later Craigie WLO simply a locative case.

Rigby/Ceres appears on the OS 2½" 1st Series (printed 1955, compiled from 6" sheets last fully revised 1912–3). It is not on the *Pathfinder* series, nor on the OS 6" or 1" 1st editions, but it is on OS 1" 7th series. Although it is at the north-west end of Ceres village, it lies right on the Cupar-Ceres parish boundary. Because of its late, and fleeting, appearance, it cannot be seen as a genuine -bý(r) name.

Eastern England was virtually the sole preserve of Scandinavian settlers of Danish origin, who moved in among the Anglo-Saxon rural communities and added their own linguistic imprint to the existing English toponymy. The different phases of settlement took place in the late 870s after many years of raiding – raiding which had culminated in the arrival of the micel here ('great host') in 865. This remarkable military force, not surprisingly, split into several warrior groupings under individual chieftains in the 870s and the Anglo-Saxon Chronicle gives us valuable, if limited, information about which group eventually settled in which locality. Such historical information is highly unusual in the whole story of Scandinavian settlement in northern Britain, although it only gives the most basic information about the process of settlement: 'in this year (876) Halfdan shared out the land of the Northumbrians and they proceeded to plough and support themselves' (Keynes and Lapidge 1972, 19). In eastern England there is very little archaeological evidence to help fill out the pattern of Scandinavian settlement. The absence of pagan graves[1] gives some indication that the micel here must have come under the influence of Christian beliefs in the decade that it raided and moved around the countryside. The firm intention on the part of the Wessex kings to bring the pagan Danes within the Christian community is clearly described in the Chronicle's account of the Danish leader Guthrum's acceptance of Christianity and baptism in the peace arrangements concluded with Alfred in 878 (Keynes and Lapidge 1972, 85). This occasion would not have had much effect on the Danish settlers in Northumbria however, and their acceptance of Christianity was perhaps a result of demands or persuasion exercised by the archbishops of York who survived the Danish takeover of their metropolitan city, although probably losing lands and wealth in the process.

The events of 876 should be seen as a starting point for the beginnings of a long process of Danish colonial settlement and endeavour in northern England to which the place-names themselves are the best witness. How this was carried out and

---

1. The distribution of all Scandinavian pagan graves in England is shown in Wilson 1976. The burials of Norse type in the North-West are examined in detail by Edwards 1992, fig. 3.

under what political organization is still barely understood but it is acknowledged that there must have been a major disruption of the traditional system of landholding as suggested by Sawyer as long ago as 1979 (p. 5). In this process a land market was created which introduced the concept of buying and selling land into Anglo-Saxon society and the fragmentation which resulted from all this disruption probably accounts for the many -by village names with a personal name as specific. The importance of the city of York as a power centre and fulcrum for trading activity which provided the wealth to finance colonial endeavours, should not be underestimated (Higham, N. 1993, 209). The Vikings had controlled the city since 866 and they developed it into a major trading centre, as shown by the Jorvik excavations which have taken place since the 1970s (Hall 1978, 1994). The richness of the archaeological evidence provides a whole new dimension to our understanding of the Danish Kingdom of York which the bald historical record of the violent doings of the kings never hints at. However, that bald historical record does tell us that one dynasty attempted to rule both York and the Viking trading centre of Dublin on the east coast of Ireland from time to time during the Viking century in Northumbria, which lasted from the mid-900s to the mid-1000s (Smyth 1978, 9). Such political links spawned their own economic and social effects, and the Irish, or Hiberno-Norse influence which is evident in north-west England and south-west Scotland is a probable result. The 'pure' Danish settlement in Yorkshire soon shades off into a more mixed Scandinavian imprint in the vast tract of upland territory between Tees and Forth, or Mersey and Clyde, which is now receiving more detailed scrutiny to follow up Nicolaisen's seminal studies of the 1960s.

The Viking kings of York may have had little desire to recreate the former kingdom of Northumbria. Indeed the unity of that kingdom had been 'smashed beyond recognition' by the disruption of the Viking Age (Higham, N. 1992, 24). It was for the dynasty of West Saxon kings to re-create a permanent new political structure, incorporating the Danish Kingdom of York within the wider Kingdom of England in the tenth century. This situation eventually allowed the Kings of Scotland to extend their southern boundary to the Tweed in the eleventh century, and the political map of medieval north Britain was drawn.

10 Scandinavian settlement in Yorkshire – through the rear-view mirror

GILLIAN FELLOWS-JENSEN

INTRODUCTORY

Over twenty years have gone by since my study of the place-name evidence for Scandinavian settlement in Yorkshire (Fellows-Jensen 1972) was first published. In the intervening period a great deal of water has flowed under the onomastic bridges, some of it muddied and opaque, some of it crystal clear and sparkling, all of it with a contribution to make to a better understanding of the place-names bestowed by Danish-speakers in eastern England. It has therefore seemed opportune to present to the 'Last of the Angles', a reassessment of the place-name evidence for settlement by immigrants from Denmark in Yorkshire, the largest pre-1974 English county.

The inspiration for my study of the Yorkshire place-names came from Kenneth Cameron's three pioneering articles dealing with Scandinavian settlement in the East Midlands (Cameron 1975). These studies were intended as a contribution to the debate on the size of the Viking armies and the density of the Danish settlement in England that had been opened by P.H. Sawyer (1958) with a breakneck assault on Sir Frank Stenton's assessment of the Scandinavian place-names in England as the record of 'a migration' (Stenton 1947, 514). Cameron agreed with Sawyer that the armies were probably small but asserted that there must nevertheless have been a considerable Scandinavian immigration into the East Midlands as a result of a secondary immigration in the course of the first two generations after the original partition of lands. He based his conclusions on a study of the topographical situation of villages with English and Scandinavian names, the quality of the land, the availability of fresh water and the nearness to rivers, roads and trackways. He considered that many of the Grimston hybrids, that is names in which a Scandinavian personal name is compounded with the Old English element *-tūn*, represented old established English villages whose names had merely been partially Scandinavianized by the Vikings who had taken them over when the land was partitioned: that the names in -*bý* represented colonization in the strict sense, and that the *thorp*s probably resulted in the main from secondary colonization.

I, in turn, applied the methods used by Cameron to the place-names of Yorkshire, exploiting in addition various other kinds of evidence, both linguistic and non-linguistic. My conclusions agreed in the main with those reached by Cameron but I became aware that the picture was more complicated than he had led us to believe. This was because in Yorkshire there was evidence both that Danes sometimes settled in English villages without changing their names and also that some villages with purely Scandinavian names must originally have been established by Englishmen before the arrival of the Vikings. I was also inclined to believe that some few of the hybrid names in -*tūn*, in particular the names whose first element is the personal name *Grímr*, might well derive from the period of secondary colonization, when land less immediately favourable for agriculture was taken under plough to meet the needs of an increasing population. It was not until some years later, however, that I felt it necessary radically to revise my interpretation of the material.

Several factors contributed to this realization of the need for revision. First and foremost there was my gradually widening knowledge of the Scandinavian place-names in other parts of Britain. I published a detailed study of the Scandinavian names in the East Midlands (Fellows-Jensen 1978b) and a similar study of the names in East Anglia, the third major English region of Danish settlement, is in preparation. Realizing that the names of Danish origin could not be treated in isolation from those coined by the Norwegians, I turned my attention to names almost exclusively of Norwegian origin in Shetland, Orkney and the Hebrides (Fellows-Jensen 1984) and to names in areas where both Danish and Norwegian influence can be identified, that is the Isle of Man (Fellows-Jensen 1983b), North-West England (Fellows-Jensen 1985a) and South-West Scotland (Fellows-Jensen 1991), as well as to the names in an area of more diffuse Scandinavian settlement where agreement had not been reached as to the national origin of the coiners of the Scandinavian names, the Central Lowlands of Scotland (Fellows-Jensen 1989–90). In the meantime, Victor Watts had published a valuable survey of the evidence for Scandinavian settlement in Durham (Watts 1988–89), and C.D. Morris had drawn attention to important documentary evidence for a Scandinavian presence in Northumberland that has left little or no trace on the place-names there (Morris 1981 and 1984). As more and more of the Scandinavian place-names in Britain were submitted to critical examination, voices began to be raised against certain of the views propagated in my study of the names in Yorkshire.

THE HYBRID NAMES IN -*TŪN*

The group of names about which there has been most discussion is the Grimston hybrids (see definition p. 170). There is in fact little excuse for my having blindly accepted Cameron's interpretation of the significance of these names. This is because as early as 1967 Bill Nicolaisen had published an important study of some names of this type which are found in south-east Scotland (Nicolaisen 1967). He had been prompted to examine the names in Scotland by his dissatisfaction with an antiquated map of the distribution of place-names in England and southern Scotland that had been published by the BBC (1957, 22). The distribution on this of a number of blotches supposedly representing Danish place-names in south-east Scotland prompted him to take a close look at the names of wholly or partly Scandinavian origin here, many of which contain Scandinavian personal names, for example *Dolgfinnr* and *Ketill* in Dolphington and Kettlestoun in West Lothian (MacDonald 1941, 6, 59). He was able to show that many of these names must have been coined by speakers of English or Gaelic and argued that even where the bearers of the personal names were men of Scandinavian descent, speaking a Scandinavian language, they are more likely to be Norse than Danish. Although Nicolaisen's argument that the personal names involved mostly point to a West Scandinavian origin is in need of modification, particularly in view of the fact that all except one of the Scandinavian personal names compounded with -*tūn* in Scotland are also of frequent occurrence in Yorkshire, he was undoubtedly correct to treat the majority of the place-names as late coinages by English-speakers (Nicolaisen 1967, 234).

It was therefore reckless of me to assume automatically that the same type of name in Yorkshire had been coined in the early years of the Danish settlement. A warning blast was sounded by Margaret Gelling in a review of my Yorkshire book (Gelling 1973). She pointed out that East Garston in Berkshire is named from *Esgar*, Edward the Confessor's staller, who held the estate in 1065 (Gelling 1974, 330). *Esgar* is an anglicized form of the personal name *Esger*, an *i*-mutated East Scandinavian form of *Ásgeirr*. Gelling therefore suggested that some of the Grimston-type names in Yorkshire may also have had a manorial significance. This explanation would make good sense, she considered, for a string of names in the East Riding (Fellows-Jensen 1972, 197–8; cf. Fig. 32). These are Folkton, Flixton, Staxton and Ganton, which lie along the course of a Roman road running from Malton to Filey. They all stand on the belt of post-glacial sand and gravel which lies at or near the junction of the chalk Wolds with the clay and alluvium of the Vale of Pickering. Each settlement has territory extending over an area of carr to the north and of wold to the south, as well as the fertile arable land on the sand and gravel. The string is only broken by the English-named settlement Binnington in the west. It is continued westwards by two English-named settlements, Potter

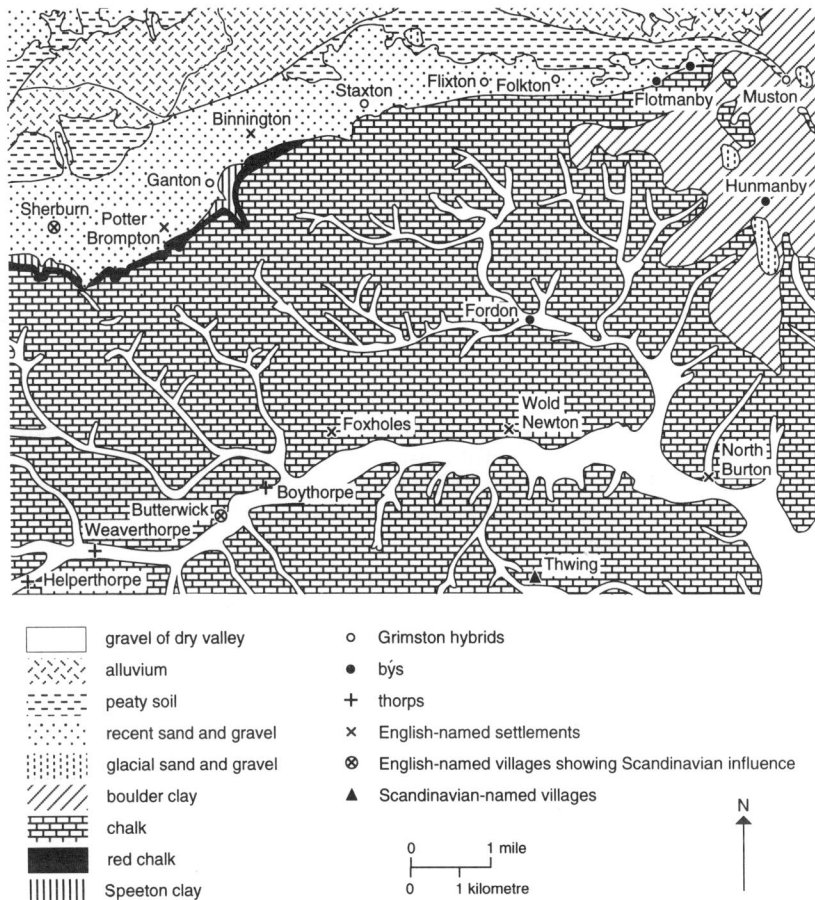

Figure 32 Geology and settlements around Sherburn, Yorkshire East Riding. Reproduced with permission from Fellows-Jensen, 1972, 197. Drawn in the Department of Geography, University of Nottingham and based upon the Geological Survey map with the sanction of the Controller of H.M. Stationery Office and permission from the British Geological Survey. Crown copyright and NERC copyright reserved.

Brompton and Sherburn. All the named settlements may have been carved out of the large estate which was perhaps known by the topographical name Sherburn, which survives as that of a parish. In Domesday Book this name is recorded once as *Sciresburne* (G(reater) D(omesday) B(ook) 303r), representing Old English *scīrburna* 'clear stream', while there are two references to it in the same source as *Schiresburne* (GDB 328r, 382r), suggesting that the name had been Scandinavianized by the substitution of initial /sk/

for / ʃ /. This Scandinavianization must have been brought about by Danish settlers in the area, perhaps by the *Folki, Flík* or *Flikkr, Stakkr* and *Galmr* who had taken over units of the old estate at some time in the Viking period. It is noticeable that the arable land available to Folkton and Flixton is much smaller in extent than that available to the other two places with hybrid names, and to the English-named settlements. Other evidence for a Danish presence in this area is provided by the *bý*-names, Flotmanby and Hunmanby, the *thorp*-names, Helperthorpe, Weaverthorpe and Boythorpe, and the originally topographical name, Thwing, and possibly by Muston – although this last name may be wholly English (**mūstūn* or 'mouse settlement'), perhaps used derogatorily of a poor settlement.

What Cameron and I had demonstrated in our studies of the Grimston hybrids in the East Midlands and Yorkshire, of course, was merely that the settlements were unlikely to have been founded by the Danes, since their favourable situations, high status and general prosperity pointed to their being old-established settlements. It did not show that they had been taken over by Danes at the time of the partitions of land in the late ninth century. A closer look at the forty-two Grimston-type names in Yorkshire suggests that most of them are unlikely to bear young manorial names. The main argument in support of this standpoint is that the personal names contained in the place-names are mostly names of extremely rare occurrence in the Danelaw. They would seem to be names that dropped out of use in Yorkshire with the death of the bearer. None of the place-names can be proved to be associated with any identifiable individuals. Since the names *Grímr* and *Ulfr* became common in Yorkshire and the names *Jóli, Múli, Saxi, Tófi, Róðulfr* and *Thórulfr* are recorded independently there in both Domesday Book and later sources, the six Grimstons, Oulston, Youlton, Moulton, Saxton, Towton, Rowlston and Thurlstone might theoretically take their names from eleventh-century tenants. The very frequency of occurrence of the particular name Grimston and the generally *inferior* situation of the settlements bearing this name, however, still incline me to look upon Grimston itself as a stereotype name bestowed upon inferior settlements and hence to treat the Grimstons as atypical Grimston hybrids. It is admittedly tempting to associate the *Toglauss* of Toulston in the West Riding (*Toglestun* GDB 307c) with the Danish jarl *Toglos* who is known to have been slain at Tempsford in 921, and it is possible that Stainton in Bank Newton was named after the *Stain* who held 3 carucates there in 1065 (GDB 332a), but there are no records of, for example, a *Skurfa*, who could have given his name to Scruton, or a *Flík* or *Flikkr* or a *Flóki* or a *Stakkr* or a *Galmr*, who might have been the manorial tenants of Flixton, Folkton, Staxton or Ganton. These men, whose names are not recorded in independent use in the Danelaw, are more likely to have belonged to the original bands of settlers than to have been followers of Knut in the eleventh century. The disparity between the personal names in the Grimston hybrids in Yorkshire and the Scandinavian personal names recorded independently in Domesday Book and later sources from that county is in marked contrast to the situation in southern Scotland, where most of the Scandinavian personal names compounded with *-tūn* are numbered among the comparatively limited range of Scandinavian personal names that occur in the earliest Scottish charters and are also names that are well documented in written sources from Yorkshire (Fellows-Jensen 1989–90, 47).

THE *BÝ*-NAMES

The most commonly occurring element in Scandinavian place-names in Yorkshire, as in England as a whole, is *-bý* (see Fig. 33). No fewer than 210 Yorkshire *bý*s are recorded in Domesday Book or earlier sources and there are a further sixty-nine which are first recorded in later sources (Fellows-Jensen 1972, 6–9). A study of the situations enjoyed by the *bý*s had convinced me in 1972 that the majority of them marked the occupation by the Danes of the best available vacant land – what Cameron would describe as coloniz-ation in the strict sense. The two *bý*s shown in Fig. 32 for example, Flotmanby and Hunmanby, which both have appellatival specifics, Old English *flotman* 'viking, pirate' and Scandinavian *hundamaðr* 'houndsman' respectively, are both in inferior situations to those of the Grimston-hybrids in the area. The belt of good arable land has narrowed very markedly west of Flotmanby, while Hunmanby lies out on the damp and intractable boulder clay.

I noted, however, that there was some evidence to suggest that several of the *bý*s were in fact older English settlements that had simply received new names. First and foremost among these were the fifteen *kirkjubý*s. It seemed likely that the name **kirkjubý* had originated as a Scandinavian appellatival description of an English village with a church and that this description must later have supplanted an older name for the settlement. Then there was a small group of names borne by settlements whose sites are so favourable that a pre-Viking origin seemed likely for them, namely Coniston (*Coningesbi* GDB 382b), Ellerby and Thirtleby in the East Riding, Selby and Wetherby in the West Riding, and Helperby in the North Riding. In addition, there were the comparatively few names whose specific is certainly an English appellative, namely Eppleby (*æppel* 'apple'), Huby (*hōh* 'spur') and Swainby (*swān* 'young man') in the North Riding and Wauldby (*wald* 'wold') in the East Riding. Denaby and two Denbys in the West Riding all contain Old English *Dene* 'Dane' but these three names meaning 'Danes' settlement' can hardly be pre-Viking formations. The evidence of the pre-Viking sculpture in Yorkshire was also considered and the presence of a piece of massive pre-Viking sculpture in a vill with a

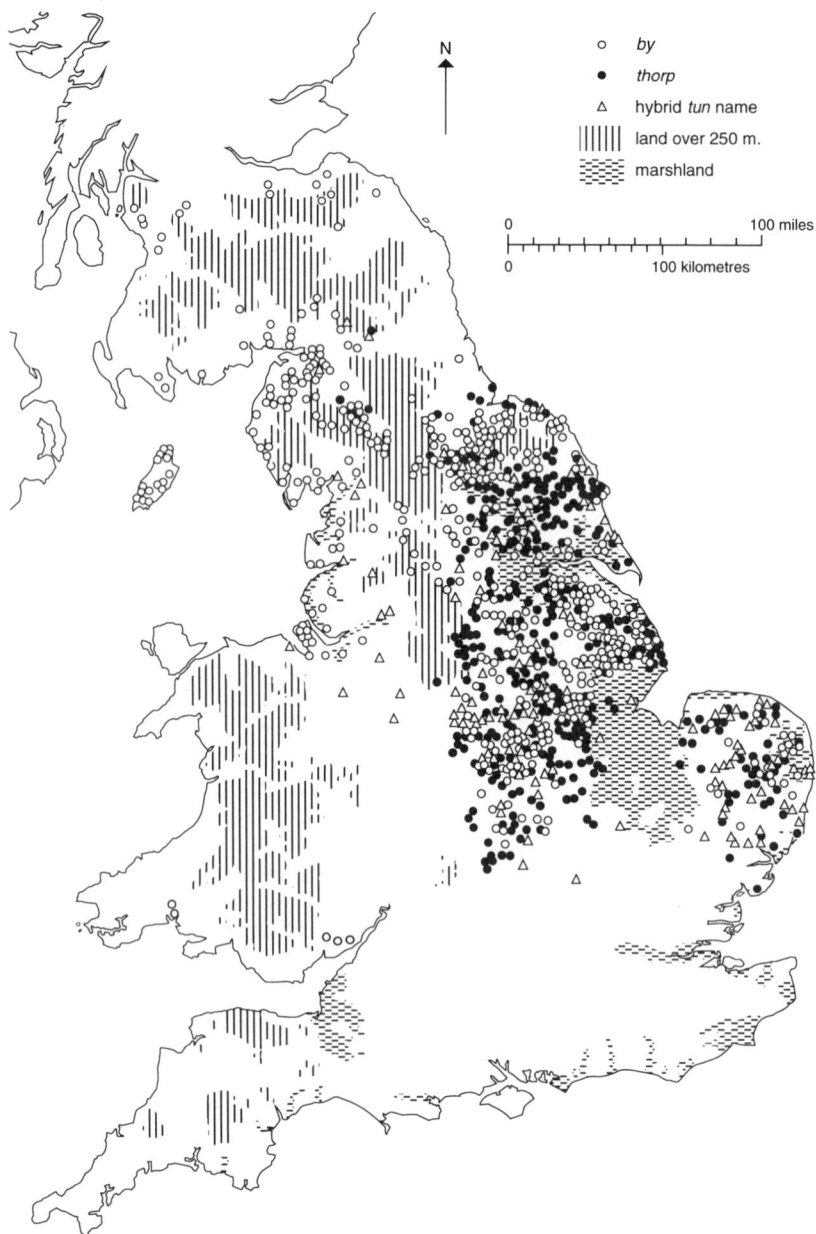

Figure 33   The distribution of *bý, thorp* and hybrid *tūn* names. The
settlements avoid land over 250 metres above sea level and marshy
areas. Based upon, with permission from Peter Sawyer, *Da Danmark
Blev Danmark*, Gyldendal og Politikens Danmarkshistorie III
(Copenhagen, 1988), 164.

Figure 34 Pre-Viking sculpture at Melsonby, Yorkshire North Riding. Reproduced from W.G. Collingwood, *Northumbrian Crosses of the Pre-Norman Age* (1927), 16.

purely Scandinavian name taken to indicate that there must have been an English settlement on the site before the arrival of the Danes. Such sculpture is, in fact, found in Easby, Kirby Hill, Melsonby (see Fig. 34) and Whitby, all in the North Riding. Remains of pre-Viking churches have also been found both at Kirby Hill and at Whitby. I have since been taken gently but firmly to task by Richard Bailey for displaying a fundamental misunderstanding of the nature of the evidence of the sculpture (Bailey 1980, 209–14). He has pointed out that there is in fact no way of knowing whether a style or a motif represents the taste of an individual lord rather than the fashion of a period. While it is true that a lord's preference for a particular style of sculpture does not necessarily reflect his nationality and the presence of sculpture reflecting Scandinavian features in a village with an English name does not necessarily mean that the village had been taken over by the Danes, it does not seem unreasonable to assume that sculpture which can be dated to the Anglian period is most likely to be found in a settlement that was already comparatively prosperous before the arrival of the Vikings and hence that the names Easby, Kirby,

Melsonby and Whitby have replaced older names. There is supporting evidence for this in the presence of pre-Viking churches at two of the vills and in the very name Kirby. That the distribution map of stone sculpture can, if used with caution, throw light on territorial organization in the Viking period and before has also been argued by C.D. Morris (1984).

My standpoint in 1972, then, was that some of the *bý*-names had probably replaced older names for existing villages, while the majority of the vills with names in *-bý* had been newly established in the early years of the Danish settlement. I was certainly disinclined to believe that *-bý* remained in currency as late as the twelfth century, as had been suggested by A.H. Smith (1925, 283) in explanation of the very few Yorkshire *-bý*s containing personal names that were introduced by the Normans, i.e. *Bagot, Bardulf* and **Gerward* in Baggaby, Barlby and Garrowby in the East Riding, *Halanant* and *Johel* in *Halnathebi* and Jolby in the North Riding, and *Fulcard* and *Hugo* in Fockerby and Huby in the West Riding (Fellows-Jensen 1983a, 53–4). None of these place-names is recorded in Domesday Book and they may thus all date from after 1065. It is certain at least that they cannot have acquired the forms in which they are recorded before the eleventh century at the earliest. I should like to explain them as the result of the sub-stitution of a Norman personal name for the first element of a pre-existing name in *-bý*, in much the same way as Scandinavian personal names are assumed to have replaced the first elements of some English place-names in *-tūn*, although I would admit that some of the names may have been coined in the eleventh or twelfth centuries on analogy with the many other names in *-bý* in Yorkshire. That analogical formations were in fact coined is suggested by a number of *bý*-names in the Central Lowlands of Scotland which have exact parallels in Yorkshire, from where the inspiration for the Scottish names can be assumed to have been derived (Fellows-Jensen 1989–90, 55).

It is in connection with the names in *-bý* in Cumberland and Dumfriesshire that the question of the Norman personal names becomes particularly pressing, for here no fewer than fifty-four per cent of the personal names contained in *bý*-names must have been introduced by the Normans. It is my opinion that these Norman names were simply substituted for the first elements of older names when the lands in question were granted to Norman settlers in 1092 or later (Fellows-Jensen 1985a, 24). The Scottish historian Geoffrey Barrow has also argued that settlement names formed in southern Scotland in the twelfth century by compounding a personal name of Norman origin with *-bý* or *-tūn* do not imply a wholly new unit of settlement and he has pointed out that in a few cases the older name for the parish has survived well into the medieval period (Barrow 1980, 40). This view has not been universally accepted, however. John Insley has stressed that there is very little evidence for the alteration of names in this way in

England (Insley 1986), while Brian Roberts has looked at the Cumbrian names from a geographer's point of view and feels that the evidence tends to support the survival of *bý* as a name-forming element for new settlements into the late eleventh and twelfth centuries (Roberts 1989–90). Whatever the correct interpretation of the situation in Scotland and north-west England may be, there is no reason to assume that the formation of names in *-bý* continued on any large scale in Yorkshire after the compilation of Domesday Book, although some of the names may well have arisen in the first half of the eleventh century. Ormesby in the North Riding was in the hands of a man called *Orme* in 1086 (GDB 331b) and it is possible that he may also have been a pre-Conquest tenant of that vill. *Ormr* is a name that occurs frequently in Yorkshire, however, and there is no reason why the name Ormsby should not derive from the tenth century and encapsulate the name of a much earlier *Ormr*.

It has been generally accepted that there was a marked difference between the nature of the first elements of the names in *-bý* in Denmark itself and that of those in names in *-bý* in the Danish settlements in England. Whereas only about ten per cent of the names in *-bý* in Denmark contain personal names, Kenneth Cameron, for example, considered that 207 *bý*s out of a total of 303, or sixty-eight per cent in the territory of the Five Boroughs contained personal names (1975, 8). My own estimate of the percentage of personal names in the Yorkshire *bý*s was more conservative, for I was convinced that a number of names whose first elements had been explained as personal names could in fact be given a more satisfactory interpretation. There seemed to be no reason, for example, to explain the first element of two Barmbys, four Barnbys and a lost *Bernebi* as a Scandinavian personal name *Barn, Barni, Bjǫrn* or *Bjarne*, when the place-names can all be explained as containing the appellative *barn* 'child' and referring to an estate established on the outfields of the parent vill by or for the children of its owner or tenant (Fellows-Jensen 1972, 14; Fellows-Jensen 1976, 451–2). Even after excluding this group of names from the statistics, however, we are left with fifty-seven per cent of the Yorkshire *bý*s having personal names as their first elements although this figure could be reduced even further if the first elements of two Holtbys and two Maltbys, for example, were derived from the appellatives *holt* 'wood' and *malt* 'malt' (explaining the medial *e* in the recorded forms *Holtebi* (GDB 381a) and *Maltebi* (GDB 380c) as a composition joint or a svarabhakti vowel). These revised interpretations have not all won general acceptance and it has to be admitted that it is hardly ever possible to prove that an appellative is more likely to be the first element of a *bý*-name than is a personal name. It is important to note, however, that when the first element of a *bý*-name has been generally accepted to be an appellative, this is often an appellative of Old English origin and this fact could be taken as confirmation of my view that the *bý*s resulted not from colonization in the strict sense but from the splitting up of an old estate into small independent units. These units received names in -*bý* and many of these names may reflect older English names that had not been recorded in writing because the unit in question had earlier been administered from, and assessed together with, the estate centre. Words of English origin may account for twenty-nine per cent of the appellatival first elements in *bý*s in Yorkshire, a figure noticeably lower than in the East Midlands, where at least forty per cent of the appellatival first elements are English, and in East Anglia, where the corresponding percentage is at least fifty. This may suggest that Scandinavian influence on the place-names was more pervasive in Yorkshire than further south.

THE *THORP*-NAMES

Place-names in -*thorp* are generally agreed to be borne by secondary dependent settlements. Kenneth Cameron argued that the *thorp*-names are a reflection of the Danes' extension of culti-vation at some time after the original settlement to less attractive land that was not being exploited at the time of their arrival in England (1975). The situations and status of the places with names in -*thorp* in Yorkshire also suggested that the majority of them were comparatively young settlements, for they tend to lie on inferior land and to be of low status or even to have disappeared. I considered that a Scandinavian settlement established on a site without a name would have been most likely to be given a name in -*bý* or -*thorp* and that it would be those of the lowliest initial status that would receive a name in -*thorp* (Fellows-Jensen 1972, 251).

A complicating factor in the discussion of the *thorp*-names is the existence of a related Old English element *throp*. Cameron had suggested, very reasonably, that the use of the Scandinavian element in the East Midlands may simply have been encouraged by the existence of the English word (1975, 48) but Neils Lund had a very different view of the role played by the English element (Lund 1976). He argued that 'there are reasons for believing that the element found in the Danelaw is the O[ld] E[nglish] word, not the O[ld] Dan[ish] one'. There are, however, good reasons for believing that the distribution pattern of *thorp* in England (see Fig. 33) does reflect the influence of settlers from Denmark, although the coining of the Danelaw *thorp*-names may have been encouraged by the existence of a stratum of English *throp*-names (Fellows-Jensen 1991–92).

An important contribution to the study of the *thorp*-names in Yorkshire was made by Margaret Gelling in a paper read to a Council for Name Studies Conference in Ripon in 1990. She demonstrated   there   that   although   there   was   archaeological evidence for intense cultivation of the Yorkshire Wolds around Wharram Percy in the early period of Anglo-Saxon settlement, there was no indication that this area was being exploited intensively at the time when the Vikings arrived in Yorkshire. She therefore suggested that the place-names of the area must point to a sharp increase in population that culminated in considerable recolonization shortly after the year 900 (see Fig. 35). Her analysis of the place-names and the vills bearing the names suggested that Kirby Grindalythe and Kirby Underdale were old settlements. They are both ancient parishes with several dependent townships or chapelries – most of which have names in -*bý* or -*thorp*. In this area there seems to be little difference between the situations of the *bý*-names and the *thorp*-names, and the assessments for taxation of the two groups in Domesday Book are similar. The striking exception to the general pattern is Fridaythorpe, which despite bearing a name in -*thorp* is an old parish and had the very high assessment of 16 carucates and 3 bovates in Domesday Book, where the median assessment for *thorp* in the East Riding is 4 carucates (Fellows-Jensen 1972, 223). I had previously explained the high assessments of many *thorp* villages on the Wolds as in part due to the generally high assessments in this area; these were probably because it was well suited to sheep-farming, an activity that was of growing importance in the eleventh century. More recently I have looked at these prosperous *thorp*-settlements in the light of a study of *thorps* from all over England. Of the 177 *thorp*-names containing Scandinavian personal names as their first elements, only 9, or five per cent, are assessed at 8 carucates or more. Significantly, all of these nine lie on the Yorkshire Wolds. This shows first and foremost that at the time of the compilation of Domesday Book, the Wolds were exceptionally prosperous but the fact that the *thorp*-names contain Scandinavian personal names suggests that this prosperity in part at least reflects an intensification of exploitation resulting from an influx of Danish settlers.

It should also be noted that the settlements bearing names in -*thorp* which are shown in Fig. 32 lie in a very narrow dry valley in the Wolds. It is likely that the exploitation of this part of the valley remained limited until the arrival of the Danes because the surrounding chalk wolds were infertile and the valley itself too narrow to provide sufficient arable land to support settlements. The appearance of so many settlements with Scandinavian names in this and other dry valleys in the Wolds was probably to be connected with an expansion of Danish settlers outwards from the Kingdom of York and the development of the chalk hills as sheep-grazing land (Fellows-Jensen 1972, 212). It is certainly the development of sheep-farming that must account for the high valuations in Domesday Book of Weaverthorpe, whose name incorporates the Danish personal name *Víðfari*, 18 carucates, Helperthorpe, whose name contains the genitive singular *Hjalpar* of the Scandinavian

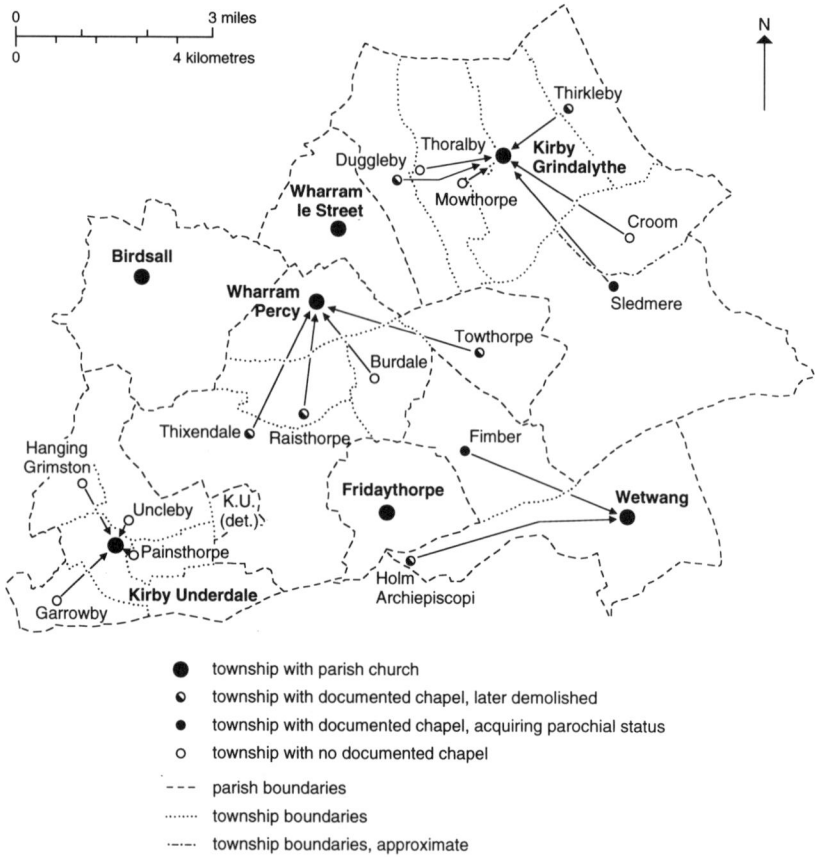

Figure 35   The settlement pattern around Wharram Percy, Yorkshire East Riding. Reproduced with permission from *Medieval Archaeology* XXVIII (1984), 91.

feminine personal name *Hjalp*, 12 carucates, and Boythorpe, whose specific may be an English appellative **boia* or personal name *Boia*, 5 carucates.

Fridaythorpe in the Wharram Percy area (see Fig. 35) contains an Old English personal name **Frīgedæg* and the name may be an English formation. There are a number of other *thorp*-names in Yorkshire containing English personal names. These *thorp*-names may, of course, have been coined before the arrival of the Danes but not necessarily so. The same applies to the comparatively few Yorkshire *thorp*-names whose specific is an Old English appellative or adjective, for example *ætheling* 'prince, noble man' in Ellenthorpe and *cyne* 'royal' in Kingthorpe, as well as to the very numerous originally simplex names in which Thorpe or Thorp stood alone. Since *throp*-names in southern and western England are comparatively rare and mostly demonstrably young, however, and the first elements of fifty-eight per cent of the compound *thorp*-names in Yorkshire are certainly Scandinavian, it seems reasonable to suggest that it was in fact Danish immigration that accounted for the creation of the majority of the *thorp*-names in the county.

This does not, of course, necessarily imply that all the settlements with *thorp*-names were originally established by the Danes. There is a certain amount of archaeological evidence to show that there was settlement on the site of some of these villages long before the arrival of the Vikings. The lowly status, inferior situations and low assessments of the majority of the *thorp*-settlements may simply reflect the fact that the resources of land at their disposal had always been limited. The names in -*thorp*, then, although reflecting Danish immigration, must be treated as unreliable indicators of areas of Viking reclamation.

THE *THVEIT*-NAMES

It might therefore be suggested that Scandinavian place-names containing an element denoting the clearing of land (*thveit*, *ruð*, etc.) provide the best indication of areas actually reclaimed by the Vikings. The problem is that comparatively few such names are recorded in early sources. In Domesday Book for Yorkshire, for example, there are only five names containing *thveit*: Hunderthwaite, Inglethwaite and Kelsit in the North Riding and Langthwaite and Mickelthwaite in the West Riding and one possible instance of a side-form of *ruð*, namely *rúð* or *ruða* in Routh in the East Riding (Fellows-Jensen 1972, 79). Several Yorkshire settlements which are not named in Domesday Book have names in -*thveit*, however. Many of these are in the north-west of the Riding, perhaps indicating an intensification of settlement in the Pennine valleys in the Viking period (Fellows-Jensen 1978a, 42).

A thorough survey of the *thveit*-names in the western half of the North Yorks Moors, carried out by a group of local historians, has revealed that there were no less than thirty-seven *thveit*-names which could be localized in the area, while there were many more names recorded in early sources which could not be localized closely (Morris and McDonnell 1990–91, 24–9). Among the compound names recorded by the group there are many whose first elements are either certainly or possibly of Scandinavian origin and these names may derive from the period of Danish colonization. The group has noted, however, that several of the names are first recorded in the twelfth and thirteenth centuries and may well have been given to land newly assarted in that period. The word *thveit* certainly survived as late as this as a place-name forming element. Two plots of land on the Cumberland plain called *Lynthwait* and *Kirkethwait* were actually described as 'newly assarted' in 1290 (Winchester 1987, 41–2).

Because the element *thveit* was adopted into the dialects of northern and eastern England and survived in independent use there for centuries, it is impossible to use the distribution of names in *-thveit* as evidence for the distribution of Danish settlement unless they are recorded in really early sources. It is interesting, however, that the distribution of the *thveit*-names recorded in such sources corresponds fairly closely with the general pattern of settlement names of Danish origin but also shows penetration into less accessible areas. It therefore seems reasonable to treat these names as evidence for the bringing of new land under cultivation by the Danish immigrants or their descendants in response to an increase in population.

MOVEMENT FROM YORKSHIRE TO SCOTLAND

The reclamation of land was not, however, the only way in which the population of the northern Danelaw dealt with the problem of land-hunger. The spread of Danish place-names from Yorkshire along the Pennine valleys into Lancashire and Derbyshire and down the Eden valley into Cumbria can be seen clearly on the map (Fig. 33). There is also evidence to show movement from northern Yorkshire into Scotland, although not apparently by way of Durham and Northumberland. Significant for a determination of the route taken from Yorkshire to the Central Lowlands of Scotland by the givers of Scandinavian names is J.T. Lang's work on the hogback tombstones (Lang 1972–74, 1984, 1994). This distinctive type of Anglo-Scandinavian sculptural monument can be seen to have originated in northern Yorkshire, probably in the neighbourhood of Brompton (Plate 16) around the second quarter of the tenth century and its popularity would seem to have spread along the Tees valley, via the Stainmoor pass, to the Eden valley and the Carlisle plain. Stylistic and iconographic affinities between the hogbacks in Cumbria and those which are found in the Central Lowlands of Scotland in roughly the areas where *bý*-names occur show that it must have been via Cumbria that the fashion spread to Scotland; but it is also significant that many of the parallel formations to the Scottish names in *-bý* are found in the Vale of York and Craven, that is exactly where hogbacks abound. These names are Bagby, Busby, Danby, Eppleby, Lazenby and Sowerby (Fellows-Jensen 1989–90, 54). It is tempting to believe that men from the Danelaw who introduced the hogbacks to Scotland at the end of the tenth century coined some of the *bý*-names there but the possibility must also be borne in mind that the settlers from the Danelaw who were known to have been planted in southern Scotland by the Scottish king and other landowners in the twelfth century may have coined these *bý*-names on analogy with identical or similar names in their homeland.

Plate 16 Hogback tombstones in Brompton Church, Northallerton. The collection of eleven hogback tombstones found in the foundations of the chancel of Brompton Church during rebuilding in 1867 are among the finest known of this particular form of Anglo-Scandinavian sculpture. Brompton may well have been a centre of production of these tombstones in the century after the settlement of north Yorkshire by Halfdan and his followers. Although their iconography is not understood they suggest that the Danish settlers of the period developed a cultural milieu peculiar to themselves, which still includes hints of their pagan background. The persistence of this tombstone art tells us that it was a strong cultural identifier for peoples of mixed English-Scandinavian and Irish-Norse origin, which they carried with them to new settlements established around the waterways of south-eastern and south-western Scotland in the following centuries. (Lang, 1972–4, 1984, 1994; Crawford, 1994.)

CONCLUSION

In conclusion, I would claim that it is correct to look upon the majority of the hybrid names in -*tūn* in Yorkshire as evidence for the taking over by the Danes of English settlements. The *bý*-names would seem to reflect the splitting up of old estates into small independent units. Most of the *thorp*-settlements would seem to have been named by the Danes or their successors, although the sites may well have been occupied before their arrival. Colonization in the strict sense would seem to be marked by names such as those in -*thveit*, which actually refer to the clearing of woodland or scrub. Population pressure led not merely to colonization within Yorkshire but to a movement outwards across the Pennines to Lancashire and

Cumbria and perhaps ultimately to the Central Lowlands of Scotland, although the names of Scandinavian origin in this last region may first have been coined by men from the Danelaw who were settled here in the twelfth century.

11 Scandinavian settlement in Cheshire: the evidence of place-names

MARGARET GELLING

There is an ongoing controversy concerning the extent to which place-names in the Old Norse languages constitute evidence for colonizing activities by Norsemen, as opposed to the renaming of pre-existing villages in the language of a small élite (Gelling 1988, Chap. 9). As regards Norse names in the Wirral peninsula, however, there has been a consensus in favour of the first option on account of a settlement in the area being documented. The Wirral names have been generally accepted as resulting from an immigration under the command of a leader named Ingimund following the expulsion of Norwegian Vikings from Dublin in AD 902 (Thacker 1987, 249; Wainwright 1948). Recently I have suggested a slightly different interpretation, according to which these names could be seen as evidence for an infiltration of Norse farmers into sparsely populated land, facilitated by the presence of Ingimund's followers who were themselves settled on land which the Lady Æthelflæd had given them nearer to Chester (Gelling 1992, 132–4).

In addition to the Norse names in and adjacent to the Wirral, there are place-names which show influence from Scandinavian speech widely scattered over the county (see Fig. 37). The aim of the present chapter is to draw a distinction between the Wirral names and these others. The former are seen as direct evidence of early tenth-century Norse colonization, the latter as evidence for the use of Scandinavian personal names, and of Scandinavian words which were adopted into the English language, at a somewhat later date.

The list of elements found in Cheshire place-names compiled by the late John Dodgson (1981) is the most comprehensive of such lists to have been provided for an English Place-Name Society county survey. It includes not only those elements which are found with a fair degree of certainty in early-recorded names, but also those which may be conjectured to have occurred in earlier forms of

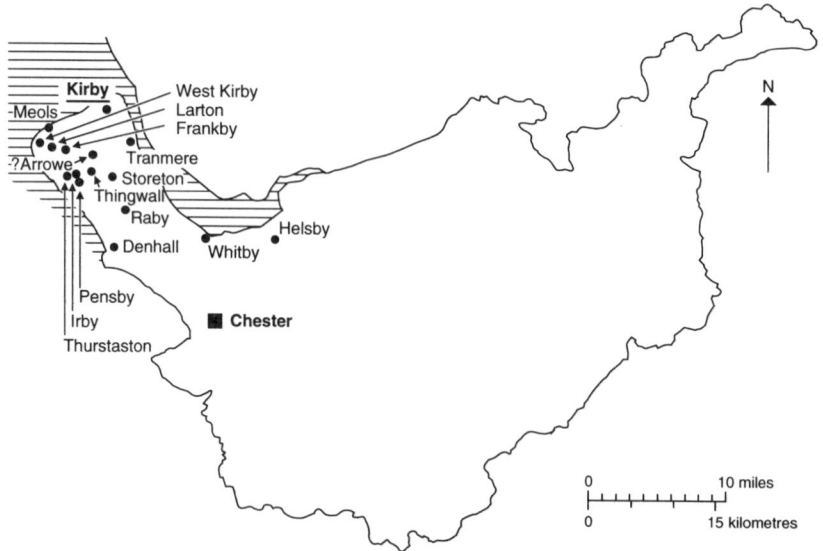

Figure 36 Place-Names indicative of Scandinavian settlement in Cheshire in the early tenth century.

names only recorded in nineteenth-century Tithe Awards or on modern maps. In order to make a critical appraisal of any item listed it is necessary to trace the names in question in the four volumes of the Cheshire survey, and as there is as yet no index this is a laborious task. Fortunately, field-names cited in the elements list are mostly provided with volume and page number. Dr Gillian Fellows-Jensen (1985a) has provided a most valuable appraisal of many of the names documented by Dodgson, but she does not discuss the field-name material or the late-recorded minor names.

A large number of the names cited under Scandinavian words in the Cheshire elements list has been checked for the purposes of this chapter, and many have been rejected as too uncertain for use. The names cited under ON *marr* 'a fen, a marsh', for instance, do not seem sufficiently early or certain in form to constitute safe evidence for the use of that word in the county, and most of those cited under ON *píll* 'a willow' are compounds in which Old English *pīl* 'stake' would be equally appropriate. Among other listed elements which have not been taken into account ON *rein* may be instanced. This word (meaning 'boundary strip') may be the ultimate origin of dialect *rean* 'furrow between plough ridges', but field-names in which *rean* occurs cannot reasonably be considered evidence for Norse settlement. As a field-name element *rean* seems to have been employed in the West Midlands in areas where the plough furrows carried water, and Wet Reans is a very common name in both Cheshire and Shropshire. An Old English form is found in

Shropshire as early as 963, in the bounds of Church Aston, which run *on bradan ræne*. Dodgson comments that in Cheshire the word occurs mainly in Wirral; but that is probably due more to the nature of the ground than to the Norse presence there.

The core of the group of Norse place-names in and adjacent to Wirral consists of eight ancient, well-recorded names in *-bý*. These are Frankby, Irby, West Kirby, *Kirby* (the earlier name for Wallasey village), Pensby and Raby – all in Wirral – and Helsby and Whitby north of Chester (see Fig. 36). Elsewhere in the county there is a single late-recorded field-name *Assheby* near Antrobus (Dodgson 1981, Chap. 2, 127). This is treated as a *-bý* name in Fellows-Jensen 1985a (p. 26), but it does not seem to me a safe example. Otherwise the generic *bý* does not occur. (Greasby in Wirral has a number of forms with *-berie, -byri, -bury* among its early spellings, and it is likely that an English name with *byrig* has been remodelled by analogy with neighbouring ones with *bý*: this is possible also for Whitby, which has two early forms with *-beria*). There are two Norse topographical names in Wirral, Meols and Tranmere. Meols is from Old Norse *melr* 'sandbank', and Tranmere (earlier *Tranemol*) is a compound of *trána* 'crane' with *melr*, or with a related word meaning 'pebbly shore'. There may be another occurrence of *melr* in a field-name *Melse Land* 1654 in Liscard, which is, like Meols, on the north coast of Wirral, but otherwise these words are not evidenced in the county. Arrowe, near Birkenhead, may be Scandinavian *ærgi* 'shieling', but it is perhaps equally likely to be a Celtic river-name (a possibility suggested in Fellows-Jensen 1985a, 61). *ærgi* probably does occur in Wirral in a field-name *Argan*, plotted on Fig. 37. Two hybrid names included on Fig. 36 are Larton and Storeton, which have ON *leirr* 'clayey ground' and ON *storth* 'brushwood' as qualifiers for Old English *tūn*. Thurstaston is the special sort of hybrid in which *tūn* is combined with an Old Norse personal name.

Thingwall (Fig. 36) is a specially significant member of this cluster of Scandinavian names, as it indicates that the Norsemen here had their own assembly-place. Raby, 'boundary settlement', may mark the southern limit of their territory. There may have been a Manx element among these settlers (Fellows-Jensen 1985a, 31, 373). An Irish element is indicated by Irby ('settlement of the Irish') and by the curious name Noctorum, from Irish *cnocc-tirim*, 'dry hill'. A colony of Danes may be referred to in Denhall, earlier *Denewell*, 'spring of the Danes'. Norse speakers in Wirral affected the pronunciation of some English names, such as Birkenhead and Gayton (which would otherwise have become *Birchenhead and *Gatton).

Turning to the evidence of the field-name material contained in the volumes of the Cheshire survey, it is immediately apparent that there is no part of the county in which field-names of Old Norse origin are of a frequency comparable to that found in parts of eastern England. Professor Kenneth Cameron's remarkable volumes dealing with the Lincolnshire wapentakes of Yarborough and

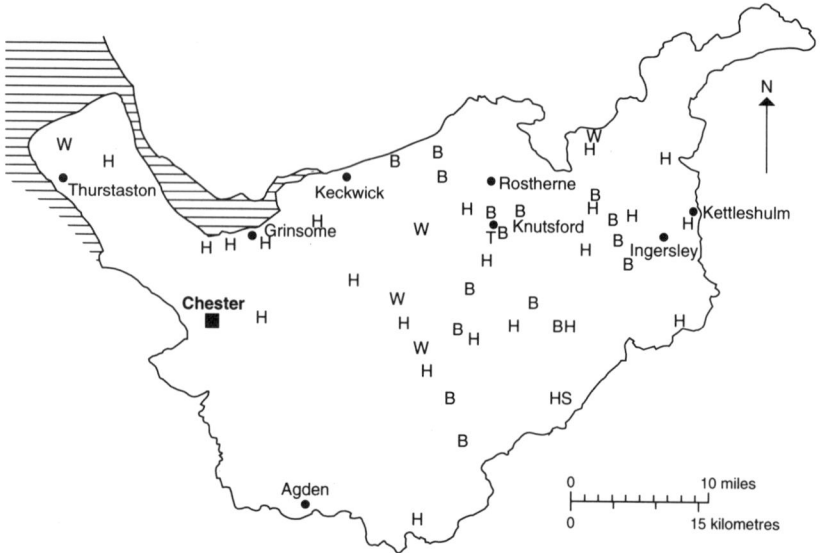

Figure 37 Early recorded names in Cheshire containing *both* (B), *holm* (H), *scale* (S), *toft* (T) and *wro* (W) and settlement names containing Scandinavian personal names.

Walshcroft demonstrate that (particularly in the former) Norse vocabulary was a major element in the speech of the countryside in the twelfth and thirteenth centuries (Cameron 1991, 1992). In Cheshire, field-name evidence for the use of Old Norse words is sparse everywhere, though the names plotted on Fig. 38 show noteworthy concentrations in Wirral and in the vicinity of Whitby and Helsby. Before considering the names plotted on Fig. 38 however, it is necessary to consider those which are shown on Fig. 37.

Figure 37 shows Cheshire names containing words which, while of ultimate Old Norse origin, were adopted into the Middle English language. Those which occur most frequently are *both* (modern *booth*) and *holm* ('island, dry ground in marsh'). There are several instances of the Middle English reflex of *vrá* ('corner'), one of *scale* ('hut', ON *skáli*) and one of *toft*. Middle English *dale*, a conflation of Old English *dæl* and ON *dalr*, has been disregarded.

It will be seen from Fig. 37 that the distribution of these terms precludes a significant association with Wirral and the adjacent area. As noted above there are concentrations of Norse field-name terms there, but (with the exception of *The Wro* 1454 in Frankby and a few field-names containing *holm*) these are formed from other words.

Figure 37 also shows the incidence of Old Norse personal names in settlement-names in Cheshire. (It would be impracticable to show possible instances of these in field-names.) Here again, this material is extremely sparse compared to its density in parts of eastern England. There are only two names of the sort which used to be called 'Grimston hybrids' in which a Scandinavian personal name is combined with Old English *tūn*: these are Agden (earlier *Agetun*) and Thurstaston. Agden is the estate of a man who bore the Old Danish name *Aggi*, Thurstaston the estate of a Norseman named *Thorsteinn*. Two more names of this type, Flixton and Urmston, lie just to the north of the Cheshire boundary in the southern outskirts of Manchester, but they are not common in any of the five north-western counties considered by Dr Fellows-Jensen. The total listed is only fifteen (Fellows-Jensen 1985a, 189–91), and this contrasts sharply with a total of sixty such names in the East Midlands, in the territory of the Five Boroughs (Cameron 1971). Scandinavian personal names are also evidenced with other Old English generics, habitative in the case of Keckwick, topographical in Grinsome, Kettleshulme, Knutsford, Ingersley and Rostherne. As noted above the generic of Grinsome and Kettlshulme is ultimately of Scandinavian origin, but the word was adopted into late Old English.

Names shown on Fig. 37 must necessarily date from after the Scandinavian settlements, but personal names such as *Aggi, Grímr, Ingjaldr, Keikr, Kettil, Knútr, Rauthr* could have been borne by landowners of the time of King Cnut, in the early eleventh century, when such names were fashionable among landowning families all over England. The main reason for considering the men commemorated in these place-names to be of Scandinavian origin (rather than English) is that the field-names and minor names of central and eastern Cheshire provide evidence that the words *both, holm* and *wro* were adopted into the speech of the countryside. The distribution of these and other words mapped on Figs. 37 and 38 stops short at the Shropshire border. In Shropshire, as in other counties south of Cheshire, there is come confusion of *holm* with Old English *hamm*, but that is the extent of Scandinavian influence once the dialect word *rean* has been excluded. No Scandinavian personal names have been noted in Shropshire. It is possible that a small number of Danish landowners who became established in Cheshire in the eleventh century were accompanied by a larger number of humbler dependants, and that the presence of these people led to the adoption of some Danish words.

The Norse settlers in Wirral who coined the names mapped on Fig. 36 must have had the Old Norse ancestors of the words *both, holm* and *wro* in their vocabulary, but they did not use them in forming settlement-names. This may have been because the circumstances of their colonization provided no contexts in which they would have been useful. These are arguably 'infill' terms, useful when small estates are being carved from the area of larger, earlier ones. The two *both* names in Knutsford, *Knutsford Booths* (now Over Knutsford) and Norbury Booths, obviously denote late, dependent settlements: the ancient centres of Lymm and Somerford also had outliers named in this way, and Booth Lane in Middlewich is named from *Bothis de Medio Wico*, first recorded in 1240. Most of the names indicated by B on Fig. 37 are field-names, such as *Bothefeld*. Settlements with names in *holm* or *hulm* are by definition located in wet land where there is a limited raised area available for buildings. Such sites can be highly desirable (as witness many Old English names in *ēg*), but they are less likely to be so in northern than in southern climes. None of the Cheshire settlements with names containing this word is likely to have been an early estate centre, and none of them is recorded before the twelfth century. The *Holme, Hulme* names plotted on Fig. 37 are in fact mostly field-names, and they are not likely to be indicative of Scandinavian speech (as opposed to use of Scandinavian words by English speakers), with the single exception of *Routheholm* 1306 in Wallasey, which seems virtually certain to have ON *rauthr* 'red' as qualifier: this has been plotted on Fig. 38. *Wro*, from ON *vrá*, is in some ways similar to the Old English word *halh*, for which precise definitions are notoriously difficult. The few Cheshire names in which *wro* occurs are not settlement-names except in the special instance of *Muncheniswra*, the site of the abbey later known as Vale Royal. There is no reason to suspect any of the names plotted on Fig. 37 of being coined by Old Norse speakers or of dating from the tenth century. The status of the settlements mapped on Fig. 36 is different. Six of them appear in Domesday Book (Meols, Thurstaston, Raby, Thingwall, Helsby, Storeton), and three others are recorded in the late eleventh century (West Kirby, Irby and Whitby). Thurstaston and West Kirby are parishes.

The minor names and field-names plotted on Fig. 38 have been selected on the grounds that the words contained in them are less likely to have been in common use in Middle English speech than those shown on Fig. 37. The commonest of such words in Cheshire names is *brekka* 'slope', a word widely distributed in Cumberland, Westmorland, Lancashire and Yorkshire. The names listed under this heading in the Cheshire list of place-name elements include some instances (such as *Cambrick Hay* 1841 in Liscard) which are best left out of account, but there are six reasonably certain examples, closely clustered in north-east Wirral and in the vicinity of Helsby and Whitby. The inclusion of ON *thveit* ('clearing, meadow, paddock') could be contested, especially as *The Place-Names of Cheshire* (Part 4 xvi) asserts that it was a living term in Bidston in Wirral in the fourteenth century in the sense 'woodland clearing'. Wirral was technically a medieval 'forest', and this may account for the technical term 'assart' being applied to newly-cultivated land there. It is very doubtful, however, that there was substantial woodland in the northern part of Wirral, and it seems more likely that the *Thwayte* names listed in *The Place-Names of Cheshire* (Part 4 312) refer to areas of grassland which had been ploughed up. Morphany, earlier *Morthwait*, the other occurrence

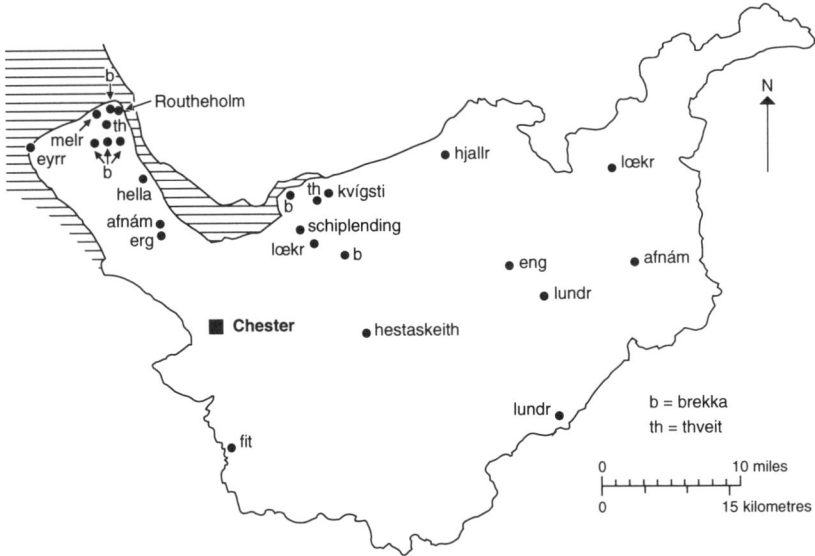

Figure 38 Norse elements in minor names and field-names in Cheshire.

plotted on Fig. 38, is a well-evidenced settlement-name in an area where 'meadow' is the obvious meaning. If the word had survived into Middle English it is probable that it would have been commoner and more widely distributed in the county.

We cannot attach precise historical significance to all the occurrences of Old Norse words plotted on Fig. 38, but a few may be picked out as particularly convincing evidence for the use of Scandinavian speech, albeit on a small scale. *Schiplendinges* in Frodsham, with thirteenth- and fourteenth-century forms, contains ON *lending*, 'landing-place'. Frodsham, on the estuary of the River Weaver, was a haven of the port of Chester. Queastybirch Hall, in the same area, preserves a well-recorded settlement-name *Quisty*, which is accepted in Fellows-Jensen 1985a (p. 58) as deriving from **kviga-sti(a)*, 'heifer pen'. *Haskethay*, recorded in 1353 in Little Budworth, is the most convincing of several possible Cheshire examples of *hest(a)skeithi*, which (despite doubts expressed in Fellows-Jensen 1985a, 133) is probably a term which Scandinavian speakers in England used for a horse racecourse (Atkin 1978).

The material plotted on Fig. 38 is sparse, but there are two definite clusters which support the thesis put forward in this chapter that significant Norse settlement in Cheshire was confined to Wirral and the area adjacent to Helsby and Whitby. The northern half of the Wirral peninsula and some stretches of the southern shore of the Mersey estuary may have been lightly settled before the early tenth century, and marshy land in both areas may have been reclaimed by the Norsemen to whom the Lady Æthelflæd gave land, or by farmers from Ireland and the Isle of Man who came to join them.

The Norse presence on the other side of the Mersey, in Lancashire, was probably a good deal denser. There is as yet no detailed survey of Lancashire place-names, so field-name material is not available for comparison. The settlement-name material is, however, presented in Ekwall 1922, and it is clear from the list of elements on pp. 7–21 of that work that these names contain a greater variety of Norse words used with greater frequency than in Cheshire.

12 Scandinavian settlement in north-west England, with a special study of *Ireby* names

MARY C. HIGHAM

For the purposes of this study, north-west England is taken as being the area which comprised the pre-1974 counties of Cumberland, Westmorland and Lancashire. The physical environment within this area is extremely varied. In the north, the mountains of the Lake District are bounded on three sides by coastal plain, and on the fourth have the important routeway afforded by the Eden and Lune valleys (see Fig. 39) – used by all incomers, peaceful or otherwise, from the Romans, via the Scandinavians, the Normans, and through to the Scots in medieval times. Further south, the Pennines present a barrier to easy communication with the east, but N.J. Higham suggests that the Ribble/Aire gap 'provided the easiest routeway south of the Tyne-Solway gap between the two coastal plains of Northumbria' (1992, 21). Both of these 'gap' routes must have been important to potential Scandinavian settlers from the Danelaw on the eastern side of the country. In relation to sea-based communications within the 'Irish Sea Province' north-west England was readily 'available' to Norwegian settlers from Ireland, Man and the Isles. The Pennine foothills would provide reasonable opportunities to Scandinavian settlers for mixed farming, as would the river valleys, with their good alluvial soils. The mosses, meres and 'islands' of higher ground on the Lancashire Plain – the Fylde in Amounderness and the area to the west of Ormskirk south of the Ribble estuary – would also have been exploited. The meres would provide fish, wildfowl and eels. The 'islands' of higher ground were quite suitable for arable cultivation, and the adjacent mosses would have been available for summer grazing (Coney 1992, 51–5).

Much of the cultivable land was, however, already settled and exploited before any Scandinavian settlers arrived. According to

Kenyon this should not have posed any major difficulties however, for, when discussing Scandinavian involvement in the North-West she comments that 'in the early decades of the tenth century [the Scandinavians] were not necessarily motivated by land hunger. . . . They were not all looking for land on which to settle and to raise crops and flocks. As later in the century, many were opportunists, looking to raise a capital sum to finance ventures elsewhere.' (1991, 114). This may well be the case, but there must have been others who did look for land on which to settle and to raise crops and flocks, and who did infiltrate into north-west England. Identifying where these people actually settled does pose problems: B.J.N. Edwards, in an excellent review of the archaeological evidence for the Vikings in north-west England (1992, 43–62), covering the area from the Dee north to the Solway, comments that 'the body of evidence is not as great as one could wish, and is distressingly deficient in some respects, particularly in the case of evidence which might relate directly to the identification of settlement'. As will be seen later, there is very little documentary evidence for Scandinavian incursions, whether peaceful or otherwise. One is therefore dependent on the evidence afforded by a study of the place-names of the area to assess the nature of Scandinavian settlement in the North West.

Place-names wholly or partly Scandinavian in origin are found all over the North West, used as names of settlements and also as names of minor topographical features, but it is not always possible to use these as reliable indicators of either the extent of initial Scandinavian settlement or that of secondary colonization. The scarcity of early documents relating to the North West means that place-names may only be recorded for the first time in Domesday Book, and probably not even then. Many names are only recorded for the first time in the twelfth and thirteenth centuries, often in monastic charters, with others being recorded for the first, and sometimes the only, time at a much later date. This means that there will always be problems of the validity and the interpretation of some of the name-forms. A long tradition of eminent scholars have worked on the place-names of the North West revising and refining ideas and interpretations regarding Scandinavian settlement in the area. One of the earliest was E. Ekwall who published *Scandinavians and Celts in the North West of England* in 1918, followed by F.T. Wainwright whose many articles were collected together in *Scandinavian England* by Finberg in 1975. In 1985 *The Scandinavians in Cumbria* (eds Baldwin and Whyte) included several papers on place-names which, together with the publication of Gillian Fellows-Jensen's important work *Scandinavian Settlement Names in the North-West* (1985a), made this a 'vintage' year for Scandinavian studies in the area, and these publications have obviously influenced recent thinking on Scandinavian settlement. There have been several papers on Scandinavian settlement in specialist academic publications since then; the most accessible and up-to-date material appears in *Viking Treasure from the North West* (ed. Graham-Campbell 1992), which includes archaeological, economic, numismatic and place-name papers.

Prior to the publication of *Scandinavian Settlement Names* (Fellows-Jensen 1985a), it had been thought that the group which had the greatest impact on the North West was made up of settlers of Norwegian descent, either from Norway and the Isles or from Ireland. Fellows-Jensen, however, has argued persuasively that 'settlers of Danish or Anglo-Danish origin from eastern England must have played a greater part in the Scandinavian settlement of the North West' (1985a, 411) than had been realized before. The distribution of the names in -*bý*, (Fig. 33) is seen as a reliable indication of the spread of Danish influence and settlers across the Pennines, particularly along the Eden valley. The valleys of the Lune, Ribble and Calder are also regarded as routeways to the coast for settlers from the east, this westward phase of settlement being suggested as beginning in the ninth century. As in the Danelaw, it seems likely that these Danish settlers took over many of the existing settlements together with old administrative divisions, retaining existing names for some settlements, adapting some names to a more Scandinavian form – and giving completely new names in -*bý* to some settlements which were also already in existence. The pattern which appertained in the Danelaw where the takeover of large estates was followed by fragmentation into small independent units does not seem to have been followed in all parts of the area under Danish control west of the Pennines; Westmorland for example, and Amounderness, remained as coherent administrative units long after the Norman Conquest. This may be because the Vikings did not hold the land for long enough to effect such a reorganization, as it returned to English control in 927 (Fellows-Jensen 1985a, 414).

Despite this suggestion of a greater involvement by Danish/Anglo-Danish settlers in the North West, beginning at a date somewhat earlier than the formerly accepted one for Scandinavian settlers in the area, the presence of Norwegian settlers is documentarily attested. The settlement in Wirral, Cheshire, after 902 by Norwegians who were refugees (albeit high-status ones) from Dublin is referred to in Irish sources and the name of the leader given as Ingimund (Wainright 1948, 132). The use of OWScand *búð* in the place-names of Cumberland, Westmorland, and Lancashire north of Ribble demonstrates the presence of Norwegian settlers in this part of the region. Secondary settlements apparently developed later in woodland clearings, -*thveit* indicating those named by Scandinavians. These 'thwaite' names are often found alongside names which demonstrate that these areas were often used by the Scandinavians for sheep farming and pig rearing. 'Thwaites' are often found in Cumberland, Westmorland and in north Lancashire but are quite rare south of Ribble. The origins of the Scandinavian settlers are not, however, a reason for this distribution, for, as

Fellows-Jensen points out 'the generic *thveit* "clearing" . . . is very common in both Norway and Denmark. . . . It occurs in place-names in the Northern Isles, the Danelaw and Normandy' (1991, 86). In the North-West, therefore, *thveit* merely indicates those areas which still had woodland available for clearance and settlement – notably the Cumbrian Fells.

Scandinavian settlement names in the North West also include two groups which originally denoted shielings. Those with names in ON -*sætr* are usually held by settlements in upland areas indicating their development from former hill pastures originally used by sheep and cattle in summer to take pressure off the hay meadows and arable lands in the valleys. The second group, with names in -*ærgi*, a Scandinavian word which is a loan from Celtic *airigh*, form part of what Crawford (1985b, 3) called 'the highly interesting and still not fully understood "ærgi" problem'. These place-names are now believed to be the result of links between the Gaelic-Scandinavian colonies in Galloway, the Scottish Isles, Man and the North West, and form a very distinctive element of the place-nomenclature of the area. It has been argued (Higham 1977, and Fellows-Jensen 1980) that the shielings to which the term *ærgi* was applied differed in some way from the shielings for which the Vikings used their native words such as *sætr*. A clue to this might be found in the Irish literature, where one meaning of the term *airigh* is 'a herd of cattle'; cattle rearing may have been their original land use, although this could have changed later. So many of them are on good quality land, at low altitude, and have names which consist of Scandinavian personal name plus *ærgi*, that this might suggest the takeover of an already-established farming enterprise, which could well have included some element of transhumance. The rearing of cattle is one of the traditional ways in which the aristocracy of the North-West supported themselves, both before and after the Norman Conquest, and the daily and yearly routine involved would have been one with which the Scandinavian incomers would have felt quite familiar. This could help to explain the presence of a significant number of *ærgi* names in the very limited number of vills recorded in the Domesday folios for the North West.

As in the Wirral, where there is strong evidence for the takeover of an already established territory by Ingimund and his followers (Vipond 1993, 9–10), it has been suggested that this type of 'invasion' best explains both the archaeological and place-name evidence for the Norse infiltration into the North West (Winchester 1985, 99). The theory put forward by G.R.J. Jones (1965) to help explain the Scandinavian settlement in Yorkshire, followed by C.D. Morris (1977) in his study of Viking settlement in Northumbria, is possibly relevant when attempting to explain the Norse infiltration of Cumbria. Jones and Morris suggested that the Norse invaders took over the seat of power of established overlords and gained access to the resources which supported that overlord – in both land and services. Winchester quotes the 'sole recorded instance' of a substantial Cumbrian landowner being displaced from his estates by Norse invaders and suggests that 'such dispossessions might have been repeated elsewhere as English overlords were replaced by Norse invaders' (1985, 99). This might explain why the major territorial divisions down the Irish sea coast of north-west England all bear names of Scandinavian origin and Copeland is seen as being particularly significant – a Norse name meaning 'bought land' (*kaupa-land*). There is evidence to suggest that money changed hands in the case of Amounderness as well, albeit in the other direction, for when King Athelstan granted the area to the church of St Peter in York, he notes that he had bought Amounderness 'with no little money of my own' presumably from the successor to *Agmund hold* who it is believed may have given his name to the district (Fellows-Jensen 1989). Here, too, there is evidence for a takeover at the top, for a *hold* was a Viking of high rank, and such men were among the leaders of the Danish army that submitted to Edward the Elder in 918 and again in 921 (Fellows-Jensen 1989, 89). Control of land and resources may have included taking over already established cattle-rearing establishments, particularly in the lowlands, and this is supported by a closer examination of the place-names. Place-names of the type 'X's farm or estate' may indicate the takeover and renaming of already-established settlements, and a significant number of the *ærgi* names, for example, do have a Scandinavian personal name as their specific, including several which are recorded as Domesday vills. The taking-over of territory with all its resources would provide an excellent 'springboard' for the further expansion of Scandinavian settlement into the upland areas, which doubtless included the setting up of shieling settlements of the *sætr* type.

THE IREBY NAMES

Another small group of names suggests that the Norse may have brought Irishmen with them when they came to the North West, to the three settlements with the place-name *Ireby* and its variant *Irby* in Cheshire, Lancashire and Cumberland (Fig. 39). Fellows-Jensen (1985a, 16) suggests that the use of the Scand *Írar* 'Irishmen, Norwegians from Ireland' in these names indicates that they were isolated settlements made up of members of one national group in an area dominated by another group. Although the number is so small, because the name was so limited in its use, the 'Ireby/Irby' settlements may provide useful insights into how land was obtained by what must have been an obvious 'minority group', whether Irish or Norse from Ireland, and perhaps how that land was subsequently utilized. The most southerly example is Irby in Wirral, Cheshire (SJ 202758). This is within the area of the lands apparently granted to Ingimund and his followers in the early years

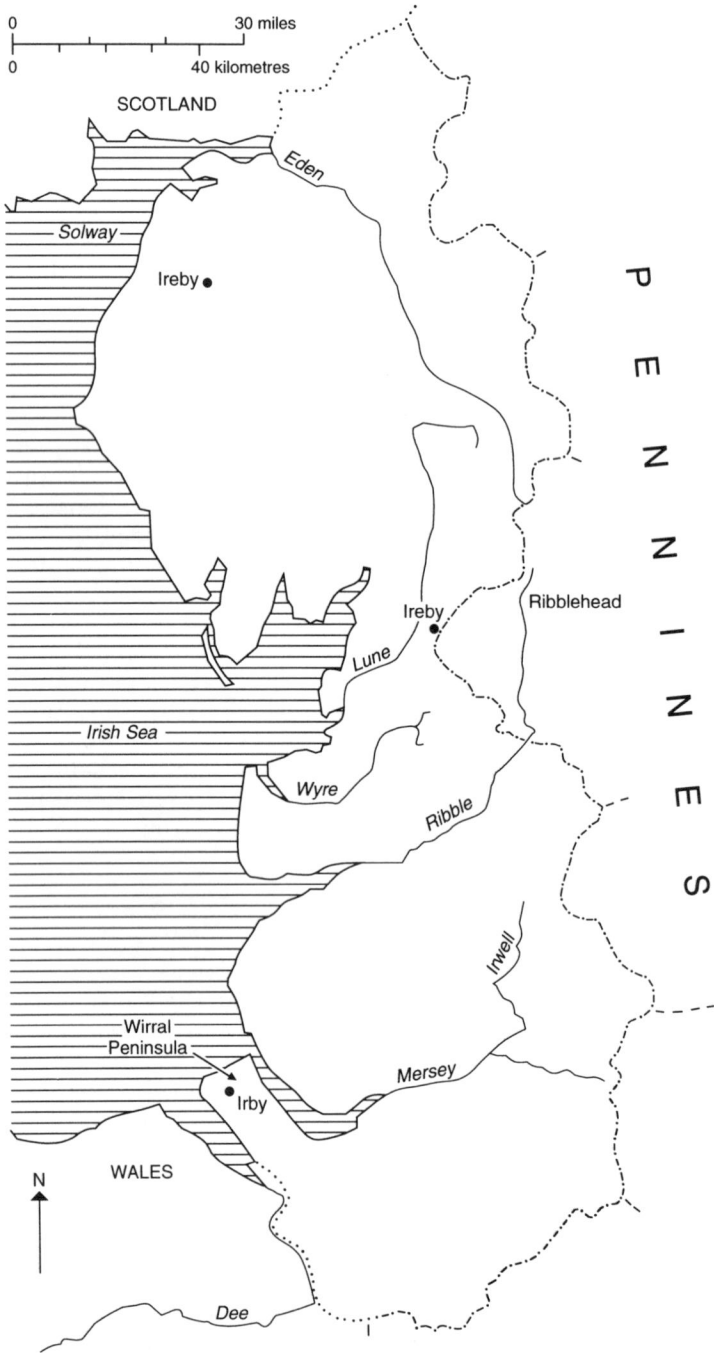

Figure 39   The location of Ireby names in north-west England.

of the first decade of the tenth century (Wainwright 1948). They had been expelled from Dublin, had failed in an attempt to obtain a foothold in Wales, and had then obtained permission to settle in Mercia from Æthelflæd, Lady of the Mercians, who granted them lands near Chester on which to settle. These lands are believed to have been in Wirral, with place-names such as Raby ('village at a boundary') suggested by Dodgson (1972, 229) as indicating the 'confines of a Scandinavian enclave' there. Even though Irby (*Erberia*) is only recorded for the first time at the end of the eleventh century (Dodgson 1972, 264), it is quite likely to be connected with the settlement of Ingimund and his followers in the early years of the tenth century, and, as the dominant group was comprised of Norsemen from Ireland, they could be the settlers who gave their name to Irby. Fellows-Jensen's recent suggestion (1992, 39) that the 'Irishmen recalled in the Wirral place-name Irby may have come from Man rather than Ireland', if correct, could presumably alter the date of this settlement, but would not change the basic assumption that these were settlers who had their origins in Ireland. As the present settlement of Irby lies on fairly heavy clay soils in a rather exposed position, it would have been a site more likely to be given to 'followers' from either Man or Ireland rather than those settlers with a higher ranking within the Scandinavian hierarchy.

Ireby in Cumberland (NY 239389), occurs for the first time *c.* 1160 in the records of Fountains Abbey, which had a grange there (Armstrong *et al.* 1950, 299). It lies to the north-east of Bassenthwaite Lake in the northern foothills of the Cumbrian Fells, in the ancient territorial division of Allerdale – yet another of the divisions in the North West which bears a name of Scandinavian origin (Winchester 1985, 99). In the medieval period, Ireby apparently had two main components – High Ireby and Low, Base or Market Ireby, these last three all aliases for the main settlement of Ireby where there was a weekly market and yearly fair by 1236 (Swift and Bullman 1965, 222). As well as this, the township has several settlements in *thveit*, indicating a strong Scandinavian presence in the area. Ireby was probably the original settlement, with High Ireby (NY 230372) to this day exhibiting features which would suggest it may have developed from a dependent shieling site. There is clear evidence for a stock track leading from the main settlement of Ireby up to High Ireby, with drinking troughs at intervals along it. This track then funnels out on to the open fell. The settlement of High Ireby has a large stone-walled enclosure at its centre, with stiles into it at several places, indicating both a need for communal access and presumably communal use, possibly as a small area for arable cultivation. A road encircles the enclosure, with farmsteads placed on the perimeter, immediately adjacent to the in-bye fields. High Ireby also exhibits a clear division between the high status farms in one part of the settlement (the eastern side) and those clustered along the road to the North

West, which are much smaller. This is very typical of settlements in the North West which developed from *vaccaria* in the medieval period (Higham 1985), but had their origins as stock-rearing enterprises before the Norman Conquest.

Ireby in Lancashire (SD 655756) was recorded in the Yorkshire folios of Domesday Book (Faull and Stinson 1986, 301 d), where it was included as a subsidiary vill of the large manor of Whittington on the north bank of the Lune, held in 1066 by Earl Tosti, and by the king in 1086 (Fig. 40). After 1086 the Domesday estate of Whittington suffered a major reverse – from a territory with *caput* and sixteen appendant vills it became a single-township parish into which two of the appendant vills, Newton and Thirnby, were absorbed, with other vills re-grouped. Ireby was alienated from Whittington and was apparently linked with the Domesday vill of Tatham (Lancashire), part of a group of vills which had been held by Ketel in 1066, but which were said to be in the hands of the king in 1086. The exact date of this affiliation with Tatham is not clear but a charter dated 1189–90 was witnessed by one Richard, 'son of Walthef, Lord of Tatham and Ireby' (Chippendall 1935, 3). What is significant, however, is that this affiliation is purely secular in nature. Although Tatham had a pre-Conquest church, the township of Ireby was not, and never has been, attached to it for ecclesiastical purposes. Whittington became an ecclesiastical parish soon after 1086, but Ireby never came under its ecclesiastical jurisdiction either.

Throughout its recorded history, Ireby has always been part of the ancient ecclesiastical parish of Thornton-in-Lonsdale in Yorkshire, the eastern fell boundary of Ireby being the western fell boundary of Thornton-in-Lonsdale, these in fact being inter-commoned until the nineteenth century. In the medieval period, Ireby, therefore, lay outwith the county of York and outwith the Honour of Burton, and yet lay within the ecclesiastical parish of Thornton-in-Lonsdale (within the Deanery of York) which was within the Honour of Burton, and within the County of York. That it went neither to Tatham (with a pre-Conquest church) nor to Whittington (with an early post-Conquest foundation) would seem to imply that the ecclesiastical connection with Thornton might well be both an ancient and a significant one. The Domesday record for Ireby could imply that this religious allegiance was a result of territorial changes made as a result of the Norman conquest of the area but a close analysis of the Domesday evidence would seem to suggest that the control of the North West had been in a state of flux for some time (Higham, M.C. 1992b) and the ecclesiastical allegiances of Ireby in the post-Conquest period probably owe more to the tenth century than they do to the eleventh. It is likely that the lands which comprised the vill of Ireby were detached from Thornton in the early years of the tenth century, when Scandinavian settlers were moving into the area.

It can be demonstrated that the territory to which Thornton (and

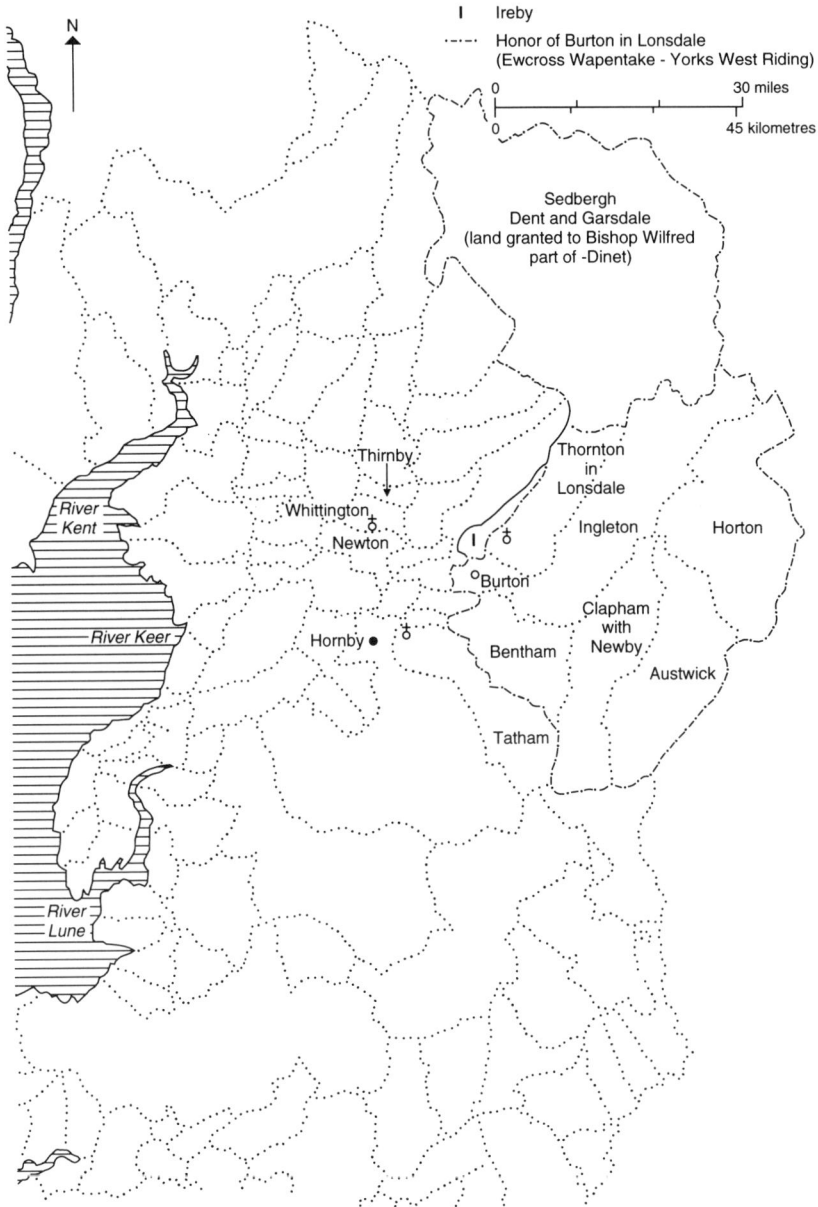

Figure 40 The Lancashire township of Ireby and its associated administrative divisions.

probably Ireby) belonged was part of a former early Celtic territorial unit, the *Regio Dunutinga* [Dinet] (Higham, M.C. 1992a and b), the northern part of which had been granted to Bishop Wilfrid for the support of his new church at Ripon by King Egfrith between 671 and 678 (Colgrave 1927, 36–7). It seems likely that this was taken over *in toto* by Scandinavian settlers in the early tenth century, and that this was the period when Ireby was detached from the vill of Thornton: a farm-name in Ireby – Anems – (ON *af-nàm* 'land detached from an estate') possibly commemorates this development. In 1086 some twenty-two vills which lay inside the bounds of the former *regio* were held by persons with Scandinavian personal names – *Orm, Ulf, Thorfinn* and *Ketel* – with the rest of the former territory being included with the Whittington entry. Indeed, the Whittington entry has the appearance of a 'temporary' administrative unit set up by William I as a direct result of Roger de Poitou's revolt against the Crown, its *raison d'être* as *caput* disappearing once Norman control of the Lune valley had been re-established.

It seems probable that, as in Cumbria and Amounderness, the area formerly *Dinet*, together with other lands in the Lune valley, was taken over by Scandinavian settlers, who took over the ancient administrative division and scandinavianized its name to one which incorporated the river name plus *-dalr*, that is, Lonsdale (Fellows-Jensen 1985b). This would explain the survival of the names Thornton-in-Lonsdale and Burton-in-Lonsdale in two townships which now have no apparent connection with the river Lune, and also confirm that the ancient territory of Dinet, and indeed the later Scandinavian territory, stretched down to the Lune – a strategic routeway from the Irish sea through to the North East of the country.

If the area around Ireby was largely under Scandinavian control, like Irby in Wirral, it would seem likely that the settlers there were probably Irishmen who had accompanied the Scandinavians from Dublin, but in view of Fellows-Jensen's revised ideas regarding Irby in Wirral, perhaps the term 'Irishman' should merely be regarded as a pre-Conquest 'term of racial abuse' – rather in the way that 'Walton' place-names indicated persons of British origin and very low social status in an 'English' context. Whatever their origins, at Ireby in Lancashire, as might be expected, the new settlers were certainly not granted best quality land, and were only granted a very limited amount. The modern village lies to the east of a series of drumlins, which would have provided the only land suitable for a small area of arable cultivation. The drumlins would have been surrounded by badly drained boggy areas, with carr-type vegetation. Even now, the valley floor gets very wet at times. The settlement itself is at the junction of the valley land and the hill grazings – pointing to the emphasis on stock rearing which probably existed in this community from the early phases of its existence. The solid geology of Ireby Fell is carboniferous limestone, which has resulted in sink holes and complex underground drainage patterns. The surface drift deposits, however, can be badly drained and could have posed problems for sheep rearing in early times because of the tendency to foot rot caused by wet pastures. It would seem probable therefore that, although with modern stock-management techniques sheep are now reared there, parts of Ireby Fell would have been much more suitable for cattle rearing in the past.

Ireby Fell was not physically separated from that of Thornton-in-Lonsdale until 1819, when the present high moor wall between the two townships was constructed. Ireby Fell itself, some 360 acres, is still not enclosed or allocated, with all tenants of Ireby estate holding in common. Only certain farmsteads in the modern settlement of Ireby have 'beast gates' on the hill – that is, the farmers of particular tenements in the village which belong to the estate have the right to put so many animals on Ireby Fell, which would support the idea of ancient rights of common pasture on the fell. These rights probably included the use of an upland shieling, the evidence for which can still be seen on the fell above the settlement, where a dry-stone walled complex known as Hurder Fold (SD 674770) survives at 350m. OD.

The longevity of the Ireby/Irby settlements in the North West, all recorded before the end of the twelfth century and probably in existence for some little time before that, demonstrates the way in which these 'Irish' incomers successfully adopted local farming practice and fitted into local tenurial structures on areas of land which had been alienated from much larger estates by new Scandinavian overlords, some of whom had taken over English settlements and renamed them. That these Ireby/Irby lands were of relatively poor quality might imply that this 'plantation' of Irishmen was an initial stage in the colonization of land which hitherto had not been fully exploited. This was followed by the clearance of woodland in areas where this survived in quantity, leading to the establishment of secondary settlements in *-thveit*. Alongside these there was the setting up of a shieling system of temporary *sætrs* in the uplands. The survival of so many Scandinavian settlement names in the present landscape, which, like the *sætr* and *ærgi* settlements often became permanent settlements early in the medieval period, indicates that there was a rapid assimilation of Scandinavian settlers into the overall economic life of the North West.

13 Northumberland and Durham: the place-name evidence

VICTOR WATTS

'Northumberland and Durham are not counties in which the evidence [sc. of place-names] for Scandinavian settlement is strong'. So in 1920 wrote Professor Allen Mawer, the author of the only reasonably comprehensive published survey of the place-names of Northumberland and Durham (Mawer 1920, xix). Nevertheless – leaving aside Durham for the moment – he proceeded to identify what he considered to be pockets of Scandinavian settlement in the Till and Glen valleys (Akeld NT 9529, Coupland NT 9331), south of Bamburgh (Lucker NU 1530, North Sunderland NU 2131), in Coquetdale (Bickerton NT 9900, Brinkburn NZ 1198, Cartington NU 0304, Plainfield NT 9903, Rothbury NU 0501, Snitter NU 0103, Thropton NU 0202, Tosson NU 0200 and Trewhitt NU 0105), in Hexhamshire (Dotland NY 9360, Eshells NY 8957), in West Allen Dale (Dingbell Hill NY 7758, Harsondale NY 8061 and Ouston NY 7752), in South Tynedale (Knar NY 6651, Knarsdale NY 6853 and Whitwham NY 6856), at various places in the Tyne valley (Farrow Shields NY 7652 and Henshaw NZ 7664, Eltringham NZ 0762, Nafferton NZ 0565 ad Rudchester NU 1167, and Pandon NZ 2564, Byker NZ 2764 and Walker NZ 2964) and at isolated places like Brotherwick (NU 2205), Cowpen (NZ 2981), Glanton (NU 0714), Glantlees (NU 1306), Ilderton (NU 0121), Howick (NU 2517), Kearsley (NU 0275), Scrainwood (NT 9909), Stirkscleugh (Hesleyside) and Thrunton (NT 0810), (Mawer 1920, xx–xxi; 1921, 12–18).

This is, and was, a very unlikely picture for, as Mawer admits himself, the suffix *-by*, the most characteristic of all Scandinavian suffixes in England, is unknown in Northumberland, as also is *-thwaite*, so familiar in the Lake District (Mawer 1921, 13).[1] The tests he based his conclusions on were not the presence of Scandinavian personal names nor the presence of certain elements

---

1. He might have added *-thorp*.

of Scandinavian origin (*bank, beck, bigging, car, toft, garth, haining, holm* etc., which early became part and parcel of the English word stock and therefore prove nothing by themselves), but the occurrence in place-names of what he believed were elements never naturalized in England in conjunction with this other evidence (Mawer 1921, 14–15).

Unfortunately, however, of the thirty-nine names at issue here alternative and preferable etymologies have since been provided for at least twenty-seven, primarily by Eilert Ekwall (1960), who saw that the majority of supposedly Scandinavian names in Northumberland consist in fact either of words early adopted into northern dialects or of purely English elements. Even Coupland (ON *kaupa-land* 'purchased land'), as he says, probably represents a common noun and, under the circumstances, it is preferable to explain doubtful names as English rather than Scandinavian (Ekwall 1924, 75).

Along the coast, then, the only remaining candidate is Lucker, *Lucre* 1195, 1255, *Lukre* 1242, *Locre* 1288, *Loker* 1290, 1346, *Lucker* from 1298, which is certainly not ON *lúkar* 'the hollows' (Mawer 1920),[2] but might be ON *ló-kjarr* 'sand-piper marsh' (Ekwall 1960). Most *kjarr* names, however, are really from its ME derivative *ker* and the specific in this name is more likely to be the Northumbrian word *luh* 'a lough, a lake, a pool'. There is to this day a pool at Lucker.

In Coquetdale only Plainfield, Rothbury and Trewhitt remain. There is no doubt about the form of Plainfield: it is *Flayn(e)* – *Flainfeld* throughout the Newminster Cartulary,[3] and seems to point inescapably to ON *fleinn* 'a dart, an arrow' and to a place where archery was practised (Smith 1956, i. 176).[4] However, Northern *ai* and *ay* spellings do not unequivocally represent ON *ei* and are not infrequently used as graphies for ME *ā* (Jordan 1934, 36). OE possessed its own word *flān* 'an arrow' which survived in regional use, particularly in Northern England and Scotland, at least until the sixteenth century (OED). Rothbury, *Routhebiria* c. 1125, was taken by Ekwall (1960) to be 'Hrōtha's fortified place', presumably referring to the conspicuous promontory fort of Old Rothbury. Christer Påhlsson has attempted to resurrect the etymology previously rejected by Mawer (1920) as an unjustifiable hybrid, viz. 'Red fort', ON *rauðr* + OE *byrig*, by pointing to the redness of the bed-rock at Rothbury (Påhlsson, 1975–6, 11).[5]

---

2. ON *lúka* means 'the hollow formed by the cupped hands' and is not known in topographical use.
3. Once erroneously transcribed as *Flanifeld*.
4. The identical place-name and identical re-formation occurs in a lost name in Levington, Cambs, *Flaynefelde* 1335, *Plainefeild* 1611, *Plain al. Flainfield* 1785 (Reaney 1943, 272).
5. Mawer's preferred solution is 'Rauthi's fort', ON personal name *Rauði*, genitive singular *Rauða*, + OE *byrig*.

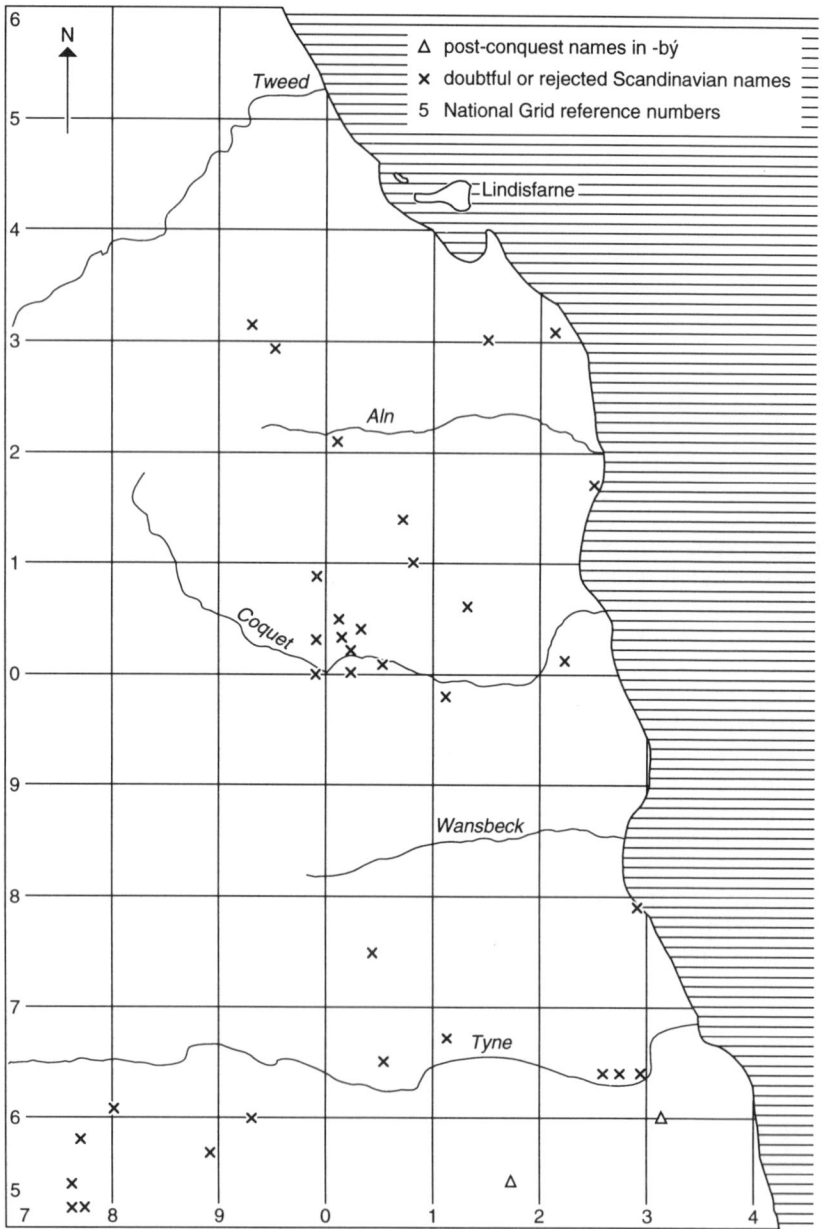

Figure 41 Doubtful or rejected Scandinavian place-names in Northumberland.

Attractive though this is, however, it still remains the case that this kind of hybrid formation is most unlikely. Finally Trewhitt, *Tirwit* 1150 × 62, *Tyr(e)wyt -wit* 1229–55, *Tirwhit* 1356, 1428, *Trewhytt* 1542, which Mawer left unsolved, has been taken as a compound of ON *tyri* 'dry resinous wood' + OE **thwīt* 'a clearing, a meadow' (Ekwall 1960) or OE **wiht* 'a bend', sc. in Wreigh Burn (Smith 1956, ii. 221, 165).[6]

In Hexhamshire Dotland, *Dotoland* [1114]1299, *Doteland* 1216 × 55, 1479, *Dotteland* [1287]1299, *Dodland* 1354, *Dotland* from 1479, is taken as 'Dot's newly cultivated land' with an ON personal name (Gelling 1984, following both Mawer 1920 and Ekwall 1960). The evidence for this name is DB *Dot, Doth, Dotus* found in Bedfordshire, Buckinghamshire, Cambridgeshire, Cheshire, Essex, Lancashire and Shropshire. It may be of Scandinavian origin, a by-name from ON *dottr* 'a lazy useless being', but it could equally well be a native coinage from OE *dott* 'head of a boil', ModE dialect *dot* 'a diminutive person or thing, a small lump'. It is not, in any case, clear that the specific of this name is a personal name rather than a topographical use of *dott*. Eshells, *Eskilescales, Eskin(g)seles, Eskinschell*, is probably 'Eskil's shielings', ON personal name *Ásketill* which has Anglo-Scandinavian reduced forms *Aschil, Astin* and *Eschil* (though not apparently *Eskin*). The evidence for Scandinavian settlement here is fugitive. In any case, settlement in south Hexhamshire was a late phenomenon, witness the name Newbiggin (NY 9460) ME *newbigging* 'new building', while Dotland, at the limits of cultivation on the edge of the high moors, would seem to be a late intrusion into poor land.

In Allen Dale, Dingbell Hill is recorded too late for certainty and in a problematic spelling, *Vingvell hill* 1386, *Dingbell Hill* 1613. To see this as an instance of ON *thing-vellir* is obviously hazardous and, as Mawer himself says (1920), it is highly improbable that a Scandinavian *thing* was ever held in this location. There is nothing Scandinavian about Harsondale, *Harestanesden* 1255, 'valley of the grey stone', – OE *hāra-stān*, genitive singular *hāra(n)-stānes* + *denu* later replaced by *dale* – but Ouston, *Ulvestona* 1279, is either 'Ulf's farm' and so an example of the so-called Grimston-hybrid formation, or English 'Wulf's farm' with Scandinavian loss of initial *W*. Farrow Shields, *Ferewith- Frewythescheles* 1279, *Farrowsheile* 1636, is thought to contain the rare ON personal name *Freyvithr* (perhaps later refashioned under the influence of ModE *farrow* 'a young pig'), but this is very uncertain. Byker

---

6. Smith objected to the absence of *t(h)wit* spellings. The objection, however, is probably unnecessary since the pronunciation [trufit] recorded by Mawer seems to imply substitution of fricative [f] for fricative [θ] as in Garfit Notts, *Gordweyt* 13th., *Gorfitt* 1637, 'muddy thwaite', OE ME *gor* + ME *thweit* (ON *thveit*) (Gover *et al.* 1940, 112), Stainfield near Haconby Lincs, *Stentvith* 1086, *Steynthweyt* 1286, 'stone clearing', ON *steinn-thveit*, and Big Forth Lancs, 'barley clearing', ON *bygg-thveit*.

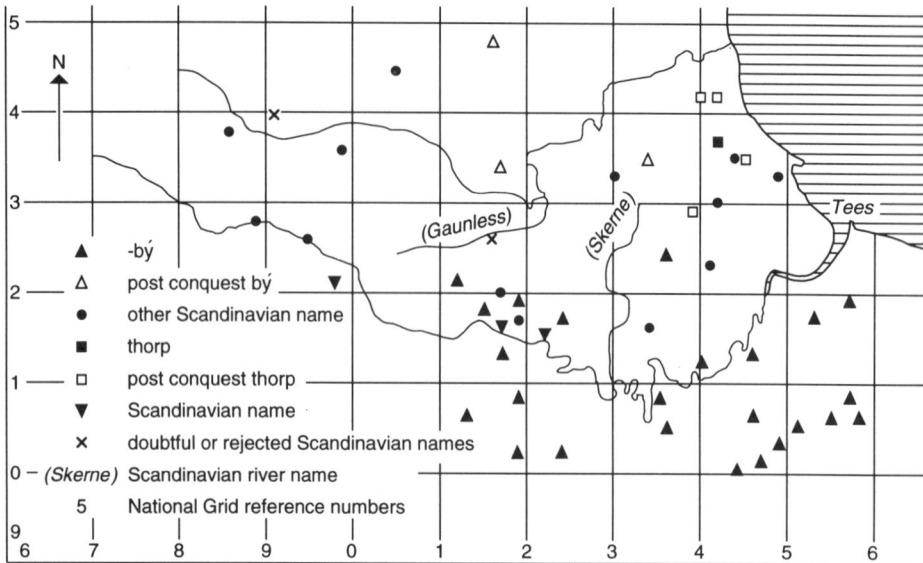

Figure 42   Scandinavian names in the Tees valley and Co. Durham.

might be ON *bý-kjarr* 'the village marsh', but both this and Walker are probably late formations with ME *ker* (< *kjarr*) if the former is not rather the elliptical ME name *Bi-ker* '(place) beside the marsh'. Mawer might, however, have added two isolated names, Gunnerton (NY 9075) *Gunwarton* 1169, 1242, 1428, which probably contains the feminine personal name *Gunnvor* recorded in LVD as *Gunnwara*, and Tarset (NY 7985) *Tyrset(e)* 1269, 1279, *Tirset* 1329, which may be another instance of ON *tyri* here with *sætr* (Smith 1956, ii. 210).

The foregoing survey, necessary in order to ascertain the evidence, has produced at most an improbable hybrid formation and a handful of Scandinavian personal names which by themselves prove nothing. It is not, in fact, the case that the place-name evidence for Scandinavian settlement in Northumberland is not strong, it is virtually non-existent (see Fig. 41).

Nor is the picture vitally different as we proceed south of the Tyne until we reach the Tees lowlands (Fig. 42). There is, to be sure, a scatter of by-names in the northern half of County Durham, but these are all demonstrably late or otherwise problematic. Follingsby (NZ 3160) *Foletesby* 1144 × 52, probably contains the OFr by-name *Folet*; Ornsby (NZ 1648) *Ormysby* 1408, is presumably named after the tenant Orm recorded here in 1183; Raisby (NZ 3435) *Racebi* 1183, is named after the donor *Race* Engaine who gave the estate to Sherburn Hospital in the twelfth century; Rumby (NZ 1734) is not recorded before 1647; and for Tantobie (NZ 1754) no early forms at all are known.[7] What is interesting about this little group of names, however, is the evidence it offers for the continued use of *by* as a formative element in the twelfth century. On a small scale the situation is not unlike that around Carlisle where in addition to *by*-names of genuine Scandinavian origin there are some nineteen *by*-names in Cumbria and Dumfriesshire compounded with names or elements of Norman origin (Fellows-Jensen 1985a, 329–32). This practice in Durham can only have been influenced by the genuinely old *by*-names of the south of the county; they have all the appearance of being late examples of new formations rather than, as is suggested for the Cumbria-Dunfriesshire examples (Fellows-Jensen 1983a and 1985a, 288), instances of the substitution of later personal names for older specifics, perhaps Scandinavian personal names, of *by*-names coined at an earlier period of Scandinavian settlement. None of these places is of any significance and if comparison is to be made with any other category of Scandinavian names it must be with the so-called Grimston-hybrids of the coastal plateau and plain.

The main sequence of *by*-names in County Durham is in the middle Tees valley from Raby (NZ 1221) to Aislaby (NZ 4012). It is this group of six names, together with a pair of Scandinavian topographical settlement names – Dyance (NZ 1917) *Diendes* 1207, 'marshland', ODan *dyandi*; and Sadberge (NZ 3416) *Satberga c.* 1150, ON *setberg* 'flat-topped hill', the meeting place of the only wapentake in England north of the Tees – and a single Grimston-hybrid (Ingleton NZ 1720, *Ingeltun c.* 1040, ODan personal name *Ingeld*), which alone can claim association with the arrangements made by Halfdan for the sharing out of the land of Northumbria in 876, primarily in Yorkshire where the sequence of *by*-names is continued, but also in the attractive Tees lowlands on the Durham side of the river (Watts 1988–9, 57).

This general picture is further strengthened by the presence of the one purely Scandinavian river name in Durham, the Gaunless (NZ 0224–2130), *Gauhenles c.* 1185, ON *gagnlauss* 'unprofitable' (replacing the r.n. **Clyde* fossilized in the place-name (Bishop) Auckland, *Alclit c.* 1040, 'the hill on the river Clyde', PrW **alt* + r.n. **Clüt*, identical with the Scottish r.n. Clyde), and by the general distribution of non-Scandinavian names whose development has been influenced by Scandinavian sound patterns. In Durham a good example is the river name Skerne (NZ 3634–2810) with initial *Sk-*, *Schyrna c.* 1190, 'clear river' from OE *scīr* (Watts 1988–9, 30, 35 and map p. 31). Outside the Danelaw this element normally gives the form Shire, as in the Hants and Sussex river of that name, or, in composition, Sherbourne/Shirburn, as in Warwickshire and, indeed, in the mid-Durham village name Sherburn (NZ 3142)

---

7. The evidence for this and the following paragraphs is set out in detail in Watts 1988–9, 17–63.

(Ekwall 1928, 361–2, 367). The Durham name is paralleled in the east Yorks Skerne Beck (See also discussion by Fellows-Jensen above, p. 173).

Elsewhere in County Durham there is evidence of later Scandinavian activity. In the east of the county we know that the Norse-Irish leader Ragnald gave the multiple estates of South Wearmouth and Eden to his henchmen Scula and Onlafbal sometime around 913 (Morris 1981, 224). But Scandinavian overlordship was shortlived. It cannot have continued after the death of Eric Bloodaxe on Stainmore in 954 and is likely always to have been curtailed in County Durham by the power of the Community of St Cuthbert. Indeed, already during the rule of bishops Cutheard (d. 915) and Tilred (d. 927), these estates are the subjects of episcopal land grants. Although the evidence must await the publication of the EPNS survey of Durham, it is clear that the Scandinavians made no impact on the minor and field nomenclature in this area. What they did apparently leave behind is a handful of Grimston-hybrids: the certain ones are Amerston (NZ 4230) *Eymundr*, Blakeston (NZ 4123) *Bleikr*, Sheraton (NZ 4435) *Skurfa*, Thrislington (NZ 3033) *Thorsteinn*, and Throston (NZ 4933) *Thór*. They are all insignificant places, none situated on the best land, five subsequently deserted, and clearly very different in kind from the Grimston-hybrids characteristic of the areas of primary Scandinavian settlement in Yorkshire and elsewhere (Watts 1988–9, 48, 53–4, 57; cf. Cameron 1971, 1975). There is also a scatter of *thorp*-names which – apart from the lost *Threlthorp* c. 1170 in Castle Eden (NZ 4237) 'the serf farm', ON *thrœll* – may best be regarded as late formations with naturalized OE or ME rather than ON *thorp* (they are Fulthorpe NZ 4042, *Fultorp* twelfth century, 'dirty thorp', OE *fūl* or ON *fúll*; Little Thorp NZ 4242, *Thorep* c. 1040; Thorp Bulmer NZ 4535, *Thorpe* 1243; and Thorpe Thewles NZ 3929, *Thorp* c. 1170).

Lastly, there are a few names in upper Teesdale and upper Weardale which seem to establish late, possibly post-Conquest, infiltration over the Pennines of settlers of Anglo-Norse origin from Cumbria. In Teesdale we have Etters Gill (NY 8830–8928) *Ethresgilebec* c. 1175, and Snaisgill (NY 9526) *Snelesgil* c. 1180, both with Old West Norse *gil* 'a ravine', a major lexical diagnostic for Norwegian settlement, compounded with a personal name which could be either ON (*Eitri, Sniallr*) or late OE (*Edred, Snel*), and in Weardale Ireshopeburn (NY 846–8638) *Ishoppburn* 1647, *Ireshopeburn* 1685, 'the stream of Ireshope, the valley of the Irishman', ON *Íri*, 'a Norwegian from Ireland'.

By contrast with Northumberland, therefore, we may say that in Durham, apart from some insignificant activity on the wet heavy clays of the East Durham plateau and near the mouth of the Tees, and sporadic infiltration in the upper dales from Cumbria, there is onomastic evidence of an arc of settlement in some density in the middle and lower Tees valley extending two to three miles north of the river from Yorkshire. Here, if anywhere, it seems possible that we may see traces of activity connected with the events of 876, although this cannot be proved. Scandinavian overlordship, as opposed to settlement, was probably established as far as the Scandinavian-named river Gaunless where, before the end of the tenth century, the peaceful exchange of land is commemorated in the place-name Copeland (NZ 1626) *Copland c.* 1040, ON, OE *kaupa-land* 'purchased land'. Even so, there remain areas along the Tees where all trace of Scandinavian or Scandinavianized names is absent, notably around Darlington and around Hartlepool. The influx of population, such as it was, outside the middle Tees valley seems to have been one of infilling of Scandinavians between and around the native population in English named vills. The two processes, Scandinavian overlordship of estate organizations and settlement both in and around pre-existing villages, led to the cultural and political mixing reflected in the Anglo-Scandinavian art throughout the county south of the river Wear (Morris 1981, 234).

Epilogue

'Place-Names in their Historical Context' has been the theme of this collection of studies drawn from widely differing parts of northern Britain. This theme is one which is essential to our proper understanding of the impact of the 'Vikings' on the history of early medieval Britain. As many of the contributors stress we lack historical sources of the period concerned which might have provided us with some direct facts about the process of colonization by those Scandinavian incomers. There is certainly some dramatic material evidence from graves for the physical remains of the Norse settlers in north and west Scotland, but very little of this material has been found in England.[1] Slow, laborious and expensive excavations can produce a wealth of information about Norse houses and settlements: but this has happened in only a few special locations of the northern and western parts of Scotland:[2] of the Danish or Irish-Norse colonizers of northern England or southern Scotland we have as yet no incontrovertibly recognized house site. Yet the place-names are there in their thousands – a vocal testimony to the presence of those men, women, farmers, chieftains, warrior-merchants and even slaves who peopled the islands, dales, *sætr* and *ærgi* hill-farms, and arable lands of the areas covered in this volume, and of the many, many other locations which remain to be studied. This is a resource which has barely been tapped, and which can never satisfactorily be utilized until a proper survey of Scottish place-names has been established and the results made available by linguists for use by historians, archaeologists and geographers. It is hoped that this volume helps to demonstrate the important place of Scandinavian settlement names throughout northern Britain, and how important it is for these names to be understood in the context of other Norse and Danish names in this wider geographical sphere.

The settlement in Orkney which the establishment of the earldom must have quickened took place at just the same time as Halfdan's

---

1. For a distribution map of the Scottish material see Crawford, 1975. For the English grave material see Graham-Campbell, 1994, 134; Wilson, 1976; Edwards, 1992.
2. For the most recent summaries of this work see Hunter, Bond and Smith, 1994; Morris, 1994.

settlement of Yorkshire in the late 870s. This Scandinavian imprint in both the Northern Isles and northern England is linked in the middle of the tenth century with the extraordinary career of Erik Bloodaxe and his wife Gunnhild who established themselves in Orkney before taking power in York. During this period Erik also had some control over the Hebrides and raided in southern Scotland. When he fell at Stainmore in 954 two earls of Orkney died with him. His widow then fled back north and 'subdued the Isles', after which their daughter Ragnhild became deeply involved with the next generation of earls in Orkney.[3] These are merely the recorded deeds of the most powerful element among Viking leaders, Norwegian and Danish, who treated northern Britain as a single field for exploitation. Of the movements and settlement of the many countless unrecorded Norwegians and Danes who similarly treated northern Britain as a land of opportunity we know little. We can however learn to use the toponymic evidence for their presence with the same broad-ranging comprehensiveness as the men and women who ranged widely throughout this territory and who put down roots in many different coastal and inland milieu. The contributors to this book show how it can be done.

---

3. For a summary of Erik Bloodaxe's career see Crawford, 1987, 61–2.

List of abbreviations

Abbreviations used for Scottish sources follow the Conventions used in 'List of Abbreviated Titles of the Printed Sources of Scottish History to 1560', Supplement to the *SHR* October 1963.

App.	Appendix
Arb. Lib.	*Liber S. Thome de Aberbrothoc* (Bannatyne Club 1845–56)
AS	Anglo-Saxon
Bagimond's Roll	*SHS Misc.* vi, 3–77, ed. A.I. Dunlop, 1939
Balm. Lib.	*Liber Sancte Marie de Balmorinach* (Abbotsford Club 1841)
BAR	British Archaeological Reports
Bellenden, *Chronicles*	*The Chronicles of Scotland compiled by Hector Boece*, translated into Scots by John Bellenden 1531 (STS 1938–41)
Bishopric	*Two ancient records of the Bishopric of Caithness* (Bannatyne Club, Miscellany *3*, 1848)
BM	British Museum
Camb. Reg.	*Registrum Monasterii S. Marie de Cambuskenneth* (Grampian Club 1872)
Chron. Picts-Scots	*Chronicles of the Picts: Chronicles of the Scots*, ed. W.F. Skene 1867
Chron. Wyntoun	*The Original Chronicle of Andrew of Wyntoun* (STS 1903–14)
CDS	*Calendar of Documents Relating to Scotland*, vol. 2, ed. J. Bain 1884
CSD	*Concise Scots Dictionary*, ed. M. Robinson 1985
CSR	*Caithness and Sutherland Records*, eds A.W. and A. Johnston (Viking Club 1909)
DB	*Domesday Book*
Dryb. Lib.	*Liber S. Marie de Dryburgh* (Bannatyne Club 1847)

Dunf. Reg.	*Registrum de Dunfermelyn* (Bannatyne Club 1842)
Early Maps	*Early Maps of Scotland* ed. D.G. Moir, 1973
EHR	*English Historical Review*
EPNS	English Place-Name Society (publications of)
ER	*Exchequer Rolls of Scotland*, eds J. Stuart and others, 1878–1908
ES	*Early Sources of Scottish History 500 to 1286*, (I & II) ed. A.O. Anderson 1922, reprint 1990
ESC	*Early Scottish Charters prior to 1153*, ed. A.C. Lawrie 1905
EScand	East Scandinavian
Fife Ct. Bk.	*The Sheriff Court Book of Fife 1515–22*, ed. W.C. Dickinson (SHS 1938)
Fraser, *Wemyss*	*Memorials of the Family of Wemyss of Wemyss*, W. Fraser 1888
G	(Scottish) Gaelic
GDB	*Domesday Book seu liber censuaris Willelmi Primi regis Anglie*, ed. A. Farley and H. Ellis Record Commission I, 1783
Inchcolm Chrs.	*Charters of the Abbey of Inchcolm*, eds D.E. Easson and A. Macdonald (SHS 1938)
Laing Chrs.	*Calendar of the Laing Charters 854–1837*, ed. J. Anderson 1899
Lind. Cart.	*Chartulary of the Abbey of Lindores* (SHS 1903)
LOE	Late Old English
LVD	*Liber Vitae Dunelmensis* ed. G. Stevenson (Surtees Society 13.1841)
May Recs.	*Records of the Priory of the Isle of May* ed. J. Stuart 1868
ME	Middle English
ModE	Modern English
Munro Writs	*Calendar of Writs of Munro of Foulis 1299–1823* (Scottish Record Society)
N.B. Chrs.	*Carte Monialium de Northberwic* (Bannatyne Club 1847)
NLS	National Library of Scotland

OA	Orkney Archives
OD	ordnance datum
ODan	Old Danish
OE	Old English
OED	*A New English Dictionary* (Oxford 1884 etc.)
OEScand	Old East Scandinavian (Old Danish and Old Swedish)
OFr	Old French
OIr	Old Irish
ON	Old Norse
OPS	*Origines Parochiales Scotiae*
Orkney Recs.	*Records of the Earldom of Orkney*, ed. J.S. Clouston (SHS, 1914)
OS	Ordnance Survey
OS	*Orkneyinga Saga*
OSc	Older Scots (from 1100–1700)
OWScand	Old West Scandinavian (Old Icelandic and Old Norwegian)
P	Pictish
par.	parish
pers. n.	personal name
p.n.	place-name
Pitfirrane Writs	*Inventory of Pitfirrane Writs 1230–1794*, ed. W. Angus (Scottish Records Society, 67, 1932)
PrW	Primitive Welsh
POAS	*Proceedings of the Orkney Antiquarian Society*
PSAS	*Proceedings of the Society of Antiquaries of Scotland* (1851–)
RCAHMS	Royal Commission on the Ancient and Historical Monuments of Scotland
Retours	*Retours Inquisitionum ad Capellam Domini Regis Retornatarum, quae in publicis archivis Scotiae adhuc servantur, Abbreviatio* (1811–16) ed. by T. Thomson
RMS	*Registrum Magni Sigilli Regum Scottorum*, eds J.M. Thomson and others, 1882–1914
r.n.	river name

RRS i	*Regesta Regum Scottorum*, vol. i (*Acts of Malcolm IV*), ed. G.W.S. Barrow 1960
RRS ii	*Regesta Regum Scottorum*, vol. ii (*Acts of William I*) ed. G.W.S. Barrow 1971
RSS	*Register of the Privy Seal, Registrum Secreti Sigilli Regum Scottorum*, 1908–, eds M. Livingstone *et al.*
St A. Lib.	*Liber Cartarum Prioratus Sancti Andree in Scotia* (Bannatyne Club 1841)
Sc	Scots
Scand	Scandinavian
Scone Lib.	*Liber Ecclesie de Scon* (Bannatyne and Maitland Clubs 1843)
SHR	*Scottish Historical Review*
SHS	Scottish History Society
SHS Misc.	*The Miscellany of the Scottish History Society*
s.n.	*sub nomine* 'under the name'
SRO	Scottish Record Office, (East) Register House, Princes Street, Edinburgh
Stevenson, *Documents*	*Documents Illustrative of the History of Scotland 1286–1306*, ed. J. Stevenson 1870
STS	Scottish Text Society
s.v.	*sub verbo* 'under the word'
TRHS	*Trans. of the Royal Historical Society*
VA	*Viking Antiquities in Great Britain and Ireland*, ed. H. Shetelig, I–V (Oslo 1940), VI (1954)
WScand	West Scandinavian

Bibliography of works cited

Adomnan's Life of Columba, trans. A.O. and M.O. Anderson, 1961, (new edn 1993)

Alcock, L. and Alcock, E.A., 1990. 'Reconnaissance excavations on Early Historic fortifications and other royal sites in Scotland, 1974–84: Excavations at Alt Clut, Clyde Rock, Strathclyde, 1974–75', *PSAS, 120*, 95–150.

Andersen, P.S., 1971, 1985, *Vikings of the West*

Andersen, P.S., 1991a. 'When was Regular Taxation Introduced in the Norse Islands of Britain?', *Scandinavian Journal of History, 16*, (2), 73–83

Andersen, P.S., 1991b. 'Norse settlement in the Hebrides: what happened to the natives and what happened to the Norse immigrants', in *People and Places in Northern Europe 500–1600*, eds I. Wood and N. Lund, 131–48

Anderson, A.O., ed., 1922 (reprint 1990). *Early Sources of Scottish History 500–1286*

Anderson, A.O. and M.O., trans. 1961. *Adomnan's Life of Columba*

Anderson, J., 1872–74. 'Notes on relics of the Viking Period', *PSAS, 10*, 554–5

Anderson, M.O., 1974. 'St. Andrews before Alexander I', in *The Scottish Tradition*, ed. G.W.S. Barrow, 1–13

Annals of Ulster, vol. 1 (to AD 1131), trans. S. MacAirt and G. MacNiocaill, Dublin 1983

Armstrong, A.M., Mawer, A., Stenton, F.M. and Dickins, B., 1950. 'The Place-Names of Cumberland, pt. 2', EPNS, XXI

Atkin, M., 1978. 'Viking race-courses? The distribution of *skeið* place-name elements in Northern England', *Journal of the EPNS, 10*, 26–39

Bailey, P., 1971. *Orkney* – The Islands Series

Bailey, R.N., 1980. *Viking Age Sculpture*

Baldwin, J.R. and Whyte, I.D., eds., 1985. *The Scandinavians in Cumbria*

Balfour, D., ed., 1859, *Oppressions of the Sixteenth Century in the Islands of Orkney and Shetland*, Edinburgh

Ballantyne, J.H. and Smith, B., eds., 1994. *Shetland Documents 1580–1611*

Bangor-Jones, M., 1987. 'Ouncelands and Pennylands in Sutherland and Caithness', in *Ouncelands and Pennylands*, eds L.J. Macgregor and B.E. Crawford, 13–23

Bannerman, J.W., 1974. *Studies in the History of Dalriada*

Barrow, G.W.S., 1966. 'The Scottish *judex* in the twelfth and thirteenth centuries', *SHR, 45*, 16–26

Barrow, G.W.S., 1971. 'The Early Charters of the Family of Kinninmonth of that Ilk', in *The Study of Medieval Records*, eds D.A. Bullough and R.L. Storey, 107–31

Barrow, G.W.S., 1973. *The Kingdom of the Scots*
Barrow, G.W.S., 1974, 'Some East Fife Documents of the twelfth and thirteenth centuries', in *The Scottish Tradition*, ed. G.W.S. Barrow, 23–43
Barrow, G.W.S., 1980. *The Anglo-Norman Era in Scottish History*
Barrow, G.W.S., 1981a. *Kingship and Unity: Scotland 1000–1306 (The New History of Scotland)*, ed. J. Wormald, 2
Barrow, G.W.S., 1981b. 'Popular Courts in Early Medieval Scotland: Some Suggested Place-Name Evidence', *Scottish Studies*, 25, 1–24
Barrow, G.W.S., 1989. 'The lost Gaídhealtachd of Medieval Scotland', in *Gaelic and Scotland*, ed. W.Gillies, 67–88
Batey, C.E., 1987. *Freswick Links, Caithness*, i & ii, BAR, British Series, 179
Batey, C.E., 1989. 'Viking and Late Norse Caithness', *The New Caithness Book*, ed. D. Omand, 67–77
Batey, C.E., 1993. 'The Viking and Late Norse Graves of Caithness and Sutherland', in *The Viking Age in Caithness, Orkney and the North Atlantic*, eds C.E. Batey, J. Jesch, C.D. Morris, 148–65
BBC, 1957. *Anglo-Saxon England*, BBC Publications no. 3637
Bentinck, C.D., 1926. *Dornoch Cathedral and Parish*
Beveridge, E., 1903. *Coll and Tiree, their prehistoric forts and ecclesiastical antiquities*
Björkmann, E., 1910, 'Nordische Personennamen in England in alt- und frühmittelenglischer Zeit', *Studien zur Englischen Philologie*, 37, Halle
Blackburn, M. and Pagan, H., 1987. 'A Check-List of Coin-Hoards c. 500–1100' in *Anglo-Saxon Monetary History*, ed. M. Blackburn, 292–303
Bradley, J., 1988. 'The interpretation of Scandinavian settlement in Ireland' in *Settlement and Society in Medieval Ireland*, ed. J. Bradley, 49–78
Brøgger, A.W., 1929. *Ancient Emigrants*
Brooke, D., 1983. 'Kirk-compound place-names of Galloway and Carrick', *Transactions of the Dumfriesshire and Galloway Natural History and Antiquarian Society*, 58, 56–71
Brooke, D., 1984. 'The Glenkens 1275–1485: Snapshots of a medieval country-side', *Transactions of the Dumfriesshire and Galloway Natural History and Antiquarian Society*, 59, 41–56
Brooke, D., 1991. 'Gall-Gaidhil and Galloway', in *Galloway: Land and Lordship*, eds R.D. Oram and G.P. Stell, 97–116
Broun, D., 1994. 'The Origin of Scottish Identity in its European Context' in *Scotland in Dark Age Europe*, ed. B. Crawford, 21–32
Cameron, K., 1965. *Scandinavian Settlement in the Territory of the Five Boroughs: the Place-Name Evidence*
Cameron, K., 1970. 'Scandinavian Settlement in the Territory of the Five Boroughs: the Place-Name evidence, Part II, Place-names in thorp', *Medieval Scandinavia*, 3, 35–49
Cameron, K., 1971. 'Scandinavian Settlement in the Territory of the Five Boroughs: the Place-Name evidence, Part III, the Grimston hybrids', in *England before the Conquest: Studies in primary sources presented to Dorothy Whitelock*, eds P. Clemoes and K. Hughes, 147–63
Cameron, K., ed., 1975 reprint of Cameron, 1965, 1970 and 1971, in *Place-name Evidence for the Anglo-Saxon Invasions and Scandinavian Settlements*, EPNS, 115–38, 139–56, 157–71

Cameron, K., 1991, 1992. *The Place-Names of Lincolnshire*, pts. 2 & 3, EPNS, 64–5, 66
Campbell, N.D., 1911–1912. 'An old Tiree Rental of 1622', *SHR, 9*, 343–4
Chippendall, W.H., 1935. 'The History of the Township of Ireby', *Chetham Society, 95*, N.S.
Christensen, A.E., 1968. *Boats of the North*, Oslo
Christensen, A.E., 1969. *Vikingetidens Danmark*, Copenhagen
Clouston, J. Storer, 1926/7. 'The Orkney *Bus*', *POAS, 5*, 41–9
Clouston, J. Storer, 1932. *History of Orkney*
Coates, R., 1976. 'Caithness Place-Names in -bster*', *Acta Philologica Scandinavica, 31*, 188–90
Colgrave, B. ed., 1927. *The Life of Bishop Wilfrid by Eddius Stephanus*
Colgrave, B. ed., 1940. *Two Lives of St. Cuthbert*
Collingwood, W.G. 1927. *Northumbrian Crosses of the Pre-Norman Age*
Coney, A.P., 1992. 'Fish, fowl and fen: landscape and economy on seventeenth-century Martin Mere', *Landscape History, 14*, 51–64
Cowan, E.J., 1991. 'The Vikings in Galloway: A review of the evidence', in *Galloway: Land and Lordship*, eds R.D. Oram and G.P. Stell, 63–75
Cox, R.A.V., 1989. 'Place-name evidence in the west of Lewis: approaches and problems in establishing a profile of Norse settlement', *Scottish Archaeological Review, 6*
Cox, R.A.V., 1991. 'Norse-Gaelic contact in the west of Lewis: the place-name evidence', in *Language Contact in the British Isles: Proceedings of the Eighth International Symposium on Language Contact in Europe, Douglas, Isle of Man, 1988*, eds P.S. Ureland and G. Broderick, Tübingen
Craig, D.J., 1991. 'Pre-Norman sculpture in Galloway: Some territorial implications', in *Galloway: Land and Lordship*, eds R.D. Oram and G.P. Stell, 45–62
Crawford, B.E., 1975. 'Viking Graves', in *An Historical Atlas of Scotland c. 400–c. 1600*, no. 13 (text 11), eds P. McNeill and R. Nicholson
Crawford B.E., 1985a. 'The Earldom of Caithness and the Kingdom of Scotland, 1150–1266', in *Essays on the Nobility of Medieval Scotland*, ed. K.J. Stringer, 25–42
Crawford, B.E., 1985b. 'Introduction', in *The Scandinavians in Cumbria*, eds J. Baldwin and I. Whyte, 1–4
Crawford, B.E., 1986. 'The making of a Frontier: The Firthlands from the Ninth to Twelfth Centuries', in *Firthlands of Ross and Cromarty*, ed. J.R. Baldwin, 33–46
Crawford, B.E., 1987. *Scandinavian Scotland: Scotland in the Early Middle Ages, 2*
Crawford, B.E. ed., 1988. *St. Magnus Cathedral and Orkney's Twelfth-Century Renaissance*
Crawford, B.E., 1994. 'The "Norse" background to the Govan hogbacks', in *Govan and Its Early Medieval Sculpture*, ed. A. Ritchie, 103–112
Crawford, B.E., 1995. *'Earl and Mormaer; Norse-Pictish Relationships in Northern Scotland'* (Groam House Museum lecture publications)
Dietrichson, L., 1906. *Monumenta Orcadica*, Christiania
Dodgson, J. McN., 1972. *The Place-Names of Cheshire*, pt. 4, EPNS, XLVII
Dodgson, J. McN., 1981. *The Place-Names of Cheshire*, pt. 5 (l:i, l:ii), EPNS, XLVIII, LIV
Donaldson, G. ed., 1954. *Court Book of Shetland 1602–1604*
Dorian, N.C., 1981. *Language Death: The Life Cycle of a Scottish Gaelic dialect*, Philadelphia

Duncan, A.A.M., 1975, *Scotland, The Making of a Kingdom*

Early Maps of Scotland, 1973, ed. D.G. Moir
  Arrowsmith Map, 1807, 'Map of Scotland'
  Blaeu Map, 1635, 'Scotia Regnum'
  Revised Mercator Map, 1595, 'Scotiae Regnum (Northern Scotland)'
  Roy Map, 1750, 'The Military Survey of Scotland 1747–55'
  Thomson Map, 1815, 'Scotland'

Edwards, B.J.N., 1992. 'The Vikings in the North West: The Archaeological Evidence', in *Viking Treasure from the North West*, ed. J. Graham-Campbell, 43–62

Edwards, N., 1990. *The Archaeology of Medieval Ireland*

Ekwall, E., 1918. *Scandinavians and Celts in the North West of England* (Lund and Leipzig)

Ekwall, E., 1922. *The Place-Names of Lancashire*

Ekwall, E., 1924. 'The Scandinavian element' in *Introduction to the Survey of English Place-Names*, pt. I, eds A. Mawer and F.M. Stenton

Ekwall, E., 1928. *English River-Names*

Ekwall, E., 1960. *The Concise Oxford Dictionary of English Place-names*, 4th edn

Eyrbyggja Saga, trans. H. Pálsson and P. Edwards, 1972

Farbregd, O., 1984. 'Gårdgrenser og Geometrisk Analyse, Teori og Metodisk Prinsipp', *Heimen, 1*, 33–50

Farrell, R.T., ed., 1982. *The Vikings*

Faull, M.L. and Stinson, M. eds, 1986. *Domesday Book 30, Yorkshire*, Phillimore Edn.

Feilitzen, O. von, 1937. *The Pre-Conquest Personal Names of Domesday Book*, Nomina Germanica, *3*, Uppsala

Fellows-Jensen, G., 1972. *Scandinavian Settlement Names in Yorkshire*, Copenhagen

Fellows-Jensen, G., 1976. 'Personal name or appellative? A new look at some Danelaw place-names', *Onoma, 19*, 445–58

Fellows-Jensen, G., 1978a. 'Place-Names and Settlement in the North Riding of Yorkshire', *Northern History, 14*, 21–46

Fellows-Jensen, G., 1978b. *Scandinavian Settlement Names in the East Midlands*, Navnestudier *16*, Copenhagen

Fellows-Jensen, G., 1980. 'Common Gaelic *áirge*, Old Scandinavian *ærgi* or *erg*?', *Nomina, 4*, 67–84

Fellows-Jensen, G., 1981, 'Scandinavian Settlement in the Danelaw in the light of the place-names of Denmark', in *Proceedings of the Eighth Viking Congress*, eds H. Bekker-Nielsen, *et al.*, Odense, 133–46

Fellows-Jensen, G., 1983a. 'Anthroponymical specifics in place-names in -bý in the British Isles', *Studia Anthroponymica Scandinavica, 1*, 45–60

Fellows-Jensen, G., 1983b. 'Scandinavian settlement in the Isle of Man and Northwest England: the place-name evidence', in *The Viking Age in the Isle of Man. Select papers from the Ninth Viking Congress*, eds C. Fell *et al.*, 37–52

Fellows-Jensen, G., 1984. 'Viking Settlement in the Northern and Western Isles – the Place-Name Evidence as seen from Denmark and the Danelaw', in *The Northern and Western Isles in the Viking World*, eds A. Fenton and H. Pálsson, 148–68

Fellows-Jensen, G., 1985a. *Scandinavian Settlement Names in the North-West*, Copenhagen

224 *Bibliography*

Fellows-Jensen, G., 1985b. 'On *dalr* and *holmr* in the place-names of Britain', *NORNA-rapporter, 28,* Uppsala

Fellows-Jensen, G., 1989. 'Amounderness and Holderness', in *Studia Onomastica, Festskrift till Thorsten Andersson, 23 Februari 1989,* eds L. Peterson *et al.* 86–94, Stockholm

Fellows-Jensen, G., 1989–90. 'Scandinavians in Southern Scotland?', *Nomina, 4,* 41–59. (A Danish version of this article, with minor changes is 'Nordiske spor i det midt-skotske lavland?' in *Analogi i Navngivning, NORNA-Rapporter, 45,* 1991, 65–82)

Fellows-Jensen, G., 1991. 'Scandinavians in Dumfriesshire and Galloway: The Place-Name Evidence', in *Galloway: Land and Lordship,* eds R.D. Oram and G.P. Stell, 77–95

Fellows-Jensen, G., 1991–92. 'Place-names in *-þorp.* In retrospect and in turmoil', *Nomina, 15,* 35–52

Fellows-Jensen, G., 1992. 'Scandinavian Place-Names of the Irish Sea Province', in *Viking Treasure from the North West,* ed. J. Graham-Campbell, 31–42

Finberg, H.R.F. ed. 1975. *Scandinavian England*

Foote, P. and Wilson, D.M., 1970. *The Viking Achievement*

Fraser, I.A., 1974. 'The Place-names of Lewis – The Norse Evidence', *Northern Studies, 14,* 11–21

Fraser, I.A., 1978a. 'The Place-names of a Deserted Island: Eilean nan Ron', *Scottish Studies, 22,* 83–90

Fraser, I.A., 1978b. 'The Norse Element in Sutherland Place-Names', *Scottish Literary Journal,* Language Supplement *9,* 17–27

Fraser, I.A., 1984. 'Place-Names of Ross and Cromarty', in *The Ross and Cromarty Book,* ed. D. Omand

Fraser, I.A., 1986. 'Norse and Celtic Place-Names around the Dornoch Firth', in *Firthlands of Ross and Cromarty,* ed. J.R. Baldwin, 23–32

Fraser, I.A., 1994. 'What is a Vik?: an Investigation into an Old Norse coastal toponym', in *Peoples and Settlement in North-West Ross,* ed. J.R. Baldwin, 69–78

Freeman, E.A., 1867–79. *History of the Norman Conquest,* 6 vols.

Gelling, M., 1973. Review of G. Fellows-Jensen, *Settlement Studies in North Yorks,* in *Notes and Queries* (April 1973), 144–6

Gelling, M., 1974. *The Place-Names of Berkshire,* pt. 2, EPNS, *L*

Gelling, M., 1984. *Place-names in the Landscape*

Gelling, M., 1988. *Signposts to the Past, Place-Names and the History of England,* 2nd edn, Phillimore

Gelling, M., 1992. *The West Midlands in the Early Middle Ages*

Gover, J.E.B., Mawer, A. and Stenton, F.M., 1940. *The Place-names of Nottinghamshire,* EPNS, XVII

Graham-Campbell, J., 1975–6. 'The Viking-Age silver and gold hoards of Scandinavian character from Scotland', *PSAS, 107,* 114–35

Graham-Campbell, J. ed., 1992. *Viking Treasure from the North West: the Cuerdale Hoard in its Context,* National Museums and Galleries on Merseyside Occasional Papers, Liverpool Museum 5

Graham-Campbell, J. ed., 1994. *Cultural Atlas of the Viking World*

Graham-Campbell, J., 1995. *The Viking-Age Gold and Silver Hoards of Scotland*

Hall, R., 1978. 'The Topography of Anglo-Scandinavian York', in *Viking Age York and the North,* ed. R.A. Hall (CBA Research Report, 27), 31–37

Hall, R., 1994. *Viking York* (English Heritage)

Heimskringla, Saga of Harald Fairhair, trans. H.M. Hollander, Oslo 1964

Heimskringla, Olafs Saga Helgi, ed. B. Aðalbjarnarson (Izlensk Fornrit, *26–28*)

Helle, K., 1993. 'Norway 800–1200', in *Viking Revaluations*, eds A. Faulkes and R. Perkins

Henderson, G., 1910. *The Norse Influence on Celtic Scotland*

Higham, M.C., 1977. 'The *Erg* Place-Names of Northern England', *Journal EPNS, 10*, 18–26

Higham, M.C., 1985. 'Pre-Conquest Settlement in the Forest of Bowland', in *The Scandinavians in Cumbria*, eds J. Baldwin and I. Whyte, 119–35

Higham, M.C., 1992a. 'The *Regione Dunutinga* – A Pre-Conquest Lordship?', *Lancaster University Regional Bulletin, 6* (new series)

Higham, M.C., 1992b. 'The Effects of the Norman Conquest on North West England', (University of Lancaster, Unpublished Ph.D. Thesis)

Higham, N., 1993. *The Kingdom of Northumbria*

Higham, N.J., 1992. 'Northumbria, Mercia and the Irish Sea Norse, 893–926', in *Viking Treasure from the North West*, ed. J. Graham-Campbell, 21–30

Hill, P.H., 1988. *Whithorn 2* (interim excavation report)

Hill, P.H., 1991. 'Whithorn: The missing years', in *Galloway: Land and Lordship*, eds R. Oram and G. Stell, 27–44

Hunter, J.R., Bond, J.M. and Smith, A.M., 1994. 'Some Aspects of Early Viking Settlement in Orkney', in *The Viking Age in Caithness, Orkney and the North Atlantic*, eds. C. Batey *et al.*, 272–84

Huyshe, W., 1914. *Grey Galloway, Its Lords and Its Saints*

Icelandic-English Dictionary, 1874. eds R. Cleasby, G. Vigfusson and Sir W.A. Craigie

Insley, J., 1986. 'Toponymy and settlement in the North-West', *Nomina, 10*, 69–76

Jackson, K.H., 1972. *The Gaelic Notes in the Book of Deer*

Jakobsen, J., 1928 and 1932. *An Etymological Dictionary of the Norn Language in Shetland*, 2 vols.

Jakobsen, J., 1936. *The Place-Names of Shetland* (reprinted, 1993)

Johnston, A.W., 1903. 'The Round Church of Orphir', *Saga Book of the Viking Society, 3*, 174–216

Jones, G.R.J., 1965. 'Early territorial organisation in northern England and its bearing on the Scandinavian settlement', in *The Fourth Viking Congress*, ed. A. Small, 67–84

Jordan, R., 1934. *Handbuch der mittelenglischen Grammatik*, Heidelberg

Joyce, P.W., 1869–1922. *Irish Names of Places*, 3 vols

Kaland, S., 1993. 'The Settlement of Westness, Rousay', in *The Viking Age in Caithness, Orkney and the North Atlantic*, eds C. Batey, J. Jesch and C.D. Morris, 340–8

Kenyon, D., 1991. *The Origins of Lancashire*

Keynes, S. and Lapidge, M., 1972. *Alfred the Great*

King, A., 1970. *Early Pennine Settlement*

Lamb, R.L., 1982. *The Archaeological Sites and Monuments of Rousay, Egilsay and Wyre* (The Archaeological Sites and Monuments of Scotland, *16*, RCAHMS)

Landnámabók, Icelandic Studies 1, trans. H. Pálsson and P. Edwards, Manitoba 1972

Lang, J.T., 1972–4. 'Hogback monuments in Scotland', *PSAS, 105*, 206–35

Lang, J.T., 1984. 'The Hogback: A Viking colonial monument', *Anglo-Saxon Studies in Archaeology and History, 3*, 85–176

Lang, J.T., 1994. 'The Govan Hogbacks: a re-appraisal' in *Govan and Its Early Medieval Sculpture*, ed. A. Ritchie, 123–32

Liddall, W.J.N., 1896. *The Place Names of Fife and Kinross*, reprinted by Lang Syne Publishers 1986

Lund, N., 1976. '*Thorp*-names', in *Medieval Settlement: Continuity and Change*, ed. P.H. Sawyer, 223–25

Lund, N., 1981. 'The Settlers: where do we get them from and do we need them?' in *Proceedings of the Eighth Viking Congress*, ed. H. Bekker-Nielsen *et al.*, Odense, 147–71

Low, G., 1879. *A Tour thro' the Islands of Orkney and Schetland*, Kirkwall

Macaulay, D., 1982. 'Place-Names', in *The Sutherland Book*, ed. D. Omand

MacBain, A., 1894. 'The Norse element in the topography of the Highlands and Islands', *Transactions of the Gaelic Society of Inverness, 19*, 217–45

MacBain, A., 1911. *An Etymological Dictionary of the Gaelic Language* (reprinted by Gairm Publications, 1982)

MacBain, A., 1922. *Place Names: Highlands and Islands of Scotland*

MacDonald, A., 1941. *The Place-Names of West Lothian*

MacDonald, A., 1977. 'On "Papar" names in N. and W. Scotland', *Northern Studies, 9*, 25–30

MacDonald, A., 1981–82. 'Caiseal, Cathair, Dùn, Lios and Ràth in Scotland II', *Bulletin of the Ulster Place-Name Society*, Series 2, 4, 32–56

MacDonald, D.A., 1984. 'The Vikings in Gaelic Oral Tradition, in *The Northern and Western Isles in the Viking World*, eds A. Fenton and H. Pálsson, 264–79

Macfarlane's Geographical Collections, Scot. His. Soc. 1906, vol. I

Macgregor, L.J., 1986. 'Norse Naming Elements in Shetland and Faroe: A Comparative Study', *Northern Studies, 23*, 84–101

Macgregor, L.J., 1987. 'Norse Settlement in Shetland and Faroe: a comparative Study' (Unpublished Ph.D. Thesis, University of St. Andrews)

Macgregor, L.J. and Crawford, B.E., eds, 1987. *Ouncelands and Pennylands*, St. John's House Occasional Papers 4, University of St. Andrews

MacInnes, J., 1989. 'The Gaelic Perception of the Lowlands', in *Gaelic and Scotland*, ed. W. Gillies, 89–100

MacKenzie, B., 1985. *The Vikings in East Sutherland* (published lecture)

MacNeill, P. and Nicholson, R., eds, 1975. *An Historical Atlas of Scotland*

MacQueen, J., 1973. 'The gaelic speakers of Galloway and Carrick', *Scottish Studies, 17*, 69–74

Marwick, H., 1922/3a. 'Antiquarian Notes on Sanday', *POAS, 1*, 21–9

Marwick, H., 1922/3b. 'The Place-names of North Ronaldsay', *POAS, 1*, 53–64

Marwick, H., 1923/4. 'Antiquarian Notes on Rousay', *POAS, 2*, 15–21

Marwick, H., 1924/5. 'Antiquarian Notes on Papa Westray', *POAS, 3*, 31–7

Marwick, H., 1926/7. 'Antiquarian Notes on Stronsay', *POAS, 5*, 61–83

Marwick, H., 1929. *The Orkney Norn*

Marwick, H., 1930/1. 'Orkney Farm-name Studies', *POAS, 9*, 25–34

Marwick, H., 1947. *The Place-names of Rousay*

Marwick, H., 1952. *Orkney Farm-names*

Marwick, H., 1957. 'Two Orkney Letters of A.D. 1329', *Orkney Miscellany, 4*, 49–56

Mawer, A., 1920. *The Place-names of Northumberland and Durham*

Mawer, A., 1921. 'Early Northumbrian history in the light of its place-names', *Archæologia Æliana*, 3rd series, *18*, 1–18

Maxwell, S., 1957–8. 'A medieval gold ring from Shetland', *PSAS, 91*, 193

Megaw, E., 1978. 'The Manx "Eary" and its significance', in *Man and the Environment in the Isle of Man*, ed. R. Davey (BAR British Series, *54*, pt. ii), 327–45

Metcalf, D., 1992. 'The Monetary Economy of the Irish Sea Province', in *Viking Treasure from the North West*, ed. J. Graham-Campbell, 89–106

Morris, C.D., 1977. 'Northumbria and the Viking Settlement: the evidence for land-holding', *Archæologia Æliana*, 5th series, 5, 81–101

Morris, C.D., 1981. 'Viking and native in northern England. A case-study', in *Proceedings of the Eighth Viking Congress*, eds H. Bekker-Neilsen *et al.*, Odense, 223–44

Morris, C.D., 1984. 'Aspects of Scandinavian Settlement in Northern England: A Review', *Northern History, 20*, 3–22

Morris, C.D., 1985. 'Viking Orkney', in *The Prehistory of Orkney*, ed. C. Renfrew

Morris, C.D., 1994. 'The Birsay Bay project: A Résumé', in *The Viking Age in the North Atlantic*, eds C. Batey *et al.* 285–307

Morris, G.E. and McDonnell, J., 1990–91. '"Thwaite" place-names on the North York Moors', *The Ryedale Historian, 15*, 24–9

Munch, P.A., 1845–9. 'Geographical Elucidations of the Scottish and Irish Local Names Occurring in the Sagas', *Mémoires de la Société Royale des Antiquaires du Nord*, 208–65

New Statistical Account of Scotland, 1845, *15*

Nicolaisen, W.F.H., 1967. 'Scottish Place-Names: 29 Scandinavian Personal Names in the Place-Names of South-East Scotland', *Scottish Studies, 11*, 223–36

Nicolaisen, W.F.H., 1969. 'Norse Settlement in the Northern and Western Isles – Some Place-Name Evidence', *SHR, 48*, 6–17

Nicolaisen, W.F.H. ed., 1970. *The Names of Towns and Cities in Britain*, compiled by M. Gelling, W.F.H. Nicolaisen and M.Richards, ed. W.F.H. Nicolaisen

Nicolaisen, W.F.H., 1975. Maps 6a-f, in *An Historical Atlas of Scotland c. 400–c. 1600*, eds P. MacNeill and R. Nicholson

Nicolaisen, W.F.H., 1976a. 'Scandinavian Place-names in Scotland as a source of knowledge', *Northern Studies, 7/8*, 14–23

Nicolaisen, W.F.H., 1976b. *Scottish Place-Names* (second impression with additional information 1979)

Nicolaisen, W.F.H., 1981. 'Bagimond's Roll as a toponymic text', in *So Meny People Longages and Tonges*, eds M. Benskin and M.L. Samuels

Nicolaisen, W.F.H., 1982a. 'The Viking Settlement of Scotland: the evidence of place-names' in *The Vikings*, ed. R.T. Farrell, 95–115

Nicolaisen, W.F.H., 1982b. 'Scandinavians and Celts in Caithness: The Place-Name Evidence', in *Caithness: A Cultural Crossroads*, ed. J. Baldwin, 75–85

Nicolaisen, W.F.H., 1989. 'Place-name Maps – How reliable are they?', in *Studia Onomastica: Festskrift till Thorsten Andersson*, eds L. Peterson and S. Strandberg, 262–8

Nieke, M., 1983, 'Settlement patterns in the 1st millenium AD: a case study of the island of Islay', in *Settlement in North Britain 1000BC–AD1000*, eds J.C. Chapman and H. Mytum, (BAR, *118*), 209–326

Njal's Saga, trans. M. Magnusson and H. Pálsson, 1964

Oftedal, M., 1981. 'Names of lakes on the Isle of Lewis in the Outer Hebrides' in *Proceedings of the Eighth Viking Congress*, ed. H. Bekker-Nielsen *et al.*, Odense, 183–88

Old Lore Miscellany of Orkney, Shetland, Caithness and Sutherland, 1907–15. 1–8

Olsen, M., 1928. *Farms and Fanes of Ancient Norway*, Oslo

Olsen, M., 1931–2. 'Orknø-Norn og Norrøn diktning på Orknøene', *Maal og Minne*

Origines Parochiales Scotiae. The Antiquities Ecclesiastical and Territorial of the Parishes of Scotland, 1851–1855. 2 vols, ed. C. Innes, The Bannatyne Club

Orkney Miscellany, 5, 1973. King Hakon Commemorative Number

Orkneyinga Saga, trans. F. Guðmundsson, Islenzk Fornrit, *34*, 1965

Orkneyinga Saga, trans. A.B. Taylor, 1938

Orkneyinga Saga: The History of the Earls of Orkney, trans. By H. Pálsson and P. Edwards 1978, reprinted Penguin, 1986

The Orkneyinga Saga, ed. with notes and introduction by J. Anderson, 1873, 1973

O.S. Map of Britain Before the Norman Conquest, 1973

Owen, O.A., 1993. 'Tuquoy, Westray, Orkney', in *The Viking Age in Caithness, Orkney and the North Atlantic*, eds C. Batey, J. Jesch and C.D. Morris, 318–339

Owen, O.A. and Dalland, M., 1994. 'Scar, Sanday: a Viking boat burial from Orkney. An Interim Report', in *Developments around the Baltic and the North Sea in the Viking Age*, eds. B. Ambrosiani and H. Clarke, Stockholm, 159–72

Påhlsson, C., 1975–6. 'Rothbury', *Journal of the EPNS, 8*, 9–11

Peterkin, A., 1820. *Rentals of the Ancient Earldom and Bishoprick of Orkney*

Pride, G.L., 1990. *The Kingdom of Fife, An Illustrated Architectural Guide*

RCAHMS, 1980. *Argyll. An Inventory of the Monuments, 3, (Mull, Coll, Tiree and Northern Argyll)*

Reaney, P.H., 1943. *The Place-names of Cambridgeshire and the Isle of Ely*, EPNS, XIX

Retours, Inquisitionum ad Capellam Domini Regis Retornatarum, quae in publicis archivis Scotiae adhuc servantur, Abbreviatio, 1811–16, ed. T. Thomson

Ritchie, A., 1993. *Viking Scotland* (HMSO)

Roberts, B.K., 1989–90. 'Late -bý Names in the Eden Valley, Cumberland', *Nomina, 13*, 25–40

Rygh, O. 1897–1936. *Norske Gaardnavne*, Christiania

Sanderson, M., 1982. *Scottish Rural Life in the 16th Century*

Sandnes, J., 1973. 'Dating av navneklasser ved Landskyld-Metoden', *Maal og Minne, 1–2*, 12–28

Sandnes, J. and Stemshaug, O. eds 1976, 1990. *Norsk Stadnamnleksikon*, Oslo

Sawyer, P.H., 1958. 'The density of the Danish settlement in England', *University of Birmingham Historical Journal, 6*, 1–17

Sawyer, P.H., 1962 (1971, 2nd edn). *The Age of the Vikings*

Sawyer, P.H., 1979. ed. *English Medieval Settlement*

Sawyer, P.H., 1988. *Da Danmark Blev Danmark, Gyldendal og Politikens Danmarks-historie III*, Copenhagen

Scott, Sir L., 1954. 'The Norse in the Hebrides' in *The Viking Congress* (1950), ed. W.D. Simpson, 189–215

Simpson, W.D. ed., 1954. *The Viking Congress* (1950)

Sjovold, T., 1954. *The Vikings Ships*, Oslo

Small, A., 1976. 'Norse Settlement in Skye', in *Les Vikings et Leur Civilisation; problemes actuels*, Bibliotheque Artique et Antartique, ed. R. Boyer, 29–37

Small, A., 1982. 'Viking Sutherland', in *The Sutherland Book*, ed. D. Omand, 180–84

Small, A., 1986. 'Norse Settlement in Easter Ross', in *Essays for Professor R.E.H. Mellor*, eds W. Ritchie *et al.*

Smith, A.H., 1925. *The Place-Names of the North Riding of Yorkshire*, EPNS, *V*

Smith, A.H., 1956 (reprinted 1970). *English Place-Name Elements*, 2 vols., EPNS, *XXV–XXVI*

Smith, B., 1989. 'In the tracks of Andrew Pictoris, bishop of Orkney', *Innes Review*, 40, 91–105

Smyth, A.P., 1977. *Scandinavian Kings in the British Isles, 850–880*

Smyth, A.P., 1978. 'The chronology of Northumbria in the ninth and tenth centuries' in *Viking Age York and the North* (CBA Research Report, 27), 8–11

Smyth, A.P., 1984. *Warlords and Holy Men. Scotland A.D. 800–1000, (The New History of Scotland*, ed. J. Wormald, I)

Steinnes, A., 1969. 'The Huseby System in Orkney', *SHR*, 44, 36–46

Stenton, F.M., 1947. *Anglo-Saxon England*, 2nd edn

Stephen, W., 1938. *History of Inverkeithing and Rosyth*

Stevenson, R.B.K., 1981. 'Christian sculpture in Norse Shetland', *Froðskaparrit, 28–29*, 283–93, Tórshavn

Stewart, J., 1965. 'Shetland Farm Names' in *The Fourth Viking Congress*, ed. A. Small, 247–66

Stewart, J., 1987. *Shetland Place-Names*

Swift, F.B. and Bullman, C.G., 1965. 'Ireby Church and Parish: History and Changes', *Trans. Cumberland and Westmorland Antiquarian and Archaeological Society*, n.s., 65, 222–39

Taylor, A.B., trans. 1938. *The Orkneyinga Saga*

Taylor, A.B., 1954. 'Shetland Place-Names in the Sagas', in *Viking Congress, Lerwick, July 1950*, ed. W.D. Simpson, 112–29

Taylor, A.B., 1973. 'Cape Wrath and its various names', *Scottish Studies*, 17, 61–9

Taylor, S. forthcoming. 'Babbet and Bridin Pudding', *Nomina*

Thacker, A.T., 1987. 'Anglo-Saxon Cheshire', *Victoria County History of Cheshire, I*, 237–85

Thomson, W.P.L., 1987. *History of Orkney*

Thomson, W.P.L., 1990. 'Settlement Patterns at Tuquoy, Westray, Orkney', *Northern Studies*, 27, 35–49

Thomson, W.P.L., 1993. 'Some Settlement Patterns in Medieval Orkney', in *The Viking Age in Caithness, Orkney and the North Atlantic*, eds C. Batey, J. Jesch and C.D. Morris, 340–8

Thurneysen, R., 1980. *A Grammar of Old Irish*, translated by Binchy and Bergin, Dublin

Vipond, P., 1993. 'Harrow Fields in Heswall-cum-Oldfield', *Journal of the EPNS, 25*

230   *Bibliography*

Wainwright, F.T., 1948. 'Ingimund's Invasion', *EHR, 73*, 147–69 (reprinted in *Scandinavian England*, 1978)
Wainwright, F.T., ed., 1962. *The Northern Isles*
Wainwright, F.T., 1962. 'The Scandinavian Settlement', in *The Northern Isles*, ed. F.T. Wainwright, 117–62
Wallace, P.F. and O'Floinn, R., 1988. *Dublin 1000. Discovery and Excavation in Dublin 1842–1981*
Watson, W.J., 1904. *The Place-Names of Ross and Cromarty*
Watson, W.J., 1906. 'Some Sutherland Names of Places', *The Celtic Review, 2*, 360–68
Watson, W.J., 1926. *The History of the Celtic Place-Names of Scotland*
Watt, D.E.R., ed., 1991. *Series Episcoporum Ecclesie Catholicae Occidentalis, VI*, pt. i, *Ecclesia Scoticana*
Watts, V., 1988–89. 'Scandinavian Settlement-Names in County Durham', *Nomina, 12*, 17–63
Waugh, D., 1987. 'The Scandinavian Element *Staðir* in Caithness, Orkney and Shetland', *Nomina, 11*, 61–74
Waugh, D., 1989. 'Place-Names', in *The New Caithness Book*, ed. D. Omand, 141–55
Waugh, D., 1991. 'Place-Name Evidence for Scandinavian Settlement in Shetland', *Review of Scottish Culture, 7*, 15–23
Waugh, D. 1993. 'Caithness. An Onomastic Frontier Zone' in *The Viking Age in Caithness, Orkney and the North Atlantic*, eds, C.E. Batey, J. Jesch and C.D. Morris, 120–8
Wilson, D., 1976. 'Scandinavian settlement in the north and west of the British Isles – an archaeological point of view', *TRHS, 26*, 95–113
Winchester, A.J.L., 1985. 'The Multiple Estate: A Framework for the Evolution of Settlement in Anglo-Saxon and Scandinavian Cumbria', in *The Scandinavians in Cumbria*, eds, J.R. Baldwin and I.D. Whyte, 89–102
Winchester, A.J.L., 1987. *Landscape and Society in Medieval Cumbria*
Wright, J., ed., 1905. *The English Dialect Dictionary, III*
Young, A., 1993. 'The Earls and Earldom of Buchan in the Thirteenth Century', in *Medieval Scotland, Crown, Lordship and Community*, eds, A. Grant and K.J. Stringer, 174–202

Index

Page numbers in **bold type** refer to figures and plates.

Towton, Yorks. 174
Tranmere, Ches. 189
Treallabhig, Coll 123
treen 134
Trenaby, Ork. 43
Trevercarcou (Br.) 130
Trewhitt, Northumberland 206–9
Trewhytt see Trewhitt, Northumberland
trolla-vík 99
Trøndelag, Norway 18–19
Trumland, Ork. 44–5
tun (Scot) 163, 166
tun (OE) **176**, 189, 191
Tune ship 19, 23–4
tunga 96
Tuquoy, Ork. 61–2, 89
Turnaig, W. Ross 99
Tweed R., Scot. 1, 169
Tyne, R., Eng. 196, 206, 210
Tyrset(e) 210

Udrigle, W. Ross 99
Uig, Coll 115
Ulbster, Caith. 72
Ulchil 164
Ulfr 174
Ullapool, W. Ross 97, 104
Ullastaðir, Ullest 84
Ullava, W. Ross 103
Ullestie, Suth. 84
Ulster 149
Unaberries, Shet. **31**, 32, 35–6
Unapool, Suth. 89
Unastaðir, Shet. 74
Unes, Suth. 86
Urmston, Lancs. 191
Usairt, Coll 123
Ustaness, Shet. 30–32, 37–40
Uttesgarth, Ork. 48

vaccaria 202
Valdres, Norway 18–19
Vale of Pickering, Yorks. 172
Vale of York 130
Vale Royal abbey, Ches. 192
vatns bólstaðr 113, 121
Vaul, Tiree 117, 121
veizla 57
Viking Treasure from the North West 197
Vikings, in British Isles 1–4, 8–10, 12–16, 19, **20**, **21**, 23–4, 44, 88, 91–2, **95**, 106–7, 124, 141–4, 168–70, 174, 180–81, 183, 196, 198–9, 214–15
see also Danes, Norsemen
Vingvell hill 206, 209
völlr 97

Wadbister, Shet. **31**, 32, 37, 72
Waldeve, lord of Inverkeithing 150–1, 161, 164
Wallasey, Ches. 189, 192
Walter, son of Philip of Lundin 162
Waltheof 150–1, 161, 164
wapentake 189–90
Warsetter, Ork. 45
Wasbister, S. Walls., Ork. 57–8
Wasbister, S. Ronaldsay, Ork. 57–8
Wathers Brae, Wathersbie, Weathersbie Tofts, Weathirsbie, Wedderisbe, Wedderisbye 156, 157
Watten, Caith. 76
Wauldby, Yorks. 175
Wear R., Eng. 213
Weardale, Co. Durham 212
Wearmouth, Co. Durham 212
Weathersbie, Fife 142, 146, 153, 156
Weaver R., Ches. 193
Weaverthorpe, Yorks. 174, 181–2
Weddersbie, Fife 142
Weisdale, Shet. 29, 30, 35n., 36
Wemys, Fife 151, 162
Wessex, expansion of 144
West. Kirby, Ches. 189
Wester Cash Farm, Fife 158–9
Westerbister, Holm, Ork. 57–8
Western Isles, Scot. 7–9, 24, 94, 104–5, 117, 148
Westmorland, Eng. 192, 196, 197
Westness, Rousay, Ork. 56–7
Wet Reans 188–9
Wetherby, Yorks. 175
Wharram Percy, Yorks. 180–81, **182**
Whitby, Ches. 189–90, 192, 193
Whitby, Yorks. 177–8
Whiteness, Shet. **29**, 27–41
Whithorn, Gall. 125–6, 131, 135, **136**, 137–9
Whittington, Lancs. 202
Whitwham, Northumberland 206
Wick R. Caith. 64
Wick, Caith. 73
Wigtown Bay, Kirkcud. 130, 137
Wigtownshire 135–6, 139
Wilfrid, Bishop 204
William Cumin, carl of Buchan 165
William de Buskeby 137, 138
William de Galliston 158
William, earl of Sutherland 88
William I, the Lion, king of Scot. 163–4
William I, the Conqueror, king of England 151, 152, 204
William the Fleming 160
William, bishop of St Andrews 164
'Windy Skail', Deerness, Ork. 48